DALO

www.**transworldbooks**.co.uk

www.transworldireland.ie

DALO
THE AUTOBIOGRAPHY

ANTHONY DALY
with
Christy O'Connor

TRANSWORLD IRELAND

TRANSWORLD IRELAND
A division of Transworld Publishers
61–63 Uxbridge Road, London W5 5SA
www.transworldbooks.co.uk

Transworld is part of the Penguin Random House group of companies
whose addresses can be found at global.penguinrandomhouse.com

Penguin
Random House
UK

First published in 2014 by Transworld Ireland,
a division of Transworld Publishers
Transworld Ireland paperback edition published 2015

A CIP catalogue record for this book
is available from the British Library.

ISBN
9781848271524

Typeset in Ehrhardt by Falcon Oast Graphic Art Ltd.
Printed and bound by CPI Group (UK) Ltd, Croydon, CR0 4YY

Penguin Random House is committed to a sustainable
future for our business, our readers and our planet. This book
is made from Forest Stewardship Council® certified paper.

MIX
Paper from
responsible sources
FSC® C016897

1 3 5 7 9 10 8 6 4 2

To my mother, for giving
me a great upbringing.

Contents

Prologue

The Pain and the Shame

'Dalo, coming from Clare, we know that days like today descend from nowhere when least expected. Good interview afterwards. If they are worth persisting with, they will do themselves justice the next day. Never give up!'

The text message from Ger Loughnane dropped in my phone the night of the 2014 Leinster final. Loughnane understands how dog-days like that can creep up on you and steal everything you believed in, everything you thought you and your team stood for. Like myself, Loughnane had experienced enough of those days as a player, the ones that make you question your very existence and sense of worth as a hurler. He had suffered the wounds to be able to recognize the scars.

On the Monday night after the game, I asked Loughnane to consider talking to the players prior to the All-Ireland quarter-final, provided we weren't meeting Clare. He agreed, but I texted him back a week before we were due to play Tipperary and called it off. In the meantime I felt I had extracted the same rawness out of myself, transmitted the same messages Loughnane would have delivered anyway.

This was my sixth year talking to these Dublin players, a lot of whom had been around for those six seasons. I probably gave two years of Loughnanesque management, of hounding and roaring at guys in trying to extract big performances from them from pure raw, savage intensity and ferocity on the training ground. You have to reinvent yourself at times, and I learned over the years from leadership development experts like sports psychologists Declan Coyle and Gary Keegan that that approach will only take you so far.

I have always had a strong belief in who I am and what I'm about, but the hammering we got from Kilkenny in that Leinster final had a destabilizing effect on everything. Just when you think your management style and the management apparatus you've constructed around you is built on concrete, it can appear like matchsticks sitting in wet sand. And then the Kilkenny tide comes along and washes away everything, the scattered debris, the flotsam and jetsam from the wreck, floating into the deepest caverns of your mind.

The questions come at you like a relentless barrage on your senses, like waves hammering against a coastal wall, the wall eroding with every one, every question, every doubt. Why did we collapse again? Why did it happen the year after another good season?

There have been plenty of bad days, but the hardest defeat during my time with Dublin was against Kilkenny in Portlaoise in 2012. We were pistol-whipped all over the pitch, dismembered by seventeen points. The 2014 Leinster final was even worse. It was another no-show. Another capitulation.

In lots of ways, I just cannot understand these no-shows. Then in other ways, I completely can. I've been there. I've played on Clare teams that have collapsed and crumbled in the same manner. As Loughnane said in his text, these days descend from nowhere. They blindside and cripple you when you least expect it.

Our defeat to Kilkenny was so bad that it had shades of the 1993 Munster final hammering to Tipperary all over it. In 1993, Clare got caught up in the hype. In 2014, Dublin got hung up on winning successive Leinster titles. The big difference between the two teams is that Dublin were Leinster champions while that Clare team was still scrabbling around the badlands of Munster hurling. Yet the two teams are almost intertwined in their circumstances, both days intrinsically connected by a lack of belief and conviction. All that was really different was the colour of the jersey.

You try and understand why these days keep happening, why we just cannot permanently change the DNA in Dublin hurling. Winning successive Leinster titles for the first time in seventy-two years would have been a huge part of that process. When we lost our footing with the summit in sight, we tumbled all the way to the bottom and landed in a heap.

It was as if altitude sickness gripped our minds and took us down. It's even more demoralizing given that we didn't even mention that target of winning back-to-back Leinster titles. When Gary Keegan came to meet the management in Parnell Park the Wednesday night before the game, he told us not to be giving any of our energy to Kilkenny. To keep our focus and concentration for ourselves. I had my notebook in my hand and I wrote that down straight away. Usually you'd be so attentive to Gary that you wouldn't take your eyes off him, but I scribbled that point on my pad as soon as the words left his mouth.

I made it all about us. 'Remember,' I said to the lads on the Friday night before the game, 'we're the Leinster champions. They're coming into our own field to try and take it off us. How proud was Jimmy Gray [former Dublin hurler] presenting that cup to Johnny [McCaffrey] last year? Are we going to watch a Kilkenny substitute go up again and collect that cup this year?' (Michael Fennelly had collected the trophy as a sub in 2009.)

And then we go out and don't fight the fight.

When we trained again for the first time on the Wednesday after the game, Ross Dunphy had a hard running session planned. We met in St Anne's Park but my gut instinct was that we needed to purge some of the pain and hurt through dialogue as opposed to throwing sweat at the problem. In any case, it was a really warm evening and the small dressing-rooms were like saunas. We could sweat out the toxins there rather than pound the hard ground.

Anybody who wanted to talk had an open forum. The sweat was flowing down my brow as the discussion broadened. The gameplan was inevitably one of the main topics of debate until Mikey Carton intervened. 'Lads,' he said, 'that was the game-plan which won us the Leinster title last year.'

Guys were looking for scapegoats and reasons to bitch but there was no hiding from the real, hard truth. 'If it was a boxing match,' I said, 'Kilkenny would have pucked us up and down Croke Park. And if I had a towel, I'd have thrown it in. As far as I'm concerned, we didn't fight the fight. That had nothing to do with the gameplan. I can take a certain share of blame for the gameplan last year against Cork, that if we had started with it, we might have been out of sight. That's the regret I have last year – that I didn't go with it from the start – but I have no regrets about gameplans or tactics this time round. My regret is that I hadn't ye ready for war.

'That's what I take responsibility for. I take absolute responsibility for that, so don't go blaming gameplans for you dropping the ball, or you going up for a fifty-fifty ball with a

Kilkenny fella and you having your eyes closed. Maybe your eyes weren't closed but he was coming down with the ball. So don't give me that.'

Nobody held back. Everybody's approach was dissected. Alan Nolan – 'Noley' – who had been our best player against Kilkenny, suggested at one stage that I had become too nice, that the players needed to see more of the madness they had first become accustomed to from me. I smiled to myself as I wound up the meeting.

'By God, it's in my nature to be that chap,' I said to the group. 'Don't worry, I can change to become that chap again. Let's also remember that the other chap was the one who won the Leinster title last year; he was the nice, cool, calculated guy. OK, if ye want the other chap, ye'll get him.'

And by Jesus, they have got him since.

Friday, 18 July 2014

Over a week later, we played Limerick in a challenge game in the Gaelic Grounds. We were reasonably happy with the performance. We scored 2-27 and won by five points. Limerick only started with four of the side which lost the previous Sunday's Munster final to Cork but we gave everybody a run and the lads who came on played well against a Limerick side which finished with a far stronger team than they had started with.

As we strolled back to the dressing-room after the game, I tipped off the management. 'Lads, I'm going to go off the rails in here now.'

Shane Martin, one of the selectors, stared at me with a quizzical look. We had played well. We'd put up a big score. There were huge positives. David Treacy scored 1-5. Conor McCormack played really well. Ryan O'Dwyer looked back to himself. Danny Sutcliffe caused rack at centre-forward. Still, I didn't care. At one stage of the second half I'd heard one of the subs behind me saying to Ross Dunphy that playing the match had been a great call by management. That we really needed a game like this.

It didn't sit well with me.

Conor McCormack and Ryan O'Dwyer were already in the showers by the time we got to the dressing-rooms so I told them to come straight back out. 'Get out. Now.'

The dressing-rooms in Limerick are designed in such a way that there are corners everywhere so I got everyone to pull in tight together, all along the middle benches. I stood behind a table loaded with water and hurleys and picked up one of Noley's goalkeeper sticks, a big yoke, from the pile sprawled across the floor.

'IS EVERYTHING FUCKING OK NOW?' I roared as I swung the stick on the table with the force of an executioner. Bottles of water and hurleys, and the table itself which crumpled on its fold-up legs, were the victims. Everyone was in shock. Paul Ryan nearly recoiled three feet.

I spoke about our brand, about who we are and what we stand for, and how we had been unfaithful to our promise as a group. I was in the middle of the fifth sentence when emotion got the better of me.

'To go out and do what we did against Kilkenny was just unbelievable. Give me days like last year's All-Ireland semi-final against Cork any time. I cried for nearly two days with the pain of not being in that final. It took me a month to get over it, but by God, give me the pain, but don't give me the shame. The absolute shame in all of us facing our families that evening was just heartbreaking.'

The shame has brought the animal back out in me. Tommy Dunne, our coach, said it to Ross that he saw the same guy he knew on the hurling pitch during those savage battles we had in Clare with Tipp, the guy with the primal desire who would do anything to win. Tommy never saw that rawness in me before as a manager because he'd only been with us for the last year, but it has always been a huge part of my character and DNA, and the wounds Kilkenny inflicted drew it back to the surface now, like pus oozing out of a sore.

When we trained again two days later on the Sunday, a week before our All-Ireland quarter-final against Tipp, I asked Tommy about the session he had planned. I suggested a couple of drills, both contested and uncontested ones, which Tommy ran brilliantly and the lads executed superbly.

'The hurling I've seen this morning is first class,' I said to the group as we gathered in our huddle afterwards. 'So don't give me the excuse next Sunday evening that your touch wasn't right or your eye was out. Yere touch and yere shooting is excellent. So this is all about the fight now. And fighting the fight.'

I've been on a war footing because I feel it's the approach we need now. If it works and we win on Sunday, I might even change tack for the semi-final because that's the kind of group they are. They're a brilliant bunch of fellas but you need to have something fresh to throw at them the whole time to keep them on edge.

They would have climbed the Sugar Loaf barefoot in the morning for me. They'd have run to Clare if I asked them to. But you need to be a bunch of wild animals to survive in this jungle. Some lads are just too lax and too laid back. That was evident in the dressing-room before the Leinster final – lads sitting down motionless, nobody talking, no energy. The mood was dead. You look at rugby players strolling down the tunnel before big games, all smiles as they hold a mascot's hand. It would be easy to think, 'How are those guys ready for war?'

They're ready because they've mentally built themselves up for war and are ready to kill anything that moves.

The lads know what is expected of them against Tipp. Mentally, they need to be ready for war and ready to nail anything that moves. They know it too, but whether or not there has been enough damage done since the Leinster final, I don't know.

Friday, 25 July 2014
Bere Island –
One task at a time
Next ball
Next game
– Be an active member
Make a difference
– Intensity, intensity, intensity, be aggressive
– Never, never assume
Never just happens
– Believe and achieve
Ready for challenge
YOUR POINTS

On the Friday night before we played Tipperary, that poster was taped to the wall in dressing-room G in Parnell Park, the last door on the left at the bottom of the long corridor. We'd gone to Bere Island for a weekend training camp the week before the 2013 league semi-final, Ross had kept all the sheets from our feedback discussions while we were there, and he stuck up some of them on the wall before training to mentally transport the lads back to that weekend.

It was savage and brutal. I had gotten ill on the way down to the camp and had to turn back, but the management graphically informed me that any exercise or form of torture the army rangers threw at our boys, at any hour of the day or night, they ate it up. We were mentally and physically prepared for any battle that weekend. So why would we go into battle again on Sunday and not remind ourselves of what we are capable of under extreme pressure and hardship?

The Leinster final was a write-off, but we are seventy minutes away from where we were last year, an All-Ireland semi-final. There is no real pressure on us. All the pressure is on Tipp. While I would have fought with the county board to try and get the game moved from Thurles, I don't really care now that we have to face them down in their back-yard. If we're up for it, we'll have a right cut off them. If we are, we can take them down.

It was a beautiful evening, one of those idyllic summer evenings on the edge of a championship weekend when you feel as alive as alive can be. I was there from 5.45 for a seven p.m. start and a couple of lads were already getting ready to rock. Alan Nolan was taking a forest of hurleys from the boot of his car. Ryan O'Dwyer and Eamonn O'Reilly, our physio, were kicking a football on the Parnell Park pitch.

By the time Ross started lining the pitch with cones, the field was flooded with bodies – guys limbering up, fellas pucking balls across the pitch, more taking pot shots at the Donnycarney church goals. When the church bells struck seven, I blew the whistle and called everyone back up to the top of the field, before leading the group to the main meeting room upstairs, above the dressing-rooms in Parnell Park.

Part of our brand is that we always believe we are the hunters, much more so than the hunted. It fits with our personality as a team. The critics and the hurling connoisseurs say that we don't have the skill and class of other teams but we have a brand of working hard together, of hunting the opposition down, of

being hard to beat. That's how we want to portray ourselves. It's how we want to perceive ourselves. It forms a central plank of our identity.

In the Leinster final we were completely unfaithful to that belief, to that identity. That day we were the hunted. And Kilkenny devoured us like wolves.

We showed the players video footage of the kill. It was embarrassing to watch, like gazelles being stalked by deadly predators. One of the clips showed three Kilkenny fellas coming in to block Colm Cronin at one stage, and no other Dublin player coming to his assistance. When Colm chased valiantly to try and get possession back, there was still no other Dublin player in sight.

Another clip showed Stephen Hiney catching a puckout and storming past T. J. Reid before Eoin Larkin came from nowhere and flicked the ball away. Hiney won it back and, hemmed in by two Kilkenny guys, got a handpass away, hoping a Dublin team-mate was nearby to assist. But there was no Dub in sight and Kilkenny came away with the ball.

'Go away and watch last year's All-Ireland semi-final tomorrow if ye want,' I said to the players. 'Feel the pain. But by God, there was no shame.'

There was nowhere to hide for any player while they were watching the screen. We always show positive images before a championship game but we could have shown positive footage this evening and only been codding ourselves. This evening was raw for a reason. 'We were the hunted against Kilkenny,' I said to the group. 'On Sunday, we need to go hunting again. To hunt down every ball as if our lives depended on it.'

We have picked our first fifteen. We're going with a dummy team for the first time in years. Tipp have enough advantages playing in Thurles so why should we give them any more? A

Tipp fella mentally prepped for Dotsy O'Callaghan might be thrown when he sees David Treacy in his corner.

Shane Martin went through our tactics, none of which were complicated. We had three match-ups in our defence, with the other three to try and hold their shape as much as possible. Colm Cronin was named at corner-forward but was to play in a more withdrawn role, with the two other lads to hold inside. The half-forward line was encouraged to engage in the middle-third battle, like half-forward lines always have done.

Since the Leinster final anyway, we have gone away from focusing on tactics and gameplans. This has to be rawer now, more primal. 'Did the gameplan win last year's Leinster title?' I asked the group again.

A few said yes, with no real conviction in their voices. 'No it didn't,' replied somebody else.

I wasn't fully sure who it was but it sounded like Gary Maguire. 'He's right,' I said. 'We won it because we fought on our backs for every ball. The plan did help, but are ye telling me that what we're after watching had anything to do with gameplans?'

Even though we were less than forty-eight hours away from the game, I wanted there to be a high energy level to the session. This evening was our first training session since the Leinster final that we didn't play a match, but the intensity level was still so evident that Conal Keaney broke Hiney's nose in a tackling drill. Hiney has already broken his nose about six times and the bridge was pushed right across to the right side of his face. Hiney's such a warrior that it won't have any effect on him. It's a sign that Keaney is well up for Sunday too.

They're bound to be more pumped by the time the session ends. Before it began, I called Johnny McCaffrey over.

'Do you remember Ed Holland?'

'Ed Holland . . . Ed Holland . . . no . . . no, I don't, Dalo.'

'The beardy fella who ran the camp in Bere Island,' I replied.

'Oh Jesus, will I ever forget him.'

'Well, he's going to be over in that corner when you're finished training.'

As soon as Johnny led the lads to the bottom corner of the field, just in front of the seated stand, Ed Holland jumped over the front wall of the stand and joined them.

I hadn't a clue what he was saying to them. I was talking to Shane Martin, Tommy Dunne and Ross Dunphy in the middle of the field, the sun glaring down on the crowns of our heads. Any time there was a break in the conversation, I would glare at the huddle, my antennae raised to try and pick up snatches of the talk, to observe the body language of the group.

At one stage I saw Ed with his head down. He was reading something from the palm of his hand and I instantly knew what it was because Ross had mentioned it to me. The lads had written letters in Bere Island; they were given certain words which they had to include in the writing. Ed was reading out one of their letters.

When they broke from the group, they all made their way back up along the sideline just in front of the stand to the 65-metre line where an ice box was perched on the edge of the field, stacked with Magnum ice-creams. It's our treat box, which the lads regularly fill before championship games, paid for with small player fines for indiscretions throughout the year. We hadn't filled the treat box before the Leinster final and Noley reminded me of it, as if it was a superstitious oversight.

As the lads made their way across the pitch to the dressing-rooms, munching ice-cream as they went, Shane Durkin approached and patted me on the shoulder.

'Some stunt, Dalo.'

'It was no stunt, Shane,' I replied. 'Ed said ye were the best guys the army ever came across down there. Ye did that camp. Ye faced whatever hardship was put in front of ye. I just wanted to remind ye of that this evening. Because we're going to war again on Sunday.'

As I pointed the car out the gates of Parnell and hit for home, the thought was on my mind: 'Is this my last time heading down the long road from training as Dublin manager?'

How do I feel? Apprehensive. Slightly on edge but full of hope and expectation too because I know how great these lads can be when they bring the fight to the battle. All I'm hoping is that we do bring that fight to the battle and then let everything else look after itself. The last thing I said to Richie Stakelum before I left was we just need to get the calls right on the side-line now because I don't think we could have done any more.

If I'm being honest, though, I'm also trying not to think of the consequences if we fail to show up again on Sunday, if we don't perform again. I'd be a liar if I didn't admit that the ramifications of defeat are not on my mind. I can already picture the press pack around me in those circumstances, the inevitable question someone will fire at me. Is this it? Is this the end of the road?

If it is, if we do lose, what is my next move? Will I miss this? I certainly won't miss the long road and the monotony of the long winter evenings, when I'm driving in pitch darkness and cold and I still have the air conditioning turned up to the max to try and keep myself sharp and awake.

On beautiful summer evenings before the championship it is easy to forget about those black winter slogs, where the loneliness and drudgery can often hang over you like a pall of dead air. It can weigh you down and beat you down but you have to endure that part of the journey if you want to picture the road stretching out to July, and hopefully into August and September.

Even on beautiful summer evenings, though, the doubts can do a number on your head. I have doubts about myself and my future, but I'm not looking beyond Sunday because I can't. It's to my detriment at times that I don't look far enough ahead in life. Others would see that as a strength, that it's important to live for Sunday, the day ahead, the next battle. To suppress any dark thoughts. To believe that we will fight our way out of this, that we will win.

Even when the questions and the doubts keep returning, I just have to bate them back, to keep believing in myself. If you don't, you just walk away from it all and say to yourself, 'That's just not for me.' That's where most of my emotion, which was smeared all across my face, came from after we won the 2013 Leinster final. There were so many times when I hadn't believed in myself, so many occasions when I had doubted myself so much.

You just have to keep believing in yourself and the group. If we pull off a big win against Tipp on Sunday, we'll have our momentum back again. We'll be playing Cork in an All-Ireland semi-final and we'll be in the same position they were last year: heading into an All-Ireland semi-final with the huge momentum of a big quarter-final win against a side which won't have played for five weeks. If we win that game, we'll more than likely square up to Kilkenny again in an All-Ireland. We certainly wouldn't lack motivation for that rematch. If you said that to anyone else outside the group, lads would be saying, 'Will you go away and get yourself checked out. Have you gone completely mad?' But what other way can you think? What's the point in all of this if you don't think that?

I often think of Ian McGeechan's famous speech on the land-mark 1997 Lions tour of South Africa, words and sentiments I often refer to. McGeechan spoke about not fearing defeat. He had known it, lived it. Defeat had been part of his life, all his life. I have regurgitated and reheated those words in so many forms to the Dublin players over the years.

'Where do ye think I'm from, lads? I have no nine All-Irelands. I was lucky to experience the golden era of Clare hurling but defeat has belted me up and down the country. Every place I have gone, I've been hammered by defeat. I hate it, but I can handle it. I can live with defeat, but I cannot live with shame.'

I don't even know if a win on Sunday will put my chin back in place. I'm still that low. I'm not even greedy enough to say that we have to win for my head to lift again. As I said, I can live with the pain of defeat. But I struggle to deal with the shame that often goes with it.

1

On the Road Again

Ballykelly, Laois, Thursday, 16 January 2014
Dublin 6-27
University of Limerick 0-17

I had just passed Newmarket-on-Fergus when the phone rang. It was Brian Lohan's number flashing on the screen. Lohan, who has been managing UL for the last couple of seasons, said he would have rung sooner only he had the Clare hurlers Conor Ryan and Podge Collins in the car with him. As soon as he'd dropped them home, Lohan almost couldn't contain himself.

'Holy Jesus, ye are gone on to a whole new level. Ye made bits of us. The clinical way ye scored yere goals was something else. How the hell did ye not beat Cork last year?'

Two years earlier, UL had hammered the shit out of us in the same field. We picked a stronger team because they had beaten Waterford in the Waterford Crystal Cup three days earlier. We were more pumped up than normal for a midweek challenge game in the middle of nowhere in January, but Lohan's comments still threw me. In my own mind, I was saying, 'Get lost, Lohan, this is a new year.'

When I landed home in Tullycrine at 11.48 p.m., I thought more about his comments. Lohan was comparing the quality he had just seen to the previous year's All-Ireland semi-final against Cork. That game was still fresh in his mind. I had been over it a thousand times but Lohan flicked the switch in my head again. 'How the hell did we not beat Cork?'

Fifteen minutes into the second half of that game I was absolutely convinced we were going to win. Maybe I was slightly naive by not shoring our defence up more in the first half. That was our game. It was our brand, our signature style. Instead we decided to go toe-to-toe with Cork in a shootout for the first thirty-five minutes. I figured they wouldn't be gone far enough ahead of us that we wouldn't have been able to lasso them back. If they had bucked five or six points clear, we would have changed the formation. We were only down one point at the break. Perfect. Time for Plan B. Time to drive on.

Danny Sutcliffe came out to the middle to get on Johnny McCaffrey's man. Johnny was to sit in front of Liam Rushe. No balls were to be hit to the corner-flags to suit our two-man full-forward line. Everyone had to up their workrate. It was obvious that they had. We were clearly more comfortable reverting to that style. We were wiping Cork out in the middle third. We had control of the game. Our system was dictating the tempo. I turned back to the lads. 'We have them,' I said. 'We have them.'

Then Ryan O'Dwyer was sent off on a second yellow card in the 50th minute. Anthony Nash nailed his second inter-continental range point from the free to level the match but they were still struggling to cope with our system. I still thought we had them. Lorcán McLoughlin ran over to Jimmy Barry-Murphy. 'They still have a loose man above.' I thought we might sneak something out of the match but the momentum had switched. It got away from us.

'We'd have won only for the sending-off,' I said to Lohan on the phone. 'We won't be getting carried away with a challenge game in January, but you're right, we are a different animal now. We are stronger. I can guarantee you, this time last year, those older fellas would not have been driving that on like they were tonight. I can see that difference. Wherever that leads to, I don't know.'

One afternoon in late autumn 2008, the journalist Jackie Cahill rang me. He was calling for the craic, to talk about everything and nothing. 'Jeez, I must meet up with you soon,' he said. It was a half-genuine call because Jackie is never switched off. If there is a line hanging around, he'll swoop like a hawk.

Before long, it was obvious he was soaring above the bait. The eyes were focused, the wings widely spanned, the talons ready to strike.

'Do you fancy taking anyone? What about the Dublin job. Would you go for it?'

'Even if I did, I wasn't asked,' I replied. 'They've asked everyone under the sun at this stage. Sure I'm probably too far away anyway.'

'Jaysus, I'd say they'd be mad keen if you were any way interested.'

Jackie must have thought he was Jorge Mendes, the soccer super-agent. He went on a solo run and called Gerry Harrington, chairman of the Dublin county board. He hopped the ball to Gerry. 'Ring Dalo. He could be the man.' Harrington was on the blower straight away.

The first thing I did was clarify that Jackie wasn't Jorge Mendes. Even if he thought he was, I wasn't on his books. I knew Dublin had been hotly pursuing Nicky English. I told Gerry that Nicky was the obvious choice for the job. He cut me off straight away. 'Jeez, if we thought you were interested, we'd have been on to you sooner.'

I was interested. Big-time. About a month earlier, Declan Ruth had asked me if I was open to an interview with Wexford. I dismissed it straight away. It would be easier to get to New York on a plane than it would be to travel from Wexford to West Clare. I couldn't face that trip, but the road to Dublin was getting shorter all the time. I knew there was some serious young talent emerging. More than anything, though, it was the methadone I was craving for my habit since I'd finished up as Clare manager.

A couple of days later, I met Harrington, John Costello and Mike Connolly in the Lakeside Inn in Killaloe. Connolly, who had been pivotal in drawing up Dublin's development squads model, showed me the hard data and the positive projections attached to the numbers. Liam Rushe, who I had never heard of, was mentioned as one of many rough diamonds waiting to be polished. Connolly's hard-drive was bursting from the volume of similar potential.

They had reams of talent coming but they needed someone who could stitch it all together. All-Irelands in the immediate future were not a priority. Dublin needed a manager who could bring enough excitement, encouragement and experience to push all their recent and irresistible underage momentum over the hill. To make a progressive hurling culture permanent. At the end of the discussion, they offered me the job.

I was excited. I desperately missed the buzz of being involved at inter-county level, but could that desire justify taking on a job which involved a round trip of 350 miles? Was it overly selfish when I had a shop and a pub to run, and a young family to rear? On the road back to Ennis, I rang my wife Eilís. We went for lunch and discussed the possibility.

'Is it mad?' she asked.

'It probably is. But I'd love to have a go at it. Expectations wouldn't be that high. It's a building process. Jeez, I'd regret it if I didn't take it.'

Regrets can contaminate your system like a virus so I canvassed solid counsel and highly respected opinion. Tommy Howard, Johnny Callinan and Fergie 'Tuts' Tuohy told me what I already felt in my gut: 'Why not? It's a great job. Go for it.' The only one who wasn't sold on the idea was Ger 'Sparrow' O'Loughlin who thought I might have lost the plot with the logistics involved.

Deep down, however, I had made my decision. The only stumbling block was the pub I ran, Murty Browne's. With the amount of travel involved, I'd kill myself if I tried to double-job full-time. I decided to put the word out there that I might be interested in leasing the pub. Before long, I was approached by a sound county Monaghan man, Dave Livingstone, who lived in Lissycasey. The deal was made. I was on the road to Dublin.

I met Vinny Teehan first. I met Richie Stakelum in the Clare Inn a couple of days later. We drank copious amounts of coffee and got lost so deep in hurling talk that we left without paying the bill. I sat down with Richie and Vinny and Ciaran 'Hedgo' Hetherton in the Citywest Hotel a couple of nights later and discussed the potential of this great journey we were all embarking on. A few weeks later, Richie also managed to recruit the highly rated coach Jim Kilty, who had trained Tipp when they won the 2001 All-Ireland.

On the day I was unveiled to the media, I made an ape of myself before I even arrived. I got lost. I knew there was a big church near Parnell Park but I confused Whitehall with Donnycarney church. I was driving around Whitehall like

Stevie Wonder. Eventually I had to call Gerry Harrington to come and rescue me.

I was far more tuned in the first time I met the players. I remembered listening to Len Gaynor and Ger Loughnane the first time they addressed the players as Clare manager. Seamus Durack was the same with the Clare U-21s one year. They all absolutely nailed their message. It left a huge impression. I needed to impart mine to the absolute maximum. I needed those Dublin players tuned in to my frequency from day one.

I was honest but as blunt as a spade. I didn't know anyone so I had no loyalty to any of them. I was looking for thirty fanatics. When I was Clare manager, we played Dublin in the qualifiers in 2005 and 2006 and I couldn't believe how naive they were. They needed to become more streetwise, more hard-headed. The only way they could learn those lessons was to get into the ring and start trading punches, to fake it until they started to make it, to at least let on that they were boxing clever.

It was easy for me to talk to them about Clare. The first half of my career was spent in the same purgatory the players in front of me had become accustomed to. I had no truck with tradition. We had been a laughing stock in Clare. On my debut, in 1990, we lost to Limerick by fourteen points. Five years later, we were All-Ireland champions. 'It can be done,' I told them. 'It can be done.'

I set the dream. Then it was all about chasing it. 'This is a boat that is just after being pushed off a port,' I told the players that night. 'I know the destination I want to reach, the steps of the Hogan Stand. I don't know where we will go in between but that is my ambition. And I will do my utmost to try and get ye there.'

When I took them for my first session, on the Astroturf pitch in Thomas Davis in Tallaght, it was pure basic stuff, lines of threes and fours. I couldn't believe how slow they were. I blew the whistle and savaged them. Then I drove them through the rest of the session like a demented beast. Their tongues were hanging when the drills were wrapped up. 'This is the way it's going to be.'

To finish up, we played a twenty-minute match. I drove it on the way Loughnane used to. Some lads looking to impress started belting each other. Similar to Loughnane, I swallowed the whistle. More of them were looking for frees.

'There will be no fucking frees here!' I roared, the exclamation mark clearly audible. 'Frees my hole!'

It was a licence to kill for some lads. Kevin 'Rasher' Ryan was leathering all around him. He was loving it. I was loving it even more. 'Aboy, Ryan!' I was roaring. He was one of the few names I knew. I was calling half of them wrong names but I appeared to be best friends with the guys orchestrating what looked like a cull.

When we went for food afterwards, I did some reconnaissance work. I was discreetly checking names and clubs. It was soon obvious that players from the same clubs were sitting together. From that night on, guys weren't encouraged to sit directly beside a clubmate.

We were all starting from base camp, but it was soon obvious that a path had been carved up the first part of the mountain. I saw Rushey for the first time the day we played the 'Blue Stars' game. He was just out of minor and was blowing guys out of his way. David Treacy blinded me the same afternoon with his skill. I could see now what Mike Connolly had been talking about. The talent was obvious. You could smell the ambition off the more experienced players. We were on a high. Then we walked into a Kilkenny haymaker.

It was only the Walsh Cup but Brian Cody put me back in my

box before I even got the chance to stick my head out the top of it. Kilkenny were not that strong on paper but Cody had them well riled up. They hit six goals and won by twenty points. I was driving down the road afterwards asking myself, 'What have I let myself in for here?'

We were never going to soar up the mountain. We began by scaling foothills. We won the Walsh Cup Shield, which was something tangible for Dublin hurling. Gradually, we got footholds on higher peaks. After a great league campaign in Division 1, a draw against Clare in our second last game denied us an outside chance of making the final. In June 2009, Dublin reached their first Leinster final in eighteen years.

On the day of the semi-final against Wexford in Nowlan Park, we drove past the Kilkenny exit and continued on down the M7. We had been to the Curragh and the Glen of Imaal on an army training camp that February and I wanted to forcibly remind the lads of that weekend. That training camp was absolutely animal. The closest I had ever seen to such brutality was Mike McNamara in his prime with Clare. I had previously dealt with Jim Maguire in the army and had requested their toughest regime. An Ulster football panel had tried to get through a similar camp two weeks earlier and Maguire sent them home a day early. He had broken them. Maguire also tried to break us.

One morning, he got the whole squad up for a gear inspection at three a.m. Everyone had been given a list of stuff to bring and Maguire brutally punished every indiscretion. A tin of peas did not pass for a tin of beans. A lighter was no substitute for a box of matches. 'Who is yere captain?' Maguire roared as he instigated the first reprisal.

Stephen Hiney's gear had been immaculately prepared but he was brought outside and put doing press-ups. Everyone else had to start running around Hiney in a circle as Maguire sought answers as to why they had failed the most basic task of the weekend. 'Ye imbeciles, tell me what went wrong!' he shouted.

None of the answers fitted Maguire's demands. 'Are ye fucking stupid? Tell me what went wrong!'

All the while, Hiney was being tortured. Maguire was standing on his back while Hiney's press-up count was extending into big numbers. At this stage, I was getting anxious. Stephen is a diabetic. You will regularly see him sipping Lucozade for a sugar boost. He is always checking his sugar levels with a needle before training, and he hadn't eaten in over eight hours. Hiney was frothing at the mouth but he just would not give in. By the time Maguire eventually let him stop, he collapsed in a puddle of sweat and had to be peeled off the ground like a piece of chewing gum. Then he joined the rest of the group for a six-kilometre punishment hike. When they returned to base, Maguire singled out Hiney for the only line of praise all day. 'I can tell ye one thing anyway,' he said, 'ye have one great captain.'

Most of the tasks the army set are almost impossible to pass, but they are looking for mental fortitude more than physical endurance. On the day of the semi-final against Wexford, I wanted to remind the players of how mentally strong they had proven themselves four months earlier. I marched them up to the top of Donnelly's Hollow at the Athgarvan end of the Curragh, where the boxer Jim Donnelly's second and most famous fight took place against George Cooper in 1814. The last time the players had been there they'd been flogged like slaves.

'Remember this place of pain,' I said. 'By Jesus, we're not going suffering again today.'

Seán Shanley planted a Dublin flag at the hollow and we walked back down to the bus.

As we drove into Kilkenny City, 'The Foggy Dew', the version performed by Sinéad O'Connor and the Chieftains, was blasting out of the radio's speakers.

Right proudly high over Dublin Town they hung out the flag of war;
'Twas better to die 'neath an Irish sky than at Sulva or Sud El Bar.

We were going to war. That day, Wexford were Britannia's Huns.

It was only after that battle I realized how much the win meant to Dublin hurling. Kevin Flynn was crying. The emotional power of the embrace between Flynn and Liam Ryan showed how deep and soulful the victory was. I was so buzzed up and so loud in my praise to the media of the performance of the younger lads that I sounded like David O'Leary praising his 'babies' at Leeds a few years earlier.

We knew we weren't ready to take on Kilkenny man-for-man in the final. We used Johnny McCaffrey as a sweeper. We definitely upset Kilkenny's way of thinking and were in with a chance until their second goal put the game beyond us. Our season ended three weeks later when Limerick knocked us out in the All-Ireland quarter-final. We were the better team but Limerick just weren't prepared to lose to Dublin that day. Their psyche and soul wouldn't allow it. Their tradition could not countenance it. You could sense it at pitch-side. It was a harsh lesson in our quest to make a hurling culture permanent.

Richie Stakelum and I went to the Horse and Jockey outside Thurles afterwards for a pint. We had massive areas to work on and develop but at least we had set a solid foundation on which to build. If nothing else, it was a good start in year one of a two-year project.

Five years on, the project was still ongoing.

Thursday, 23 January 2014

I was reading an interview with Mick O'Dwyer recently. He has always said that driving is one of his hobbies. The fact that I didn't sit behind a wheel until I was twenty-six means that there is still probably a novelty factor there for me, but I actually like pointing the car east and gobbling up the miles like PacMan. Not to the same extent as Micko, but the long road can grant you the head-space a crammed day too often cannot sanction.

It was tougher in the early days but the roads have got better and the journey shorter. I'm rarely home after midnight. Even when I am, there is still light on in the pub. When I finish up with the hurling, that's where I will be returning. I have been so lucky that Declan Keane, a former Cooraclare footballer, has done such a brilliant job with the pub, but that reality alone makes the long road and the long nights easier to reconcile.

The only time I ever found it a drag was this time last year. I had taken on a role with the Limerick Institute of Technology freshers. My eldest daughter Orlaith was not well. On the night Limerick beat us in the league, I told Richie Stakelum that I felt the end was in sight. I even wondered if five years had been too long to stay. A Leinster title obviously changes perspectives, but when Richie and I recently spoke on the same subject, I told him the main reason I was enjoying it so much again was because of how well the boys were reacting. How much they were driving it on.

Maybe I'm buzzed up on how pregnant with promise this

27

season is, but that doesn't mean you can just switch off and hit autopilot. In this gig, you can never take anything as a given. We beat UCD in the Walsh Cup quarter-final two nights ago but I wasn't that happy. UCD were well up for it but I felt we were slack. Maybe it was because we beat UL so easily, but I could smell complacency in the air like sulphur.

We were always going to beat UCD, but that should never have mattered. What we have striven for over the last few years is to be the best we can be. To get the most out of ourselves. To completely ignore the jersey we are playing. Whether it is in training or a challenge game, or Kilkenny in a Leinster final, it is all about us. On Tuesday night, we were unfaithful to that promise.

Addressing that concern was my priority tonight. I was so conscious of delivering it properly that I didn't go to bed until 2.45 this morning. I was always a good sleeper but taking over the bar messed up my rhythms over a decade ago. If it was a busy weekend, sleep was a write-off. I never got that rhythm back. My mind is always racing. I had the TV turned off at one a.m. but I didn't lay down my head until I had gone through all my notes.

It doesn't matter how little sleep I get, I never get tired on the road. I was a little later leaving home this afternoon, which meant the roadworks at Newlands Cross put an extra strain on my time, but I pulled into the car park in Bray Emmet's at 5.54 p.m. The club is in Wicklow but the pitch is actually in county Dublin. As soon as the session began at seven, I had my game-face on.

It was cold, just above freezing. The breeze swirling in from the Dublin Mountains would cut you in two but there was no rain and the pitch was in good condition. Tommy Dunne was controlling the session but Ross Dunphy had a significant impact at intermittent stages. The first sign of slackness I saw, I pounced. Tommy was running a drill, and when he blew the whistle I marched straight into the middle of the pack.

'Lads, if fellas think I came up from Clare tonight to announce the team for Sunday, yere fucking codding yereselves. Some lads are taking it easy on each other. Robbie Mahon and Shane Ryan, do ye think what went on down there was good enough? Seánie McClelland and Matthew McCaffrey are below in another group murdering one another. Different lads are watching every group. Every single ball you cop out of, I'm watching it. Because if I don't see you, it is coming back to me.'

By the time the session ended just after 8.30, we got everyone back into the dressing-room. The one room we use is so medium-sized that the two physio tables swallow up most of the ground space, but we herded the thirty-seven players and every member of the backroom into that dressing-room. Everyone was squeezed together like groceries on a small shelf. There was barely standing room for management. We have the luxury space of a massive meeting room upstairs where we eat, but this is how we do things.

That policy stemmed from the first time I met Gary Keegan, director of the Irish Institute of Sport. After we collapsed in the 2010 championship, Richie got his email address and asked if he could speak to us. Richie and I met Gary in his office in Abbotstown that autumn and were blown away by the intensity in the room. When we got back to the car, Richie said that the sweat was running out through him. I lifted my jumper and my shirt was saturated. It was like we'd just done a 10K run.

Gary is so intense. His manner is very polite but there is an intensity in the air with him. It was so powerful that we adopted that policy. Even when we are in Parnell Park, we bring the squad into the smallest dressing-room to try and create a compelling emotion and dynamic.

When everyone was assembled, I took off my baseball cap. My starting point was something selector Shane Martin had reminded me of on the way home Tuesday night.

'When Katie Taylor is fighting a poor opponent, does she win 19-17? No, she performs. It's about how Katie performs. I know it's the one word that kills ye but ye were amateurish on Tuesday night.

'Lookit, there is no us and ye here this evening. I am just explaining it from our side of the fence. In how we facilitated yere training session tonight. I collected Christy O'Connor in Ennis today at 3.30 p.m. The three keepers were on the field for a goalkeeping session with Christy at 6.15 and they burst their holes. I saw it, and Hedgo filmed it. Tommy Dunne did the hurling in conjunction with Ross and it was all top class. [Nutritionist] Crionna Tobin was on the sideline all night and will be upstairs afterwards monitoring everything that ye all eat. There are a few of ye which she hasn't got around to yet, not through her fault, but because of ye. Two fellas failed to show up on Monday night, the captain and vice-captain, Mr McCaffrey and Mr Keaney. Ye have both given her yere reasons but I wasn't overly impressed with it when she was ringing me on Monday night. I know the two of ye apologized to her before the session, but not showing up on Monday night without letting her know was unprofessional. And if anyone in this room can accuse us of being unprofessional in our approach tonight, let me know.'

I had five bullet points on my sheet of paper, all of which were addressed in a calculated fashion. David Treacy had pulled his hamstring playing with UCD twenty-four hours after lining out with us. 'Tray, you dodged a bullet. It's only a grade-one tear. If it was a grade-three tear, your season was in tatters. You need to be more tuned in than that, man, come on.'

The bottom line was that we all needed to return to the values that made us who we were. With so many new players currently on the panel, delivering that message properly was critical to how we moved forward together as a group. After hockeying UL, we got ahead of ourselves. We thought we were better than we are. Tonight was about getting back to basics. About meeting the standards demanded. Following the example set by this Dublin hurling squad as an entity.

'Are we clear, lads?'

'YEAAAHH!'

2

Pat Joe and Paschal

I was eight years old when I attended my first Munster final in 1978. I went with my brother Michael, but my brother-in-law, Colman Glynn, who is married to my sister Patricia, drove. 'We'll pull in for one here, Colman,' Michael said when the Five Alley bar outside Nenagh loomed into view. When we went inside, half of Clare was already there.

My first time in Croke Park was the 1981 All-Ireland semi-final. The Clare minors were playing Galway and our neighbour, Victor O'Loughlin, Sparrow's brother, was playing centre-forward. Victor was a hero to all of us in Madden's Terrace. The memory of seeing him play in Croke Park stayed with me for years and set huge future ambitions for us all in Clarecastle.

Clare were beaten again but the day was even more of an adventure than 1978 because Michael brought me up on the train. There were seventeen years between myself and Michael but he was always a huge presence in my life. He got married to Maureen late in life and we spent a lot of time together at home. He was a fierce Fianna Fáil man, a huge Eamon de Valera supporter. He was a great historian and was always fascinated with that period of Irish history when Dev was the man. With him around, I'd no chance. I vote Fianna Fáil.

Michael was always very good to me. He bought me my first bike but I was spoiled anyway because I was the youngest of eight, four boys and four girls – Michael, Marian, Patricia, Paschal, Lucia, Martin, Stephanie and myself.

My father Pat Joe was originally from the Quay Road in Clarecastle. He married Mary Keane from the Pound Road, the old road in Clarecastle, and they got a house in Madden's Terrace in the middle of the village. When I captained Clarecastle to the 1994 county title, I was the only player on the squad with two parents from Clarecastle.

My father won two championships, in 1945 and 1949. He played in the 1948 and 1956 county finals too. He hurled for Clare in the late 1940s and early 1950s. He played in the full-back line and was reportedly tough and rugged, but he came from good hurling stock. His brother, my uncle, Haulie, was a legend around Clarecastle. He hurled with Ring and Mackey on Railway Cup teams. Haulie also captained Clare to win the league title in 1946. His brother John, another uncle, was actually the captain, but he had gone off injured. John ran a clothes shop in Ennis for years and was another much-loved figure in the county. 'He was all things to every man,' the great Clare hurler Jimmy Smyth once described John to me.

The whole county, though, was close to Haulie. He was almost a folk-tale around the village. He was a councillor who ran his own pub for years. I obviously never saw Haulie hurl, but I heard the folklore of his deeds and feats on the field.

The one outstanding memory I have of Haulie was waking up in the early hours of an October morning in 1977 and seeing him crying at the end of my bed. Mickey 'Dart' McMahon, Sparrow's uncle, was alongside him and they were bawling like babies. I have no recollection of asking them what had happened. I never thought to ask the reason for their presence. I just remember the commotion of seeing the two lads in a state. It was like an apparition, and it made no sense to me. I just closed my eyes and drifted off.

My father had passed away in his sleep. He had been down in the village for a few pints that evening with Packie Tuohy and 'Danno' Moloney. He went home early and complained to my mother of having indigestion. A massive heart attack claimed him a few hours later.

When I woke up the following morning, I remember my mother roaring crying. There was a huge crowd in the back kitchen and I didn't want to go in to her. That is one of the most vivid memories I have of that October morning. She wanted me near her but I didn't know what had happened.

I only found out when my eldest sister Marian and her husband Pat O'Rourke sat me on the stairs that evening and tried to explain it to me. It was all a blur. Pat was going to the shop and he asked me if I wanted anything. An Action Man was my only request. Later on, Pat arrived withan Action Man figure in a sparkling new box.

I never went to the funeral. Mary and Paddy Brennan were great friends of the family and I was dropped down there around eleven a.m. after everyone left the house. I saw the coffin being lifted out past Brennans' window at the bottom of the terrace, next door to O'Loughlin's. Clubmen were shouldering the coffin and Mary Brennan ran past me to close the curtains. I remember that distinctly.

I feasted on chocolate cake and sweets in Brennans' all evening but I was empty. I could sense that something was missing. I was too young to realize it but I needed to say goodbye to my dad. It is still a regret that I have in my life.

I struggled so hard to come to terms with my father's death.

I kept thinking that I'd meet him again, that he wasn't really gone. At night, when the house was dark and quiet, I was afraid to go downstairs to the toilet in case I would run into him. I was mortified of seeing his ghost. I just hadn't fully grasped that he was dead. That sense of larceny, which is what death effectively is, remained with me because it triggered a sequence of horrible nightmares a couple of years later. One night I had it in my head that my grandmother was after falling out the window and I was going downstairs to catch her. After waking up roaring and shouting another night, I somehow made my way to my sister Patricia's house in St Joseph's Terrace, half a mile down the road. I was only ten.

A couple of days later, my mother brought me up to the Friary church in Ennis. One of the friars put holy water on my head, crossed candles across my throat and blessed me. 'That's it,' my mother said to me afterwards, 'you won't get any more of those nightmares again.'

It was probably my first introduction to sports psychology. If you think something good is going to happen, if you visualize it happening, it is easier to believe that it actually will. I never really had those nightmares again.

It offered balm to an open wound, but the deep scar left by my father's death remained visible for years. Any time a teacher mentioned the family or fathers in a general sense in the class-room, I found it hard to deal with. My cheeks would inflame. I would feel all hot and bothered, even agitated.

Nobody would ever consider me to be shy, but I think what-ever inherent shyness is in me can be traced back to the time when my father died. I didn't always like meeting people because I was afraid they would start speaking about him. There was a stage when I became a little rebellious from feeling isolated because of those feelings. I gave some smart talk to Mrs

Brooks one day in school and she complained to Michael because she didn't want to tell my mother.

I honestly couldn't say what I was feeling because I was so young, but it felt like guilt. Maybe that was because it was never fully explained to me what had actually happened. It was like, Daddy has gone to heaven and we'll leave it at that.

Not long before he died, I got an infection. I could vividly remember my father bringing me home from the hospital, wrapped up in a blanket and his warm embrace. I was craving that connection. But I knew not to ask my mother about my feelings because she was barely able to lift her head.

My godfather, Joe Horan, who had been reared by the Brennans when his family emigrated back to the UK, was very good to me around that time. He brought me everywhere. He even taught me how to swim.

Our headmaster in Clarecastle, John Hanly, knew that my father's death had had an impact on me. He had been good friends with my father. When I got to fifth class, he gave me the keys of the school, an honour that was usually only bestowed on boys in sixth class. You would always get £20 off him at Christmas as well for doing the jobs a key-holder was expected to do: turn on the heating in the school on a Sunday evening; have the door opened for the other teachers in the mornings. Living near the school was a prerequisite before even being considered for the responsibility but nobody got it for two years.

As I got older, I began to think more about my father. Maybe I would have got some form of finality from his death if I had been at the funeral. I cannot say that I would have been able to process the grief as an eight-year-old but it would have at least scratched an itch that tore at me for so long.

It really hit me when Eilís's uncle, Jimmy, passed away. When we took over the pub in Tullycrine, Jimmy had moved in with us. He had lived on the premises but we built on a little apartment for him out the back. When he passed away, my three girls were in the mortuary. They were very upset but they were all grieving for Jimmy. I remembered thinking that it was good for them because it accentuated the fond memories they had of him.

Orlaith was eight at that time and I find it hard to imagine her not remembering me if, God forbid, I dropped dead in the morning. I know it's a different time now and you have more opportunities to connect with your parents through holidays and other pursuits. But it's still difficult for me to picture her struggling to remember who I was in later life if I was taken from her at that young age.

Part of the difficulty we experienced as a young family after my father's death was also down to the reality of our circumstances. We lived in a small council house. We survived on a widow's pension. My mother tried to cope in the best way she could but it was a struggle for her. She was forty-seven at the time. Apart from bingo and the odd wedding or funeral, she never really went out. For a full year she wore black, like the widow in *The Field*.

My father's death had an awful effect on her. He died in the bed beside her. She always had a nervous disposition anyway and the shock of that exacerbated it. She is still more tuned in than any of us but my mother has literally been in mourning since losing my father thirty-seven years ago.

At the time, she just had to keep on going. Things were very tight but she was a great provider. She had an account in a small book at the local shop which she would settle every Friday. She had the widow's pension and my father had a council pension. It didn't amount to a whole lot but my mother always made it stretch as far as she could. I never wanted for a hurley with Hanly in school, and, luckily, four of the lads were already working at the time and were able to help out my mother. They all paid their keep. I don't know what other people think of us but the one trait I always felt we had as a family was decency.

My brothers and sisters were always very kind to me. Michael was incredibly generous. He had a decent job but he also brought in a few extra bob from fishing. It was a custom passed on to him, Paschal and Martin from my father. Hurling was my father's passion but so was fishing.

Fishing was always a part of Clarecastle's heritage because the river Fergus runs right through the village, meandering its way around the quay before connecting to the mouth of the Shannon eight miles down the road in Newmarket. Salmon drift-net fishing was always popular in the village and my father would often drain every hour of the day at the river.

They couldn't fish before six a.m. on a Monday because the licence wouldn't allow it. They were also only allowed to fish a certain part of the river. My father had a drift-net licence, where you would let the net drift off the boat and hope the salmon would swim into it. A good run could snare forty salmon, which was a huge haul. At the time, salmon was around eighty pence a pound and there could be a heap of ten-pound salmon among the catch. It was a great source of income for young families. The restaurant owners would be waiting at the quay to buy the fresh fish. It often provided my mother with enough money to purchase the school uniforms and books we needed.

If the river was flush with salmon, my father would come home and sleep for a few hours, then get up and with a few sandwiches and a bottle of cold tea head back down for the rest of the night. After heading off to work in St Joseph's Hospital and retirement home, where he was a caretaker, he would come home and fish again that night.

He worked hard, but he was a trooper for the cigarettes as

well. That was just the tradition in the 1950s and 1960s. He could have smoked up to fifty or sixty fags a day. There were no health warnings back then. It was almost cool to smoke. My mother once told me that if you were courting a fella and he didn't smoke, he was deemed a bit of a yahoo.

The nicotine probably didn't help his health, especially when there is a history of heart disease in the family. There were nine in my father's family and heart disease and cancer claimed eight of them. My mother was the only girl in her family but her three brothers were all clean-living. One of them, Mickey, never married or drank or smoked and is still in great health in his mid-eighties.

My mother's father, Jack, was a drummer in the famous Tulla Céilí band. He once played with them in Carnegie Hall in the 1950s. My uncle Chris even wrote a book on the band's history. Another of my uncles, Sean 'Flash' Keane, who we buried in 2013, also played drums for the band. He was a massive clubman and a much-loved character around the club. He played in goal for the Juniors for years before becoming Junior/Intermediate manager for decades. Flash's dressing-room speeches were legendary, but that side of the family were the pioneers and musicians, clean-living and aesthetically minded. So I always say that I brought the baldness from the Keanes and the hurling from the Dalys.

My uncle John was only fifty-three when he died of a heart attack in 1973. Haulie, who never smoked, squeezed a few more years out of life but a heart attack also claimed him in 1991 when he was sixty-nine. It also took my brother Paschal. He was just forty when he passed away.

In our house, there were three small bedrooms upstairs. My parents slept in the smallest one, a little box room. I was in a cot in that room until I was about three. My three brothers were in one room, my four sisters in the other one. When it was time for me to receive my pass to the big bad world next door, Martin had to shove over in the double bed to make way for me.

Paschal and Martin slept with their heads at opposite ends of the bed before Paschal left for England when he was nineteen. That wasn't long after my father died. He had left school early and there wasn't much work around at home. I wouldn't have really known him at that time. He was eleven years older than me. In his eyes, I was the baby. But as we got older, we became great friends. I would travel over to England to visit him; he would come home every year for two weeks to go fishing. He loved the pastime as much as my father had.

Paschal died the night before the 1998 All-Ireland hurling final. We had been beaten by Offaly in the semi-final after a three-game saga that eventually turned into a fiasco, but I had no intention of moping around or feeling sorry for myself on the weekend of the final. I went to Dublin on the Saturday with my great friend Tadg Collins.

My phone rang the following morning at 9.30. It rang about ten times before I realized it was easier to answer it than break it against the wall or let it wreck my head any longer. The number was our house phone in Madden's Terrace. It was my brother Martin.

'Come home,' he said. 'Paschal is dead.'

I just hung up straight away. It was one of those old mobile phones from the 1990s that were as chunky as a hand grenade. It was as if it had just detonated in my hand and completely concussed me from the shock.

I didn't know where I was. I lay back down on the bed but sleep was not my priority. I stared at the ceiling for fifteen minutes, my brain trying to compute what I had just heard. I wondered if it was Paschal Russell Martin was referring to. Paschal Russell was about fifty but had only just finished up playing junior hurling. It would have been a major shock in the village if he had passed away. I was great friends with Paschal, but then I realized that Martin would surely have rung me back to clarify if it actually had been Paschal Russell.

I redialled the number. My sister Stephanie answered. She was bawling crying. I asked her what was wrong.

'Paschal is dead,' she said.

My brother had died during the night. Paschal had worked for British Rail and had been on call. He was repairing tracks in the centre of London at some ungodly hour when his heart just gave up. His wife Anne spent three hours with him in the mortuary before the news was broken to the rest of the family.

It was a lonely place to go. If we had been in the All-Ireland final, he would have been home for the game. He would have been staying with my mother. Maybe it would have happened anyway at that time but you would always wonder. If you thought any more about it, you could drive yourself crazy.

Tadg drove like one of the guys from *The Fast and the Furious* on the way home. At one stage I remember saying to him that there was no point in the two of us being dead as well. We hardly spoke a word. I said to him that I couldn't believe this was after happening, that I would only really believe it when I got home.

I asked Tadg to drop me home in Ennis, where I lived at the time, to meet my wife Eilís. She didn't want to go down to the house on her own so we went together. When I walked in the door, everyone was sitting in the front room. Most of them were crying. That's when it fully hit me. I knew then that Paschal was really dead.

My mother was in the corner and I went straight over to her.

I hugged her and started bawling crying. I was hysterical, like a child. I might have cried in the past after losing a county final, or been upset at a funeral of a club member, but I had never let go like this. The tears flowed out of me like a flood. I grabbed my mother in a bear-hug and was holding her so tightly I was almost squeezing her delicate frame. Michael said to me afterwards that my entry was the worst moment of that day. Something had clearly snapped inside me, something which echoed back over two decades.

Michael, Martin and Patricia went over to England for his funeral because Paschal had his own family, along with a whole community of friends in Camden, who wanted to say goodbye to him before he was buried in Clarecastle, twenty yards away from my father. I wanted to be there, especially for Paschal's wife, Anne, and his two kids Tomás and Clare, but my mother needed someone to be with her for the week and Michael felt that it would be best if it was me.

When Paschal's remains were finally brought home six days after he'd passed away, the undertaker Joe Daly asked us if we wanted the coffin to stay open or be closed before the wake began. We were slightly nervous about the passage of time but I certainly was hopeful that the coffin would be open. I just desperately wanted to see my big brother.

It was a very sad moment for me, but when I saw Paschal, he looked just like the Paschal I had always known. Still my big brother. Still my buddy. A large part of my heart lay in that casket with him.

Paschal loved life and always tried to do the best for his family. You love life and you try to live it to the fullest, but nobody can hit harder than life itself. Life gives so much but it can also take in an unforgiving and devastating fashion. A couple of years ago, my young cousin David, Chris and Janette's son and

Philip's brother, had just finished his Leaving Cert when he went off to the Oxegen music festival and came back complaining of feeling sick. A diagnosis in the Galway Clinic a couple of days later confirmed he had leukaemia. He passed on the following year.

Life just keeps on moving, with or without you. Paschal's family are still in London. His beautiful daughter Clare has a young son now, little Henry, whom Paschal would have been so proud of. Paschal's death has left a terrible void in all of our lives. We all still miss him desperately, but life just moves on. And you have to move on with it.

A week after we buried Paschal, our first child, Orlaith, was born. I called in to my mother's house that day to be with her. She was crying, welled up in a ball of emotional grief and happiness. She had just buried her son but now had a new baby granddaughter.

I hugged my mother tightly and whispered to her gently. 'There's one gone out of the world and another one after coming in,' I said. 'That's just life.'

It just is.

3

Murty's Gang

Martin Sheedy, my clubmate and great friend, tells a great story about the morning after the 1991 county final. We had beaten Scarriff on the October Bank Holiday Sunday but Martin was working in the airport in Shannon from nine till five. He knew he would get away at lunchtime and that the craic would only be kicking off again around that time anyway. He was hanging but he didn't have to wait long for the cure.

As soon as Martin walked into the locker-room, he spotted Pat Joe 'Cock' McMahon, who had started his shift an hour earlier. Cock had a damp dishcloth across his forehead, a large gin and Coke in a Coca-Cola plastic cup, the *Racing Post* in his hands, his shoes and socks off and his toes being glazed by a two-bar electric heater. Cock was curing himself and picking out his horses for the day, but missing out on the fiesta in the village was still killing him. 'Who would be inside in this fucking place on a Bank Holiday Monday for double time?'

Cock had a thousand different lines and I heard nearly every one of them. He was Sparrow's uncle, a massive hurling man and a great friend to all of us. When I lived at home, he had this habit of calling the Monday morning after a big game. My mother went to ten a.m. mass every day and Pat Joe would always arrive at one minute to ten. The door would open and he'd roar up the stairs. 'Douge, get up out of that bed, your mother has a rasher and an egg left out for me.' Like a lot of people in Clarecastle, Cock called me Douge. All I know is that it was a nickname which was also somehow attached to my father. I'd be shook from the night before, telling Cock to clear off, but I still always came down. 'Make coffee, Douge, and make it a good one,' he'd say to me. 'You can go back to bed but I'm hanging.'

Every village and parish has its own unique personalities who add to the character of the place. The identity of a people is framed and cultivated by them because we often measure ourselves against these great characters who grew up down the street. In Clarecastle, we mostly measured ourselves against the great hurlers who went before us, but our spirit and personality have been formed from that singular amalgam of character, history, friendships and madness which glues it all together.

Hurling will always define who we are, but one game will never fully define the true character and personality of a parish of people. Hare coursing may seem like a sub-culture, but Ennis and Clarecastle Coursing Club is one of the oldest clubs in the country. Cock's brother, Mickey 'Dart', always had dogs. So did Sparrow's family. We never had dogs when I was young, but Haulie was one of the head honchos of coursing in the village because he did so many stints as the club's chairman and secretary. My brothers Michael, Martin and Paschal were all engrossed in coursing. The sport is often portrayed as cruel and barbaric, but two greyhounds chase a hare by sight, not by scent, and dogs are tested on their ability to run, overtake or turn a hare rather than hunt it down for lunch.

From when I was six I would tag along with Michael and Martin and the sport soon became a passion similar to theirs. If nothing else, it was a chance to get a bottle of Coke and a bag of Tayto on a Sunday evening. The club would always run our coursing meeting around Christmas, so from 1 November we'd be gone every Saturday and Sunday trapping the sixty or seventy hares that we needed.

When Michael got older, he had this dog with Danno Moloney called Too Hasty. Paddy 'Conjurer' Moloney reared the dog and it was my job to feed him. He would ate you alive but it was my first emotional investment in a dog because I felt partly responsible when I used to watch him run.

Being brought to a couple of the annual National Hare Coursing meetings in Clonmel in the 1980s inflamed my interest. The Clonmel meeting is the Mecca for the Irish coursing public because it's the sport's All-Ireland final. The fire dimmed once hurling took over and I started making Clare teams, but it began blazing again in the latter part of the 1990s. The craic was always deadly for Clonmel and I couldn't resist it any longer. I would be minding myself in January so I could let myself go for a couple of days in early February. I wouldn't tell Loughnane, but he knew that I'd slipped away for a day or two. Tony Considine knew as well, because he would sometimes go, but they always turned a blind eye.

'How was Clonmel?' he would ask when I arrived back on the Thursday night for training.

'Ah Jeez, Tony, I just went down for an auld look.'

The buzz every February in Clonmel is electric. Naturally, it's not everyone's fancy. You'll have the tiny band of animal rights protesters outside the gates with their placards and megaphones airing their usual argument: 'Shame on you for what you do.' They are entitled to their view, but I have mine. 'Ah, it's not too bad,' I'd often say when passing the protest. 'Sure, come on in for an auld look and see what ye think.'

The supporters are often more of a danger to themselves than any hare. The place is so packed that you nearly have to book a hotel a year in advance. One year, thirteen of us slept in a room with two single beds. Victor O'Loughlin decided that the wardrobe was going to be more comfortable than some corner of the floor he might be able to claim. He squeezed into the cabinet like a contortionist, and the power of a few pints knocked him out. He got a far better night's sleep than me because I was sharing a single bed with Colin 'Higgy' Higgins and Neil Casey.

My brother Martin can't handle that anarchy any more. He normally does just the one night, but I can never get enough of Clonmel. On the evening of the 2014 Walsh Cup final, I headed south after the match for my fifteenth successive yearly spin.

The place was rocking but I was feeling sick, and singing a few songs didn't do much to soothe a sore throat. I was miserable when I woke on Sunday morning and couldn't even look at breakfast. I drove on to try and fight the virus that was trying to take over my body but it was no use. By early evening, with the party raging downstairs in Hearns Hotel, I was wrapped up in bed with more layers than an onion.

I was sharing a room with Barney Lynch, Leonard McNamara and Tommy Howard, but my bags were packed before they woke the following morning. I was at home in bed in Tullycrine before that day's coursing began. Beneath damp sheets and thick duvets, I had to make do with following final day on Twitter.

Sparrow won a duffer stake, a local meet, once in Cooraclare. It didn't qualify him for Clonmel but we knocked some craic out of it. The prize money was one grand and we drank a fair share of it back in Navin's pub in Clarecastle, rocking into the village as if we had won the All-Ireland club.

For anyone involved in coursing, getting a dog to Clonmel was always the dream. It was something myself and Tommy Howard had often spoken about because Tommy's late father-in-law, George Gallery, was a renowned trainer and breeder from Clarecastle. One night after club training, Tommy told me that George had a litter of pups coming from Cillown Blond, a super bitch, who had been bred to Hilltown, the Irish Derby and Champions Stakes holder and the top stud-dog coming on the scene.

'Jeez, we'd never get one of them,' I said to Tommy.

'Leave it with me,' he replied.

We were having a pint in Navin's a few weeks later when Tommy delivered an update. 'That bitch had seven or eight pups,' he said. 'We might be in business.'

We were. Tommy asked if Michael would come in with us so we opened up a bank account and named ourselves the ATM syndicate – Anthony, Tommy and Michael – which I felt had to be a winner. We named the dog after the pub, with a rider attached – 'Murty's Gang'.

He was reared by George Snr and his son George Jnr but they had too many of their own dogs to train so Old George recommended Gerry Holian, an up-and-coming trainer from Athenry. Initially, Gerry didn't know what to make of Murty. He didn't want to gallop or hardly get up in the morning, but Gerry still decided to run him in a trial in Loughrea on the third coursing day of the season. Once the dog saw the hare, he was transformed into a speed machine. He went up the field faster than any pup. Only one cup dog went up faster than him. We knew then we had something on our hands.

Gerry knew it too, because he didn't run him again for nearly two months. The boys in Clarecastle were calling him the glass-case dog. Eventually, Gerry said he'd run him at the Limerick city trial stake in mid-November. He fizzed like champagne in the first round but was flat in the second. When we went over to the van afterwards, Gerry was doing his usual Grizzly Adams impersonation, holding the dog up to his face and speaking to him like he was a little baby. 'The clock-man has you gone back, Murty. Sure we'll see what the clock-man has to say in the morning.'

Coursing is a bookie's dream because the other dog, the hare, the slipper and the judge can all beat you. We'd got word that the bookie Martin Crowe was giving generous odds on Murty the following day and we put a wallop of cash on him. He wiped the field, and we wiped poor old Martin Crowe. We were through to Clonmel. The dream had come true.

We went back to Clarecastle and celebrated it like a county final. Even my great friend Michael O'Shea from West Clare was there. Mick and myself often enjoy a soothing Guinness together in Murty's. Everyone was delighted for us, but they couldn't help slagging me.

'The first dog ye ever bought and yere heading for Clonmel.'

'I'm ten years buying pups and I can't even get a duffer.'

'Well, they couldn't take the luck out of you anyway, with the hurling and the dogs. Christ, you're one poxy bastard.'

I was ready for all of them. 'Not only are we through to Clonmel,' went my war-cry, 'but we'll rattle it.'

We had to make a decision as to whether we would rest Murty or run him in cup competitions. There is this famous stake in Abbeyfeale, the Corn na Féile, which is made up of sixteen qualifiers for the Derby in Clonmel. It's the third biggest coursing cup after Clonmel and the Irish Cup. Michael was so excited because he never thought he'd have a dog running in the Corn na Féile. Gerry felt he'd win it.

The meeting was on the week after Christmas 2001, the day after Ollie Baker got married in Athlone. Excitement and adrenalin got me out of bed that following morning because I was dying. Murty ran well and qualified for the final rounds on the second day. We had him heavily backed from the outset at 5-1 to win but another dog, Tooned Up, was clocking the best times and went into the final as favourite. We hit the bookies hard again before the race and Gerry turned into the dog whisperer once more. 'Those clock-men have you written off again, Murty,' he said, speaking to the dog with the same affection Ron Burgundy showed to Baxter in the film *Anchorman*. 'But you'll show them, Murty.'

Then Gerry turned to me. 'Dalo, this dog will take a bit of beating because he is jealous. It's like you playing a National League game and playing a Munster semi-final. You'd be a bit more jealous for the championship game.'

Murty won by a length and a half and propelled us into dreamland. There was a picture taken below in the snow in Abbeyfeale, which is still hanging in Navin's pub, where I have my hands around the dog like it's my child. Dinny Goold the bookie elbowed his way into the shot. 'I'm going into this picture because I nearly have shares in this dog with all the money ye have taken off me,' he said.

Those couple of days were magic. I was as lucky as an Irish leprechaun. All I was missing was the stupid green hat and red beard. This fella asked me afterwards if I'd buy a ticket for a hundred euros to support the Abbeyfeale Coursing Club. 'Of course I will,' I said to him as I pulled a ball of cash out of my pocket and bought one. Tommy and Michael bought one ticket between them. 'Ye'll have no luck for being so mean,' I said to them. 'We're after winning the Corn na Féile, taking three thousand euros out of the place in winnings, plus the bag of cash from the bookies.' As sure as Christ, a couple of weeks later I got a call to tell me that I had won the draw as well.

The party back in Clarecastle went on until New Year's Day. As soon as the year turned, the countdown to Clonmel was on. Murty had been installed as the favourite but one of George Gallery's dogs, Cillown Harbour – Murty's brother – had won a really hot trial stake in Miltown-Malbay and was also hotly fancied for Clonmel.

A relation of Cillown Blond (a son of Cillown Glory), Duke of Hearts, had also qualified, but there was drama everywhere we turned. Three weeks beforehand, a man from Cork came to us with a bid to buy Murty. The prize money for winning Clonmel was €33,000 but he made us an offer of €25,000, long before Murty even went up against a field of sixty-three other top-class dogs. We had a meeting but never even entertained the deal for one second. Money was only a minor issue in any proposed transaction. We were living out our dream.

The draw in the Hotel Minella in Clonmel before the festival began was like a Champions League affair in Zurich. Our priority was to avoid Cillown Harbour, but the Corkman who had made an offer on Murty had since bought another top dog, which he renamed Judicial Affair. Lo and behold, Judicial Affair was drawn against Murty's Gang in the first round. There was a gasp among the crowd – it was akin to Real Madrid being pitted alongside Barcelona. You couldn't have made it up.

At the preview evening on the Friday night, Micheál Ó Muircheartaigh interviewed me with a line of questioning as if I was getting ready for an All-Ireland. I was far more nervous than for any game I'd ever played because I had absolutely no control over what was about to happen.

In his opening race, Murty set the tone for what was to follow. He went toe-to-toe with Judicial Affair before taking off once he met the rising ground. He never looked back.

It was still like someone was writing the script. Cillown Harbour was in one semi-final, with Murty meeting Duke of Hearts in the other. Once he met the rising ground again, Murty turned on the afterburners and scorched home. Cillown Harbour also won through, but at a huge cost. The hare wouldn't go home and came back down the field six times. The dogs got thirteen turns compared to the one in the other semi-final. Cillown Harbour was carried off the field.

Murty's times were better and he was far fresher, but he never got the chance to prove as much against his brother. We met Patricia, Tommy's sister-in-law, beneath the stand. She told us that the family were very upset. They'd got to a Derby final and had a big decision to make as to whether they would run the dog. Old George ruled it out straight away. The family were still immensely proud to have bred two brothers to meet in the Derby final in Clonmel. Eventually, Patricia came over to Gerry Holian's van and said that Cillown Harbour was not running. 'It's still a great achievement for us all,' were her words. 'It's a fantastic day.'

I hugged Tommy and we made our way back to the stand. We were not gone far when Michael arrived to meet us. 'Well,' I said, 'we're the Derby champions.' We hugged and broke into tears.

It was an anti-climax, and it actually took away from the dog's achievements in his life. He was named Greyhound of the Year and Coursing Dog of the Year but he never got the credit he deserved. Tooned Up won the Irish Cup the following year. Judicial Affair was the fastest dog in the country the same season. They were great dogs, but Murty's Gang had something different. He wanted it more than any of them.

We were tempted to run him in the Irish Cup in Limerick, which had a winning prize-money pot of €64,000, but we decided against it. We opted instead to rest him for the early part of the following season and then go for the Irish Cup.

But Murty ran for the last time in Kilrush six months beforehand. He went up against Ningaloo in that semi-final and ran faster than ever before. His absolute raw pace took him so close to the hare that when the hare veered in under the escape, Murty hit the thatch of grass with an unmerciful thud. I thought he was dead. So did everyone else. He was just slightly injured, but our decision was made. He had been unbeaten and we didn't want to take any more chances. We put him out to stud.

He returned to his brother Cillown Harbour, but they growled at each other every day of their lives. They never got on. It was as if they knew. It was like they were both saying to each other, 'I'd have beaten you anyway.'

Cillown Harbour produced the finalist of the Oaks in Clonmel the following year, while Murty later sired a classic winner, the son of Sandy Sea, who won the Irish Cup. Murty had his way with thirteen bitches that season but the pups never amounted to any success. Eventually he threw Murty's Blaze, which was a great dog for us. He was beaten in the final of the Corn na Féile and was well fancied for the Derby until he got sick two weeks beforehand. He won three cups before being narrowly beaten in the semi-final of the Champions Stakes by Boavista, who was part-owned by the actor and former soccer player Vinnie Jones.

The line has been going strong ever since. Murty's Destiny was the fastest dog in Ireland in 2006 and he went to Clonmel as one of the favourites that season. Murty's for One was another very good dog. Murty's Blaze had nineteen bitches at stud in 2013 and maybe another Derby champion will be among one of those pups.

I'm still involved in another couple of syndicates but some of the coursing diehards think I'm only a come-day-go-day guy. I'm just so caught up with hurling that I cannot make the same number of meetings. Even our own coursing meeting last year clashed with the U-16A final, which Clarecastle were involved in. Naturally, I went to the hurling. Hurling will always be my first love, but there will be six foot of clay on top of me by the time I'm finished with the dogs.

When we were presented with the cup and crowned Derby champions in Clonmel, I sent out an open invitation in my acceptance speech. 'We'll see ye in Johnsey's in Oola for one,' I said. 'And we'll see ye all in the village.'

Half the country seemed to take up that offer. Clarecastle was like Mardi Gras. Navin's was packed like Copper Face Jacks on an All-Ireland final night.

Up the road in Madden's Terrace, Cock was on his deathbed in his sister Helen's house, Sparrow's home place. Riddled with cancer and in his final days, he called Sparrow's brother, Fergie.

'Fergus, get my suit ready, I'm going down to the village.'

Fergie couldn't believe what he was hearing. 'PJ, you're going nowhere. You can't move. You're only after getting morphine twenty minutes ago, don't be codding yourself.'

'Fergus, Douge is after bringing home another All-Ireland and I'm going down to celebrate with him. Get my suit ready.'

Fergie got Cock up and got him dressed. He drove him the short distance down the road but he couldn't make his way into Navin's with the crowds. In the cold February air, he sat outside on the windowsill. Mrs Navin, who was alive at the time, was a great character and friend of Cock's. She was a lovely person and was always minding him, giving him a glass of Guinness when he'd had too many. She handed him a naggin of brandy and slipped it into his top pocket.

'You wouldn't give it to me when I wanted it, you oul bitch,' he said to Mrs Navin with a smile.

After a while, word filtered through that Cock was outside. I couldn't believe it. I had heard in Clonmel that there wasn't much left in him. I was just hoping that he'd hang on, that I'd get to see him once more. I ran out the door and there was Cock, dragging on a cigarette, sipping his brandy, luxuriating in the final days God had granted him.

I put my arms around him and wrapped him up in a huge hug. He was gone to nothing but we sat down on that windowsill for a priceless and precious half hour. We laughed and we cried, we cried and we laughed. Eventually I turned to Cock and just looked him in the eye.

'Cock, let yourself go now,' I said. 'Don't fight it no more. Fair play to you for coming down tonight, but don't suffer on. Let yourself off.'

'You're right, Douge.'

Cock went back up to Helen's house and told her about the golden time we had just spent together. 'I had a great chat with Douge below,' he said to her. 'Tell [Dr] Bugler to bring plenty of morphine. I'm not going fighting this no more.'

The party was still in full swing the following evening at five p.m. when the news came through. Cock was gone.

He had let himself go.

4

The Hard Road

Tuesday, 11 February 2014

Five days before our opening league game against Galway and you wouldn't put a dog out. The weather has gone haywire. The eighth storm to hit the country since 18 December is forecast for the south tomorrow. It has been the wettest January and February I can remember. Pitches are like paddy fields. There have been some nights during training when you'd think you were stuck in a biblical plague.

Every team has had to deal with the collateral damage of nature's power and rage. Nowlan Park even lost the roof of its stand. The roaring and shouting and baiting they did against Tipp last year must have loosened the screws and hinges. Pitches and facilities and trying to cram in some decent hurling training are ongoing issues for everybody. We're in St Anne's Park in Clontarf and we're damn glad of it. The pitch is in excellent shape considering that raindrops have been hammering off the sod like golfballs all afternoon. The only reason we have been able to swing a session here is because Hedgo lives just up the road. His daughter plays football with the club and his street cred is good.

I smile ironically when people say it to me about the comfort I must have up in Dublin. They probably think I'm like José Mourinho swanning around Cobham. Here we are, on the edge of a public park, or begging John Henderson to let us in to Bray, or in the dark every Tuesday night at this time of the year in O'Toole Park.

None of the top teams are training in their county grounds at the moment but at least they have more centralized alternatives. We don't have the same access to Parnell Park, but it doesn't matter much anyway. The Thursday night before the 2011 All-Ireland there were weeds – tracers as we used to call them – growing up through the grass. It was a throwback to when we were young and we'd go off picking mushrooms on summer mornings. You would push the mushroom down the trace of the stem before pulling it out at the base. People on their way to work in Shannon would often stop on the side of the road and buy them fresh off us. Richie Stakelum had a different term: he used to call them trawneens. As we plucked them from the ground that Thursday night before we played Tipp, I said to Richie, 'Imagine the contrast between this and Thurles.'

Gary Maguire caused a major stir last year after we played Wexford. He publicly stated that it looked as if a herd of horses had been let loose on the pitch. Gary said we were playing 'second fiddle to the footballers', and some people threatened to resign over the accusations.

What happened a couple of weeks back was a disgrace. Our match against UCD in the Walsh Cup was called off because Parnell Park was unplayable. We never opened our mouths and played the following Tuesday. We looked for Parnell that week-end ahead of the Walsh Cup final but were refused. Then the footballers sauntered in and played three thirty-five-minute periods against Cork. The pitch now looks like a herd of elephants was let loose on it. And this on the same ground where we have our only two home league games, both of which are against the last two All-Ireland champions.

With the atrocious weather, Parnell Park will be like something you'd see at the National Ploughing Championship. Then by the time we get to May, it will be as bare as a desert. It's grand for football but it's not conducive to fast hurling.

We've often just had to make do. Back in 2010, we got Trinity College's grounds in Santry Avenue. Joe Morgan had the hurling field in great shape for us but we'd often have to clear bottles and cans off the pitch from some party the previous night. We were in the middle of a match one evening and this fella drove across the pitch on a motorbike. He must have thought they were re-filming *Eat the Peach*.

John Costello will always do his best for us but there is only so much he can do when there is no centralized training facility or one ideal hurling venue which we could have continuous call on. I keep having this vision of Tipp and Kilkenny training below on a carpet. Clare, Cork, Limerick, Wexford, Galway are also mostly based in their main stadium. Meanwhile, we're training in public parks. Lads are running after loose sliotars like pet puppies. There's no atmosphere during training matches. I'm like Bruce Springsteen after one of his concerts – hoarse and sweating like an animal. At least Bruce has a microphone. Half my audience can barely hear me.

We went down to Castlemartyr in Cork last May for a training weekend. We did a couple of sessions in Carrigtwohill and there was a beautiful sward of grass on the main pitch. As the bus pulled into the ground, I could hear this collective gasp. We walked the pitch before the first session and lads wouldn't have been any more in awe of a patch of grass if they had smoked it. We went in to Páirc Uí Chaoimh that Sunday morning and the pitch was immaculate. I remember saying to Conal Keaney that Wexford Park will be as good. And it was.

We really are dependent on the generosity of certain clubs. Clondalkin have been very good to us. So have Castleknock, only they don't have dressing-rooms. The physio tables would be lined up along the sideline. Depending on the weather, the physios might not even need lotion when they are rubbing lads – there is a constant flow coming from the sky.

In recent winters we had the use of Balgriffin Inis Fall/ Innisfáil's pitch on the road to Portmarnock, but the footballers got first call on that place last winter. It's not a whinge against the footballers because the county board have been very good to us in plenty of other ways. The facilities just aren't really there. For the clubs, having a quality clubhouse and gym is almost prioritized ahead of a decent pitch. Maybe that's because there isn't the same emphasis on the club championship.

I got an awful shock one night when I went to watch Faughs and St Vincents in Tymon Park. It was on in pitch number seven. The grass was half a foot long. The place was so open that if something kicked off, there could have been a riot. All it was missing was a big tent. It was like a circus instead of a championship match. How is a championship going to develop in those conditions? How are good players going to improve?

Dublin has so much going for it as a county – numbers, clubs, enthusiasm. In trying to make a hurling culture permanent, though, Dublin hurling has got to stand up for itself more. To demand the best for Dublin hurling as an entity, as a thriving culture. In that organic system, a pervasive and continuous culture of winning will grow stronger all the time.

The Dublin footballing tradition will always thrive, but that doesn't mean that the hurlers should accept their place in that perceived natural order. You risk falling out with people but you have to challenge that natural order if you want to improve.

When I was involved with the Dublin U–21s in 2010, I had a run-in with Pat Gilroy over releasing Rory O'Carroll. We had a few heated phone calls. We both got it off our chest in the media. He was just minding his corner in the same way I was minding mine.

Similar to Gilroy, I wouldn't have known Jim Gavin before he took over the footballers. Martin Kennedy had agreed to return as strength and conditioning trainer with the hurlers before Gavin wooed him. Kennedy is a businessman. But he is also primarily a football man and he understandably saw the footballers as a more attractive option. Winning an All-Ireland last year franked his decision, but Dublin hurling has got to make its culture strong enough to withstand that emotional urge.

Tomás Brady left the panel last year to join the footballers. When Ciarán Kilkenny returned from Aussie Rules at the outset of 2013, somebody close to him told me that he was very keen to play hurling and football. I made contact but never actually met Ciarán. There was more talk again at the start of this year that he might hurl but it was widely reported at the time that Gavin ruled out the possibility of dual stars.

There always seems to be a complication with hurling when the dual-player issue raises its head. Some people were annoyed that I didn't make a stronger push to enlist Cormac Costello and Eric Lowndes when they finished up as minors. That is just not my way. I invited them to our first meeting and asked them to hear what we had to say before they made any decision. Just before the meeting was due to start, I received almost identical texts from both that they were going with the footballers. You wouldn't need to be a genius to work out that they were probably given a directive.

That's fine, but there are right ways to do these things. Be straight. Be upfront. Of course you want the best for your group, for your crowd. You want the best players. There are complications when they are dual players but let them make up their own mind.

Every serious player wants to play on the biggest stage, but it has to be about more than just the big summer Sundays in Croke Park. The glamour of the football team will always be an irresistible counter-attraction but you have to follow your heart. Play the game you really love. If you love both, let your heart guide you, not the lure of greater glory.

If I have achieved nothing else in my time with Dublin, I hope my most important legacy is not the medals won or glory gained. It will be about the attitude instilled, the standards demanded. The example we set as a squad. The culture of excellence which defines Dublin hurling. A culture that in time will hopefully be on a par with football.

Anyway, I've enough worries rummaging around my head without being overly concerned with pitches and dual players and the footballers wrecking Parnell Park. We have to drop seven players tonight and the thought of doing it has been sitting in my stomach all day like acid.

It's the one part of this job I cannot stand. When I was Clare manager, I'll never forget telling Tyrone Kearse he was dropped off the panel. He is my cousin, and I always had great time for Tyrone. I had coached him all his life. When I delivered the news that night, he was hurt and emotionally upset. So was I.

That was an extreme case because of my Clarecastle connection to Tyrone, but letting guys go is never easy. Some lads have had an issue with getting a release letter at the end of the season but my feeling is that when the year is over, a new panel is in place. I never felt the need to go ringing a fella. On a couple of occasions, fellas rang me instead. Davy Byrne called at the end of 2010 and told me I was making a big mistake. He was a great guy, a super trainer. He told me that he still had a lot to offer, but I just felt that he didn't fit our plans. He was hardly willing to accept it and I was genuinely upset for a day or two afterwards.

Delivering bad news never gets any easier, but when we picked the extended panel before Christmas, we went for characters. The seven guys we dropped tonight were all disappointed but they were strong enough to take it on board. To a man, the seven of them thanked us.

Sunday, 16 February 2014, Pearse Stadium
Galway 0–28
Dublin 1–12

Holy Jesus.

Half an hour in, my head was spinning like a tumble drier. We were getting leathered all over the pitch. Galway were cutting us to pieces, opening us up like pathologists. And yet, you would not believe the shit that was flying around inside the tumble drier.

The strain of viral pneumonia which buried me below in Clonmel has been in my system ever since. I missed two sessions that week but I crawled out of bed on the Saturday for a challenge game against Offaly. The following day, I travelled to Ballinasloe to do some scouting work on Galway in the Interprovincial semi-final between Connacht and Munster.

On Tuesday morning, I texted David Treacy to enquire if he was playing for UCD in their Fitzgibbon Cup match that day against Mary Immaculate College. He was starting at number

11 so I jumped in the car and hit for the capital. Tray was our only player on show but he had missed four weeks' training and I wanted to check his form.

I got frozen above in Belfield. It snowed solid for twenty-five minutes. When the game was over, I hung around the lobby of a hotel for three hours trying to warm up. I read one newspaper about three times. I was in Clontarf at 6.15 for a 7.30 p.m. start. On the way home, I felt like death warmed up. By Thursday, I looked it.

Still, I pointed the car east and started gobbling up the miles. I was gone through the toll bridge in Limerick, which is normally the point of no return, but I got a weakness near Birdhill. I rang Dr Chris Thompson and he told me to cop myself on and turn around. He had admitted twenty-eight people to hospital in the previous two weeks with viral pneumonia. It was rampant. 'Not only will you give it to three or four lads in the dressing-room,' said Dr Chris, 'you'll kill yourself coming back down that road.'

When I got home, I rang Richie at 8.45 p.m. to check how the session had gone. I spoke to Shane Martin ten minutes later and he reaffirmed what Richie had just told me. It was reportedly a great session. Tommy Dunne had kept it to one hour and five minutes to keep them fresh for today.

And yet, coming up to half-time, missing Thursday night's session was hammering away inside my head like a woodpecker going to war on the bark of a tree. 'I let them down. That's the reason they are flat now. Was I soft in myself? Should I have kept going?'

I knew I would have made bits of myself if I had, but the tumble drier was at full heat throughout the day. Galway is only up the road from Clare but I drove to Dublin last night and came down on the bus with the lads this morning. Seán Shanley, the vice-chairman, drove my car to Galway so I could just skip home afterwards.

Sometimes, I ask myself if I am being over the top. Should I have just met them in Galway? Is that me not allowing more control? Then when I do, I'm afraid that we don't have enough players to assume the leadership and drive it forward. Players need to be able to realize that they don't need to be molly-coddled, but I just could not believe how flat we were. How could there be a twenty-five-point swing from last year's Leinster final? With the nature of the hiding and the importance of scoring differences in this league, we effectively lost three points today.

When the match was over, I let the lads have their shower before I said anything. I was entitled to savage them but I didn't. I barely raised my voice when I started speaking.

'Lads, I don't know why we do half-baked days like this. Rushey, Peter [Kelly], Conal, half-baked is no good. A half-baked Liam Rushe is no good. He is beaten. And you were beaten. Why do ye turn up half-baked?

'We only have a few games in the year. Championship could be over in two days, as has been the case in the past. Why do ye allow yereselves to be mentally unprepared? Are we just cheating each other here? Are we just turning up for training? We are trying to make this thing as professional as we can and yet, when it came down to it today, we were bullied everywhere.

'We knew this crowd were going to be up for it after last year. Yet one team decided, "I'm going to show this fella." And the other team decided, "I'm going to take it." Guys going around looking for excuses. This blame game drives me demented. Fellas getting on to [referee] Johnny Ryan. Let me get on to Johnny Ryan.

'How can we go from our last competitive game, where we

were in tears leaving Croke Park, to what we produced out there? We were good enough to win the All-Ireland last year. I have no doubt in my mind about that. We had a bit of bad luck. But how can we go from that to what we did to ourselves and our families out there?

'Do I have to call ye cowards to get a reaction from ye? I can take being beaten. I just cannot understand why you just fucking give up.'

Ever since the 1993 Munster final, I can't stomach these days where you allow yourself to be annihilated. Why can't we be beaten by five points? Why can't we go down fighting? And yet, when I'm asking those questions, the woodpecker is back, rattling away inside my head. How honest was I today in my own performance?

We promised the lads two years ago that we would reward performance. We took Tray off at half-time but, if I'm being totally truthful, he had been better than Conal Keaney up to that point. Keaney always has the potential to go in full-forward, grab one and stick it in the net. That is often why big-name players get left on. But I still felt very uneasy going to Tray and telling him he was coming off. Even now, I regret it.

There is never anywhere to hide from a day like this. When I faced the media scrum afterwards, I was waiting for one inevitable question. Eventually the *Irish Independent*'s Colm Keys asked it: was I concerned if another opening-day defeat, similar to 2010 and 2012, would preface another barren year like those two seasons?

'I wouldn't think like that,' was my response. 'If I did, I wouldn't get out of bed in the morning.'

For now, we have more pressing concerns than any projections of doom. In hindsight, it was a mistake to train in Clontarf on Tuesday night. That might sound like a contradiction but the muck and dirt of O'Toole Park would have been a better acclimatization process for the mud-pie we've just played on.

I sent Hedgo over to chairman Andy Kettle and Seán Shanley to ask them for the use of Parnell Park for the coming Tuesday evening. Kettle said it was unlikely, given the state it was in. I was bulling because the footballers had wrecked it in the first place. I went back to Kettle with the same request. My tone was light-hearted but it was also underlined with a deadly seriousness.

'Give me the auld form there and I'll sign it and be gone. Sure I'm not far from Clare here.'

Half afraid that the boys might think I meant it, I changed tack. 'What went on out there is no excuse for anything but we need to get into Parnell, even for one of the two nights this week. The footballers have no match there so we have to get first call on it. It won't be great for the Clare match but at least we'll be used to it. The pitch will probably be in complete shit for the Kilkenny match but I don't mind that either.'

Kettle said the weather was promised good and that he'd come back to me. I wasn't long back in the car when he called to say we were good to go for Tuesday night.

The drive home was a nightmare. A thousand things went through my head. You'd be concerned with the performance but thank God there isn't a three-week break and that we have a match on Sunday. Clare are coming to town and are on the crest of a wave after beating Kilkenny today. The Dublin crowd will rock up to Parnell Park. There will be a big Clare crowd. It's a huge game for us, but at least fellas can go out and show now that they have some pride.

When I got home, after eight p.m., I put a post up on our Facebook page. 'Lads, I know ye are still on the road. When I walked in the door, all my three girls were worried about was who was going to get through on *The Voice*. I guess life goes on. But we have to stand up next week. And I believe we will.'

5

Clarecastle

I won my first medal playing for Madden's Terrace against Main Street. We played hurling, football and soccer before a winner was declared. Sparrow was manager, events promoter and medals presenter. He collected 50p from all of us and bought the medals above in Ennis.

Sparrow lived six doors down from us. He was three years older than me but Madden's Terrace was stocked with boys for whom hurling and sport were the passion in our lives. We lived right in the middle of the twenty-four-house terrace, at number 16, and if you include the haul of handball titles the Frawley brothers won, that small nest of houses bagged over twenty All-Ireland titles.

My father put down a path through the middle of our lawn. The O'Loughlins grew cabbage and turnips on their patch while they had a shed out the back for greyhounds, but the Healys had a full lawn and we made the most of that luxury. Stephen Maloney had a field out the back – Stevie's we used to call it – but the grass was usually too long for hurling. Jimmy Flynn, a landowner up the road, owned the field and we'd often have a go at cutting it with a fleet of lawnmowers. If we heard Jimmy coming in the tractor, we'd leg it.

The river Fergus was just beyond that field so we spent most of our time playing in the tennis courts at the end of the estate. After the council first erected those courts, the nets lasted only a couple of months. The ground was perfectly tarred and we ripped those nets to pieces with sliotars and footballs. Tennis balls might have appeared, but rackets never did.

Sparrow was our God. He was the chief organizer of everything, a real wheeler-dealer, a mighty man for arranging matches against the other areas in the village – Church Drive, Main Street, St Joseph's Terrace. The hurling matches were animal, deadly serious. If you needed a goal, it was all in around the square, dust flying everywhere. For the puckout, Sparrow would always have his paw up. If you had to mark Sparrow, you had no hope. He wasn't big but he was always deadly skilful.

There were four teams in Sparrow's league and it could go on for a month – a mixture of soccer, hurling and football. Some kids from the smaller estates dotted around the village would play with the other teams as isolated players but we were never short of numbers. Main Street would come up to us every so often to get leathered. They never had too many skilful fellas but they were mad for road. You could end up marking a fella thirteen years of age when you were eight. If Sparrow told you to pull, you pulled. 'He's a bit windy, that fella,' he'd say.

No matter what happened, Sparrow always ended in credit. He'd collect 50p off us for medals that cost him 20p. He was an entrepreneur from the word go. In his mid-teens he held the distribution rights for the Catholic papers but his margins were so good that he could sub-contract to willing apprentices like myself.

Sparrow built his commercial empire any way he could. He

would run the greyhounds out of their back shed for a few hours to stage music hall shows. A sheet was draped over the clothes line as a curtain, drawn back to reveal a brilliantly improvised stage. Performers sparkled in their mother's head-scarves and make-up. Patrons paid two pence at the door.

We tried anything, but hurling was always our game. In Clarecastle, it was our culture and our heritage. Hurling was, and still is, our one true religion. It's our love and our celebration and our identity. That's what we talk about, dream about. It's our primary source of community in the village.

I grew up during a time when Clarecastle couldn't win county titles but that didn't diminish our culture and the realization of who we were and what the black and white jersey stood for. Our fathers hurled. Their fathers before them hurled. We hurled. It's what we always did. It's what we do. We hurl.

The tradition was passed down to us like a family heirloom, but our headmaster in Clarecastle primary school, John Hanly, stitched it into the fabric of our souls. He embedded it so deeply that it seeped into the marrow of our bones. Jesus, he loved the game. He was so into it. He taught me for fifth and sixth class, and if there was a break in the clouds on a bad day, it was an opportunity to hurl. 'Come on,' he would say, 'let's go.'

We got a great coaching education from Hanly. When the GAA first started coaching courses in Gormanstown College in the 1970s, he was one of the tutors. He instilled that love of hurling in us, but he was strict too and there was no messing with him. 'Yes sir, I understand sir,' you would say to him. Hanly is in his eighties now and we still call him sir.

When he turned eighty a couple of years back, myself and Tommy Howard called down to him with a bottle of whiskey. We were just about to open it when his daughter called to bring him to mass. We'd still meet up the odd time because he'd take a pint and a small one, but he doesn't get out too often. When we do talk, the fanatic in him still shines through. He'd still be nagging me, telling me where I'd be going wrong with the Dubs, and how to go about putting it right.

The passion Hanly instilled in us also strengthened our identity. We were always really clannish, a bit like a cult that you daren't turn against. Even when I went to secondary school in St Flannan's, the majority of the lads from the primary school went there. The first day we went as first years, about twelve of us set off on our bikes down the road – the cult in convoy.

There was a Clarecastle corner in the front building, just in front of the noticeboard, right beside the trophy cabinet. I don't know if it's still there, or whether the teachers tried to break it up, but it was a tradition that continued for years after I left. We'd meet there for eleven a.m. break and reconvene at the same spot after coming back for lunch at 1.20. If anyone crossed the boundary and transgressed into our corner, they'd get pucked on the back of the head. If some fella from Barefield or Ennis strayed out of bounds, we'd pull him into the pack before hunting him with a warning: 'Get out of here and don't come back.' If some fella from Shannon or Newmarket lost his bearings, we'd make sure he didn't make the same mistake again. 'If you don't keep out of this corner, we'll kill you overnight.'

We even had a notorious reputation among the staff. We would gather to talk hurling but we felt like a law unto ourselves. We were always late back for classes. We were definitely always late back from mid-morning break because the group nearly always had to be broken up by a teacher before we'd scatter like a flock of pigeons. 'Get out of here and get back to class. Yere the same every day.'

I loved Flannan's so much that I found it very hard to leave the place. Having repeated the Leaving Cert and being disillusioned with a computer course I took up in Moylish – now Limerick Institute of Technology – I landed back in Flannan's after Christmas for a third crack at it. 'Jeez, you must be fair thick,' one classmate said to me as I took up a seat at the back of a history class.

It was the hardest thing I ever did in my life.

I always wanted to be a PE teacher. It was the reason I repeated the first time, but the points went up and I fell just short. I also needed to get four honours in the one year to get the council grant which would have paid my fees and accommodation. The reason I went to Limerick was because I wouldn't have to move out of home.

I hated that computer course. Because I got a C in honours physics, I transferred into electronics. Fr Willie Walsh, our hurling coach, was a good teacher and he brought some of the hurlers in for extra tuition on a Saturday. It stood to me for the Leaving but I had no real interest in physics or electronics. I could hardly even change a plug.

I was completely disillusioned. Someone told Willie and he arrived down to the house one evening and we went for a spin in the car. We drove to Gort, just inside the Galway border, and drank two pints. I just told him that I hated college. I suppose I was missing Flannan's and the stability and the status I had enjoyed there. So Willie challenged me. 'Have you the moral courage to go back and repeat again?'

The prospect didn't appeal to me, but I had to face reality. 'Yeah, I do have the balls for it,' I said to the future Bishop of Killaloe. 'I will go back.'

Flannan's couldn't have been more accommodating, but it was a horror-show. Guys who had done the Inter-Cert when I had done the Leaving the first time were now in my class. I had a half day four days a week but I was miserable. Every chance I got, I was running home on the bike for fear of being seen around the place. My friends were moving on to their second year in college or to the next stage of their apprenticeships, dating dolls and earning money. I felt like the Bill Murray character in *Groundhog Day*.

I was back in school for two weeks when my mother spotted an ad in the local paper for a job in what was then the Cork-Limerick Trustee Savings Bank. She told me to apply, so I did. I got called for a second interview. A few weeks later, I got the letter to say that I had got the job. So I finally left Flannan's for the last time. There was no going back.

My father hurled with Clare and Clarecastle, and his sons carried on that tradition. Michael won a county senior title as a sub in 1970. He's the guy standing in the back row, on the extreme left of the team photograph, still claiming he should have started. Paschal was a decent player. He played for the Clare minors before he emigrated. Martin was hard and tough. He played an U-21 final once against Broadford and there was holy war. Broadford would fight with their fingernails but Martin was stuck in the middle of it, so he probably started the row. Johnny Corbett, who played with Éire Óg, called to the house one Friday evening to collect money from my mother for a milk round and I answered the door. 'I'm glad Martin didn't answer anyway,' he said to me. Johnny must have had a run-in with Martin in some game and was half afraid that he'd deck him.

He is still very active in the club. When Clare hosted the Féile na Gael in 2010, he took over as Féile secretary and gave the job more time and commitment than he was probably expected to give. I didn't expect any less of him. Growing up, I saw how much hurling meant to him. I also saw how much it meant to him to support me. During the early part of my career with Clare, I had no car and Martin drove me everywhere. When I was younger, any match he ever went to, he brought me with him.

Hurling was our religion and our passion, and that fusion and Martin's enthusiasm made it an obsession for me. When I was growing up, nobody had jerseys like young kids wear now. You never had a jersey, just a T-shirt. When Paschal was U-16, they won a county title and some fella had enough money to sponsor the team and allow the lads to keep the jerseys. My brothers used to keep their gear in the hall press and I was forever sneaking into that press and putting on the jersey. I'd quietly head out the back and visualize myself bringing honour to the black and white.

Once you were old enough to head to the pitch on your own, you never looked back. I was always down at the pitch, especially when the seniors were training. We didn't even have a proper pitch at the time; we trained for the 1978 county final in Catherine Devine's field, a patch of land loaned to us by a local family. When I first made the senior panel nearly a decade later, we used to train in 'The Pump Field', which was owned by Barney Lynch's parents.

We lost that 1978 final to Newmarket – again – but we lost a lot more than a game that day. Clarecastle were trailing by three points late on when Johnny Callinan flicked a ball back across the square that appeared to be going wide. Dermot Fitzgerald doubled on it and rattled the net. Callinan still swears that the ball was in play but it was waved wide. Fitz argued the decision and a scuffle broke out with an umpire, which resulted in Fitz spending a short time in jail.

Dermot wouldn't hurl with Fr Harry Bohan's Clare team that won two leagues in the late 1970s but he was a smashing club player. The Fitzgeralds were a great family. I won a Munster club title alongside Dermot's sons Robbie and Dermot Jr, in 1997. Dermot had always made a huge contribution to the club, but that episode had a terrible impact. I remember it as being an awful time in Clarecastle. The first night Dermot spent in prison, I went down to the chip shop in the village and everyone was outside. It was like somebody had died. There were nearly black flags hanging out of windows because Dermot was such a popular and well-liked figure around Clarecastle. My mother was always giving out about lads fighting at matches but even she said it was very wrong.

It nearly broke us. The club deteriorated so badly that a motion went before the AGM in 1980 opting to go back to Intermediate. Johnny Callinan said if it was passed, he was joining Claughan in Limerick, where he was working at the time.

People were just broken. They felt guilty that they weren't able to do more to protect one of our best players. We spent a full five years in purgatory before Michael Slattery eventually led us out of our misery. Five years seems like a long time for scars to heal and wounds to close but that's how deeply it cut into the club.

Slattery had played on the club team in the 1960s and early 1970s. He had refereed the 1973 All-Ireland final. He ran a huge freight company in Shannon and was a wealthy and ambitious man. My brother Martin worked for Slattery and he'd smuggle me in with the team. He was like a raving lunatic in the dressing-room, but I was in awe of him. Slattery was one of those guys who just got things done. He knocked heads together in 1983 and was a huge unifying force. The senior team trained harder than they ever had and Slattery packed the panel with young players. We reached the Clare Cup (league) final and the county semi-final and were finally on the road again. We got to the county final a year later and were leading with five minutes remaining until Sixmilebridge got two late goals. The 'Bridge went on to win a Munster club title that season. We consoled ourselves with the belief that we would soon be joining them.

Slattery pulled out after we lost the 1985 semi-final but his fingerprints were all over the team that won successive county titles in 1986 and 1987. In the same two seasons, Slattery coached us to successive county minor titles, which laid the foundations for the successful teams of the 1990s. His legacy in Clarecastle was huge. His influence on me was massive.

He had a way of identifying your weaknesses and subsequently addressing them. When I was seventeen, my legs were like knitting needles. To improve my speed, Slattery said I had to make my legs stronger. He showed me a basic squat drill that you'd still see the Dublin fellas do now. I just needed weights. Tommy Hegarty, who played in goal for us, was doing an apprenticeship as a fitter and had access to steel and metal. Hego arrived to training a couple of nights later with two rough-and-ready dumbbells.

Every night before I went to bed, for more years than I can remember, I would do fifty or more of those squats following Slattery's instructions with Tommy Hego's wedges of steel. Those exercises didn't make me run like Usain Bolt but they made my legs stronger. I never had much pace but I got quicker and the progress made me mentally stronger. People started saying that I was well able to read the game. That stayed with me. It wasn't that a couple of dumbbells developed greater intuition. Greater leg strength gave me greater confidence. It enabled me to survive at a higher level because a higher level often looked far beyond me.

In my early teens, there were two accusations consistently

levelled against me – that I was too slow and too soft. The latter term is always like a slap in the face. Even as a fourteen-year-old in Clarecastle, it was the ultimate put-down. In a club that prides itself on manliness, where toughness is a badge of honour, being called soft is like getting hit in the jaw with a baseball bat.

I wouldn't have ever said I was afraid, but I wasn't aggressive. I was shy. I was small and light. When I was fourteen, we played an U-15A semi-final against Wolfe Tones from Shannon and my brother Martin decided to find out if I was as windy as everyone seemed to think. He was manager and he put me on this real hard, tough player – Alan Keane was his name – that everyone else was afraid to go near. Martin even handed me my brief four days before the game. I put down a week of dread but I got stuck into Keane. I knew that I had to put my head down and get through it. I felt afterwards that I had turned a corner.

The turn just didn't seem to lead anywhere. I never made it near a Flannan's U-15 team. I was corner-forward on the Dean Ryan (U-16) side. I was absolutely useless and was taken off in the final we lost to Midleton in 1985. I couldn't make the mid-Clare U-16 team the same season. There were four guys from Clarecastle on the panel and they won the Munster final. I never felt hurt like it. The misery was exacerbated the following year when I couldn't make the Flannan's Harty panel.

I was tormented with hurt, but the feeling became my companion because it drove me on a crusade. I never left a hurley out of my hands for twelve months. I was eating the weights Tommy Hego had made for me. I grew a few inches but I added more power to my frame. I was almost living in the handball alleys in Flannan's. At seventeen, all the other lads were discovering drink and women. The joke with me at the time was that I was in a serious relationship and was sleeping with someone. That someone was a thirty-six-inch plank of ash.

Drink was of no interest to me. I was obsessed with hurling and getting better at it. When we met Kilmaley in the 1986 county minor semi-final, I played the best match I ever played. Fr Gardiner from St Flannan's was at the game. I had really turned a corner. And this time, it was leading somewhere.

Nineteen eighty-seven was a great year for me. I made the Flannan's team which won the Harty and All-Ireland. I captained Clarecastle to the minor league and championship double. I played for the Clare minors. I also won my first county senior title with the club. It was the year which kept on giving.

The only negative was losing my place on the Clarecastle senior team after getting roasted in the quarter-final against Tulla. One of the corner-backs, Frank Roughan, emigrated to Australia a couple of days after we won the final against Feakle, which reopened the door for me. The week before we played Midleton in the Munster club championship, I marked Sixmilebridge's Gerry McInerney in the league semi-final. Magow was the best forward in Clare at the time and I thought I did well on him but management didn't feel I was ready for Midleton's physicality and scoring power. So they put Callinan, a career forward, corner-back on Ger Fitzgerald and Fitzgerald took him for 1-3. I still often remind Callinan about that day. In hindsight, maybe it was better for me that I didn't get to experience Fitzgerald's company. He was a big strong man and Midleton were embarking on a run that saw them crowned All-Ireland champions the following March. That day, they ran a drag with us.

I always fondly think of 1987 as my breakthrough season but there was one barrier I never got the opportunity to clear. We didn't think we had any right to beat the Cork minors but we would have if we'd really believed we could. It stuck in my gullet all year. I gagged on the thought because if we had beaten Cork, we'd have met Tipp in the Munster final.

I was mad for a run at Colm Egan, who was from Kildangan in Tipp. He had been in Flannan's in 1986 but he left after doing the Leaving. I heard back from a few people that he often expressed surprise at how well we had done in 1987 with 'the likes of Daly playing'. He never rated me. He even said it to Fr Gardiner. I played for the Clare U-21s for three years but we never met Tipp. If we had, I'd love to have asked Egan, 'Do you rate me now?'

6

This Is Our Town

Monday, 17 February 2014

The day after the Galway game in February 2014, management had a conference call during the day. We were trying to get to the bottom of what had happened twenty-four hours earlier but it was worthless without the input of the players. We needed to peer inside the soul of the group, so we called the Tuesday-night session for 7.00 instead of 7.30. We went upstairs in Parnell Park and I told everyone to pull the chairs around in a circle.

'Right,' I said, 'let's have it out.'

There can often be too much bullshit talked at meetings like this, but you knew from the minute Richie kicked it off that this wasn't going to be a fake exorcism. It was real and straight and the truth was delivered to some lads between the eyes.

Conal Keaney was the first to speak. 'We talk about our brand, that we're a working-man team and we bring that to our game,' he said. 'We might have had a brand last year but in my opinion at the minute, we have no brand. We have nothing. We don't even deserve to say we have a brand.'

Then Mark Schutte brought up the fact that the bus had been

late. I have worked with Hedgo since November 2008 and in all that time Sunday was the only occasion he got his times wrong. We were there for 1.15 for a two p.m. start and it was the first time he has ever made a mistake. He is absolutely meticulous. I was a little annoyed with Mark, but Gary Maguire did my job for me and went down his throat. There was some other discussion about not having done enough video analysis work on Galway and I was afraid the meeting was going down that road of apportioning the blame to side issues as opposed to the core issue of being outfought and outworked on the pitch.

Then Richie rerouted back to a point which Alan Nolan had made the Thursday night before the match, the session which I missed. He had stood up in the middle of the field in Bray and scolded guys for not challenging each other hard enough in the drills. We thought everything was going great but Noley had identified the root cause of the virus before it was fully exposed in Pearse Stadium. Richie asked Noley to elaborate on what he had said six days ago. 'I think it's been going on for two months,' he said. 'Fellas are codding Ross and youse the management. It's not like two years ago where there was real codding going on but I can smell an element of it again.'

Deep down, some lads had to be admitting as much to themselves. You could read it in the body language. The truth was written across their brows and the hunch in their shoulders. It got guys thinking.

The next two speakers were the most constructive of the evening.

'Are guys mentally preparing themselves a week beforehand for what is coming in these matches?' asked Niall Corcoran. 'I don't think they are.'

Conor McCormack took up that theme of mental slackness. He told a story about a Leinster club game Ballyboden had played a couple of years ago. 'We spoke beforehand about this guy on the opposition and we felt he would shit himself on one of our hard men. He ended up man-of-the-match. We didn't respect him and we paid the price for it. We didn't respect Galway after the Leinster final last year and they were wired. They came out to ram it down our throats. And they did.'

There were a couple of other contributions before I spoke. Hedgo apologized for the bus being late. Eamonn O'Reilly, our physio, spoke about getting back forms that everyone was expected to fill out, which detailed their training loads, especially the guys in college. That was my cue to come in.

'Just on that, Eamonn, have you got all those forms back yet?'

'Dalo, I have ninety per cent back now. In fairness to lads, I know the others are on the way.'

'Hang on, when did you first request this?'

'Five to six weeks ago.'

I cut loose. 'Hold on a minute here now. Conor, your point about respect is well made. But what kind of respect is that for Eamonn O'Reilly, who has been with us for the last three years? Is that respect?'

As I was saying it, I was looking across at two lads who I knew hadn't returned their forms. I was eyeballing them. One of them dropped his head in shame. He had no defence because he had been cleaned out on Sunday.

I didn't want to single out Mark Schutte because he is a super guy but I had to corner him. 'I'm not blaming you now, Mark, but people were going to go down the road here of blaming the bus being late. Ideally we would have liked to be there twenty-five minutes earlier. But did that bate us by thirteen points? Mark, I'm making this clear now, I'm really not having a go at you. But where is the respect for Hedgo and all he has done for ye? [Logistics and kit man] Ray Finn was below in

Salthill at ten-thirty a.m. He sent us back a photo of the pitch and the weather. Where is the respect for Ray?'

I had my stopwatch with me. The meeting had gone on for half an hour before I opened my mouth. When I finished, the clock was at thirty-seven minutes. I might have gone too hard on them but I had been simmering for most of the evening and I eventually boiled over.

'I'm after blowing a gasket there and I meant to say nothing tonight. I'm sorry, but guys need to get their heads out of their holes. We codded ourselves that we were going well against UCD and Wexford in the Walsh Cup. Both of those games could have been lost. Despite what ye all might think, we weren't flying it this time last year either. We were lucky to beat Offaly in the first round of the league out here. Don't cod ourselves either, Loughnane said we were playing constipated hurling below in Wexford Park last June. Now we're after getting the greatest kick in the bollix straight away. Thanks be to fuck we don't have three weeks to stew. Thanks be to God the All-Ireland champions are coming to town on Sunday.'

Before we started training, the stats from the game had armed me with enough ammunition to shame them into embarrassment. Thirty balls went in to our inside-forward line, fifteen of which were uncontested. Jenny Coady, our statistician, said there wasn't a Dublin player in sight for eight of those balls. And that doesn't even contain our stats for shots for points. Damning, damning stuff.

When we played a game during training, fellas went at it like lunatics. Nobody got a free puck. 'Don't bullshit me from now on about too much space,' I said to them all afterwards. 'Nobody got anything easy because fellas wanted to tackle tonight.'

A few of the U-21s had come in to make up the numbers and their manager, Joe Fortune, sat in the stand to observe each individual performance. We spoke on the pitch just after the session concluded. 'There will be no fear of ye for Sunday,' he said.

I hope not.

Sunday, 23 February 2014

The night before the Clare game, Tommy Hegarty, my old buddy from Clarecastle – the guy who had made me those dumbbells, a neighbour I had hurled with since I was a child – sent me a text looking for directions to Parnell Park. Hego is part of the Clare backroom team, like so many others I have known throughout my life.

After I arrived in Parnell, I passed the Clare dressing-room. Seánie McMahon and Fergie McDonagh were at the door so I walked in. 'Well, what way are ye?'

I went upstairs to write my stuff down on a flip chart and to run something by John Costello. I asked him if it was protocol to applaud the All-Ireland champions on the field because I wasn't fully sure if that ritual was only followed on the opening day of the league. Costello said that was how it played out with the footballers in two of the last three years but I didn't want to load any bullets in Clare's gun for later in the year so Costello went down and made the offer to Pat Fitzgerald, the county secretary. The gesture was appreciated but kindly declined.

Before the game began, Hego was doing the hurleys near me so I went over and squirted him with water.

'If you open your mouth, I'll kill you,' I said to Hego as I was trying to hold in the laughter.

'Get away from me,' he said as he tried to avoid the shower.

I was well used to them by this time, but games with Clare were naturally still a little strange. The first time I managed Dublin against my own county, in 2009, we had the chance to officially relegate Clare from Division 1. Mike Mac was manager of that team. Ollie Baker and Alan Cunningham were part of his backroom team, just as they had been part of mine a few years earlier in Clare. A lot of the players who had played under me were still around, including Niall Gilligan. The night before the game, I was staying in the Louis Fitzgerald Hotel and the Clare boys were down the road in the Citywest. I texted Gilly to come down and join me for the craic.

Johnny Callinan also texted me beforehand with a reference to Denis Law, the Manchester United legend, whose back-heeled goal for Manchester City in 1974 appeared to have relegated United, although they would have gone down anyway. 'The Denis Law theory?' I replied. 'Sure, I'm a Tottenham fan.'

There are always more angles than a compass. On the week we played Clare in a qualifier clash in 2010, I did a photo-shoot with Sparrow, who was then the Clare manager. Coming to Ennis for a qualifier in 2012, though, was a whole different ordeal. I knew I was facing into an emotive tornado. And I walked into the teeth of it.

We based ourselves in the Temple Gate Hotel, right in the middle of Ennis, which rests on the site of a nineteenth-century Convent of Mercy. When my father played in the 1949 final, the teams togged off in the Convent before being marched up side by side to Cusack Park – like making a journey from the church to the battlefield. That was something I wanted to invoke, but I emptied everything out of my locker that day. I was facing down my own people. When we spoke in the Temple Gate beforehand, I told the players that my long-dead father had graced the same place before a big game, he had made the same journey that we were going to make now. We were going to march up through the town, through my own people. It was not in my

DNA to bring a team to Clare to go to war against them. But I told the players, 'By God, I am willing to do this for ye.'

When we left the hotel to make that journey by foot, I led the posse. Some people were half shocked. Others were seeking a response, but they knew not to look at me twice. I was charged up on a cocktail of emotion and tension. Michael Carton once said to me that it was one of the most surreal experiences of his life, and he has accumulated a fair few of them in his job as a fireman. Martin Flanagan, the old groundsman in Cusack Park, told me afterwards that the hairs stood on the back of his neck when he saw me leading the Dublin lads in the gate. I was so emotional that when we got to the dressing-room I had to compose myself for five minutes.

At the other end of the tunnel, Clare were dialling up their own emotion. 'They're after walking up through our town,' was the war-cry in their dressing-room. 'Who the fuck do they think they are?'

Our defeat that evening was even harder to take given that we were six points ahead when Clare had Nicky O'Connell sent off early in the second half. I know Cusack Park better than any man. The crowd were turning against Clare. We had inter-cepted one of their short handpasses and drove it over the bar. You could hear the groans from the stand. We did some crazy things with the ball, but after the sending-off it was as if the Park had been transformed into the Türk Telekom Arena in Istanbul, where Galatasaray play. And we felt like Fenerbahçe on the run.

When I visited the Clare dressing-room afterwards, I stood in front of clubmates, close friends and former team-mates. I distinctly remember looking at Brendan Bugler. 'I know you've had your doubters,' I said to him. 'But when Clare needed you tonight, you were the man. I'm delighted for you.'

It was like being in a twilight zone. I was happy for everyone in that dressing-room, especially Fitzy, but that feeling did nothing to tranquillize the pain and devastation coursing through my body. Before I made the short trek down the tunnel I had taken off my runners and was in my bare feet. One reporter subsequently made the analogy in his report of me having been crucified by my own people.

In many ways, that day was a point of resurrection for Clare and Dublin. We went on to win our Leinster title the following season. After winning their first championship match in four years that beautiful summer's evening in 2012, Clare shot through the light and won their All-Ireland a year later.

When Clarecastle were planning their part in Clare's home-coming in September 2013, the protocol was mapped out with military precision. Having the six of us from Clarecastle who were part of Clare's All-Ireland winning panels in 1995 and 1997 on the stage was a central part of the evening's celebrations. It was the club's way of stitching the storied past with the glorious present, but I was still uneasy about the whole event.

I wasn't sure if the balance was right. Sparrow was MC for the evening but many of those Clare players had not performed for him when he had been manager. I had also agreed to go back with Dublin. It was nothing negative against Clare, I just wasn't convinced that we should have been on the stage. 'Look,' I said to Johnny Callinan, 'this is about 2013. This is not about us any more.'

A huge crowd had been gathering all evening but I just made it to Clarecastle before the Clare bus. I had come from a Dublin hurling championship double-header in O'Toole Park and just had time for one pint in Powers before the bus pulled in. When it did, we were on the stage and some of the lads started chanting my name. It was a nice touch and I really appreciated it. Cian Dillon and Fergal 'Bruiser' Lynch even managed to arrange a pint with me through a series of choreographed hand-signals.

As I watched the new generation surf the huge tidal wave of human emotion, I was transported back to those eternal nights when we were carried over the bridge on the river Fergus and into the bosom of our own people. For a couple of seconds, my mind started drifting back and I was trying to imagine how the people felt during our homecoming, especially in 1995. We were way behind schedule and the Gardaí were trying to keep us moving. I remember Leonard McNamara saying to a cop, 'This bus is going no further until those six boys get off.'

When we were being shouldered up through the village, I spotted John Hanly. I saw Johnny and Eamonn Callinan up on a shed alongside O'Meara's shop, opposite his mother's pub where Johnny grew up himself. You could see how emotional Callinan was. I got emotional too.

It was brilliant to rekindle all those memories. Yet no matter how pure those feelings actually were, I couldn't deny the hard questions I was asking myself. Could I have been part of it? Why am I off with another county now? Why am I not in charge of this great young bunch of Clare players? It's like a break-up of a loving relationship. It is sad when it ends. To extend the analogy, you are happy when you hear a couple of years later that the girl you broke up with is getting married. You just wish she was marrying you.

The only reason I had those thoughts was because Dublin were so close. We could have been in the final. We could have been All-Ireland champions. I found the drawn 2013 All-Ireland final, especially the build-up, very difficult. I was training the Clarecastle minor team. The anticipation and excitement around the club was dripping off the walls like wet paint. Hype had enveloped the county like a warm blanket. Songs were booming out over the airwaves. Everywhere was decked out like Mardi Gras. It reminded me of the 1990s. Yet all I was thinking was, 'My team should be there too.'

If Dublin had been meeting Clare, it would have been a complete circus for me. I probably would have had to leave the county for a time to prepare properly. But being spared that prospect didn't alleviate the torment I felt on the day of the game right up until the throw-in.

Every minute was almost a checklist. Would we be in Portmarnock beach now for a walk? What would be going through my head? What would I be saying about Clare? If I met my clubmate Jonathan Clancy during the warm-up, would I give him a hug? What would I say to Davy Fitzgerald? Arrrgghh.

All the remorse and regret had been fully flushed out of my system by the time of the replay. I was able to enjoy the whole day far more. I went bananas at the final whistle.

I basked in the warm afterglow with the Clare supporters that night. Yet by the time I got to Mulligan's on Poolbeg Street, my hard-drive was already rebooting itself. In my own mind, I was planning how to take Clare down. I was thinking, 'We'll have to try and come up with a way of stopping that Clare style of play.'

In Clare, I'd like to think that my passion and love for my county is positively acknowledged and ingrained in the psyche of Clare people. But as Dublin manager, you just have to close off part of your own mind. To try and be as professional as you can, to completely immerse yourself with your own crowd. Now, my own crowd are Dublin.

Clare have their All-Ireland now. They want more, but for the moment they have what we desperately crave, what every part of our being aches for. Winning a Leinster title has only sharpened that desire. This new season has presented us with the chance to heal the hurt we're all still feeling since last year's All-Ireland semi-final, but our opening-day league hiding by Galway picked at some scabs and reopened old scars.

The journey just continues. The battles keep coming. It seems almost ironic, yet apt, that Clare arrive in town now with their swords and shields at the ready. We need to be ready too.

The performance proved that we were.

7

Go Out and Live It

When Clare reached the 1986 Munster final against Cork, the players were lavished with gear-bags and T-shirts. Tommy Keane, who captained the team, never bothered with either. Tommy arrived down to meet the bus in the Abbey Street car park in Ennis, his shirt open almost down to his navel, his socks and togs tucked into his two boots in his hand. He shouted back to whoever dropped him off and said that he'd 'be back home by Tuesday'.

Tommy was wired. No nerves, no hang-ups, he went down to Killarney and hurled a stormer against Cork. It takes all sorts, but Tommy was some character. I played Junior with him a couple of years later. We were playing Kerry in a challenge game in Parteen one evening and there was no sign of Kerry arriving. We didn't know whether to go home or train, and eventually this bus pulled up. 'Harden yereselves, boys, they're here,' roared Tommy. It turned out to be some Parteen under-age team coming back from a challenge game.

There were some amount of characters around Clare hurling at that time, and that was the scene I joined when Sean Hehir – 'The Hack' as he was known – brought me into the senior panel in the autumn of 1988 for some tournament game. We won and got presented with these weird-looking goblets, which are still in my mother's house. I wasn't on the panel when the league rolled around the following year but my form in the local U-21 championship was good enough to earn a recall before the 1989 championship game against Waterford.

John Hanly, my old headmaster, was a selector, along with the late Paddy Duggan from Éire Óg. Duggy was kind of a legend around the county. He was a lunatic in the dressing-room. He had trained me at minor level. He had also trained the Clare minor team to win their first Munster title in 1981. A Galway jersey was famously torn up in the dressing-room before they played Galway in that year's All-Ireland semi-final. It was standard procedure. When I played with the Clare minors, against Cork in 1987, Duggy was the trainer and he tried to tear up a Cork jersey beforehand. It must have been some thick woollen jumper from the 1930s and Duggy couldn't rip the fabric apart. So he threw the jersey on the ground and started jumping up and down on top of it.

The set up was all over the place, but that's just how it was at that time in Clare – run a few laps and play backs-and-forwards. A couple of guys selected in the half-back line for the Waterford game had only just got off the plane from a three-week US tour with the De Beers Inter-firm hurling team, which had won a rake of All-Ireland Inter-firm titles. They were full of porter, but The Hack had already stirred up a hornets' nest when he dropped Seán Stack off the panel. Stack had been a legendary centre-back with Clare for over a decade and was still a God in Clare. The Hack had soldiered alongside him on the Clare half-back line for years, but he had no truck with sentiment.

The four Clarecastle lads – Sparrow and his brother Victor, Barney Lynch and I – travelled to the game in Sparrow's blue

Fiesta. It was a sweltering hot day but the pre-match meal was a cup of tea and a slice of brown bread and jam. We weren't exactly dining at hurling's top table but we played like we ate – brown bread and jam. We got the shit bate out of us.

The players and management were going down the tunnel at half-time when a famous Clare follower from the old days, 'Spinner' O'Shea from Ennis, was shouting down at Hanly, 'John, will you go in full-forward.' Hanly was striding into his sixties at that stage. Sparrow was beside him and he thought it was a reflection on his performance, even though the ball had hardly gone near the full-forward line.

We skipped the team meal afterwards and decided to go home by Newport, an alternative route back to Limerick through the mountains. Just as we pulled into Ryan's in Newport for a pint, we spotted Spinner traipsing in behind us in his little car. He pulled up beside the blue Fiesta, rolled down the window and started making small talk.

'Ah Jeez, the selectors were cat,' he said. 'I don't know what they were at.'

He hardly had the words out of his mouth when Sparrow went nuts. 'Get out of here you little fucker,' he roared, the spittle splattering from his lips. 'Get out of here or I'll break your fucking jaw.' We nearly had to pull Sparrow back in through the window.

Spinner had an auld banger of a car but he sped out of Newport like he was driving the Batmobile.

That was as much fun as we knocked out of the day. At one stage in the second half, The Hack had turned to me and told me to get warmed up. I was delighted and mad keen to have a go at it, even though we were fifteen points down. Then I heard Hanly intervening, telling Hehir not to bring me on. He was still minding me but I was bulling with him. The only one who got anything from the day was Barney. He was thirty-two by that stage. He had played football for Clare for years and had finally got a shot with the hurlers. Mossy Walsh asked him after the game to swap jerseys. 'Will you shag off,' Barney said. 'I'm after waiting thirty-two years for this jersey. I'll hardly get another one after today.'

The Clare minors got to the All-Ireland final for the first time that summer. St Flannan's and Shannon Comprehensive contested the Dr Harty Cup final. They were the first shots of a revolution waiting to ignite, but there was still this sense of malaise and apathy at senior level.

There was always a certain clique of gear-merchants hanging around the place. The same guys would be complaining for three weeks if they failed to get the wife or girlfriend in for the team meal after a league game. Then you had the county board, who were on a whole different level. They'd be grabbing jerseys off you after championship matches as if we were all living in Siberia and they needed the extra layers for the winter. I never put in for expenses in those days because I didn't have a car, but you were entitled to three hurleys. One year, John Ryan, the treasurer at the time, sent a letter out to everyone who claimed expenses, with his own amendments made to the cheque. The letter included a photocopied article from the old *Cork Examiner* on some auld fella in Cork who used to make Christy Ring's hurleys. 'Good Hurlers Don't Break Hurleys' was the headline at the top.

Tony Kelly took over the team in 1990. TK himself was a polished figure. He taught in Ennis National School and was a really professional guy. He was talking to us about sports psychology before we even knew what the term meant, but most of the players had no ambition or interest in making themselves better players.

We were training one evening in Tulla and TK addressed us on the benefits of 'intestinal fortitude'. He was speaking about Pat Cash and how he attributed his Wimbledon singles title the previous year to 'intestinal fortitude', as if it was a new backhand stroke that had bagged him a load of baseline winners. TK was trying to get the best out of lads but the general attitude of the players was a joke.

We went up to play Down in the league in February 1990 and some of the players went on a massive piss-up in Dundalk the previous night. I had three pints, but there was an all-night party in one room. The first three balls that dropped on top of one of the wing-backs the following day may as well have been raindrops because he certainly didn't see them. On the way to the game, the lads down the back were trying to sober him up with flasks of coffee.

We got promoted out of Division 2 but we lost a league play-off to Kerry, who had been promoted from Division 3, two weeks before the championship. It was a disaster because the winners got a trip to London, which was as good as it got in those days. Myself and Sparrow couldn't even go back to Clarecastle afterwards. We drove through the village, went to Brogans in Ennis and buried ourselves in the bunker of a booth at the back of the bar. John Power sent us down two pints because he knew we were in hiding.

After losing to Kerry, trying to lift momentum and confidence before our opening championship match against Limerick two weeks later was like trying to raise the *Titanic*. Limerick arrived in Ennis and bate the shite out of us.

When I worked in the bank with Martin Coffey, the manager, Clare hurling was on its knees and Coffey often mentioned one name that might help drag us off the ground – Len Gaynor.

Coffey was a north Tipperary man who knew plenty about Gaynor, a hard man and a good hurling man – just what we needed. When Gaynor was appointed Clare manager in the autumn of 1990, I was thrilled.

As soon as he arrived, all bets were off. Nobody had a reputation in Clare at the time but Gaynor probably didn't know any of the players anyway because we'd been hammered in our two previous championship matches by an aggregate of twenty-nine points. That's the form of a crowd of jokers. So he herded sixty names out for a trial and you dared not miss it.

We went upstairs in the clubhouse in Newmarket afterwards for tea and sandwiches and a formal introduction to Gaynor. The standard line in the dressing-room after the two previous championship matches was that we had to put respect back in the Clare jersey. Gaynor got to his point straight away. He wasn't there to get respect back. 'I'm here to win a Munster championship.'

It was refreshing to hear someone talking in those terms. When I was in St Flannan's, I always felt that the hardest part of winning a Harty Cup medal was getting on the team. If you made it, you always had a chance of getting that medal.

We would go down to hurling fields all over Munster and knock North Monastery, Midleton CBS, St Finbarr's Farranferris and Thurles CBS out of our way. They were stocked with county minors and we didn't give a damn. In the 1987 All-Ireland Colleges final, we played a star-studded St Kieran's team and hammered them.

Hanly first started bringing me to Flannan's matches when I was in sixth class. Flannan's won the first of successive All-Irelands that year in 1982. I was in first year when they retained it in 1983 and those players were heroes to me. You'd get a half day on a Wednesday to go to the match on the bus. The craic was deadly. The atmosphere in some of those games was Fenerbahçe–Galatasarayesque. We'd be on the hill singing songs and roaring abuse at Teddy McCarthy and his buddies from the North Mon. It was epic stuff. All you wanted was to be out there when your turn came.

An influx of Limerick and Tipperary minors infused the college with a stronger sense of belief but there were always loads of good Clare hurlers on Flannan's team. We had an animal side in 1987. On the same day we hammered St Kieran's, Shannon Comprehensive walked away with the All-Ireland B title in the curtain-raiser.

We played Cork in the Munster minor championship in Kilmallock a week later and lost by five points. We were as good as Cork but we never performed. We arrived in a minibus; Cork pulled up in this fleet of black limousine taxis. We were intimidated before the match began, before the Cork boys even got out of those cars. Those players who had meant nothing to us when they wore North Mon or Midleton jerseys suddenly seemed better and bigger hurlers when they had the Cork jersey on their backs.

We just didn't have the same level of belief in a Clare jersey. There was also this theory in parts of Clare – I think it was more begrudgery – that Flannan's was making Clare minor teams too soft. Flannan's had a reputation of being clean, pure ball-players. You were encouraged to be hard but dirt was never tolerated. Jeez, you'd be mortified if you were ever sent off for Flannan's. Even at that age, I knew that theory was pure rubbish. But I was sure of one thing: Clare teams were too soft.

Gaynor was a former Flannan's man. When he addressed us, he said that he had never really liked being a boarder in the school. He had been sent there for an education but hurling was his way of expressing himself. It was his way of telling us that no matter how unhappy or uncomfortable you felt in life, you could always be somebody's equal on a hurling field. He believed that hurling was the perfect forum for expression, for liberation.

'Go out and live it,' he used to say. 'Do your livin' best.'

That's something I took with me throughout life. When I'd go off the rails as a young fella, 'Are you doing your livin' best?' I'd ask myself. 'You're doin' your best to kill yourself, you eejit – get back on track.' And I would get back on track. From that first meeting, Len Gaynor was a huge influence on me.

Gaynor always loved coming to Clare. He was big into set-dancing and traditional music. He knew we were even more passionate about hurling than music but he could never understand why we didn't fully express that passion. Part of that reason, he believed, was that we had a soft underbelly. He said that he could always detect that softness any time he played against Clare. He mentioned the 1967 Munster final and how Clare had effectively rolled over to Tipp.

We weren't going to roll over with Gaynor around. I had great time for TK but his manner was more precise, more technical, too nice. 'The highest hurley wins possession,' he would say. When Gaynor came along, it was rawer, more primal. There was loads of hardy hip-to-hip stuff. 'We want to see splinters of ash flyin' up into the stand, lads' was one of his favourite lines.

There was real steel in Gaynor. He introduced serious discipline. There was no messing around. When we started winter training, the animal in him came out. Mike Mac deserves massive credit for the physical shape we were in by 1995 but it was Gaynor who had begun the beasting process in the winter of 1990. We trained in Crusheen with bales of hay. We would sprint in soggy ground, running towards someone else carrying square bales. When you got to within throwing distance, you'd fire the bale at them. They would have to catch it and sprint with it to the other side. If you didn't catch it properly, the hay would either knock the head off you or burn your puss. If you had your mouth open, you'd be chewing the cud later on in the session like a heifer.

The training got more scientific in the winter of 1991. Ger Loughnane and Louis Mulqueen were part of the backroom team that season and Mulqueen introduced us to weights training for the first time. I really tore into it. I got physically stronger, but I mostly focused on leg weights to try and improve my speed. When we were on the training ground, Gaynor did a lot of the running with us himself. He was an athletic guy and he wanted us to be fitter than we had ever been before.

We didn't win a championship match in our first two years under Gaynor but we were definitely going somewhere. We drew with Cork in the sixth round of the league in 1991 and there was a right good crowd in Ennis that day. I went up town for a few pints that evening and there was a real buzz around the place about how the team had performed. We lost to Limerick in the championship by three points in May. We went down to Waterford the following year after a replay.

Coming home from that defeat, Sparrow retired for the fourth year in a row. Not a word was said between Thurles and Newport until we stopped for a soothing pint. On the next leg of the journey, Sparrow opened his heart.

'Did you see me after the game?' he asked.

'How do you mean, Gerry?' I replied.

'At the final whistle – I waved goodbye to the old stand. A last farewell.'

On the road home, we came to the conclusion that we'd never

win anything, but that was just the general mood of the time. By 1993, after five years of misery, we were finally ready to start winning championship matches again.

8

Fearless Defiance

Saturday, 15 March 2014

On the night Dublin played Kilkenny in the 2014 league, I was strolling around the pitch in Parnell Park with Richie while the lads were doing their warm-up. I looked up to the top of the stand and saw Nicky English in the TV booth alongside Dave McIntyre. Nicky was doing co-commentary on the live broadcast for Setanta Sports, and I was half tempted to send him a text and ask him how he had enjoyed his annual trip to the Cotswolds.

At the start of the year, I told the lads that the only night of training I wouldn't make was the Tuesday of Cheltenham. I had missed more sessions in the meantime because of the viral pneumonia, but that day was clocked in the calendar from the previous November. The 'Clarecastle snooker society' had decided to go to that month's Cheltenham meeting but I couldn't make it because the Clarecastle minors were in the county final the same weekend. Given that most of us hadn't been to Cheltenham in years, we made a promise to ourselves to go gung-ho for it in March. We would travel to the festival in the early 2000s. Nearly every year we would team up with my great friends from north Cork city, Pat Bozynski, Ken Healy,

Aiden O'Callaghan and Brendan Cronin. The craic was always 90 with those lads on board.

The snooker society first began in the early 1990s. There were originally nine members – myself, Sparrow, Fergie 'Tuts' Tuohy, Tommy Hego, Alan Neville, Padraig Russell, Nigel Moloney, Mikey McNamara and Tadg Collins. We used to have monthly meetings and our own tournaments. Tuts reckoned he was as good as Alex Higgins. He was just madder than the Hurricane. We started paying in £20 for trips away but the group gradually got smaller and there are only four of us paying in now. Fellas got paid off when they departed but the spirit of the group never left us.

When we met up in Dublin airport before flying on the Monday evening, Tadg handed me my boarding pass and an envelope of cash drawn from my investment in the snooker society. It was a great couple of days.

When I arrived back, I spent a lot of Thursday preparing for that evening's session. The previous Sunday we lost to Waterford and only scored 1-10, with the goal coming in the dying minutes. Heading to Cheltenham the following day wasn't ideal timing but I wasn't concerned with the performance, despite the result.

On that Thursday I took out my notepad and wrote down in green biro the points I wanted to get across to the players. After the session in Bray, I elaborated on those notes.

Allowing for conditions, we played better against Waterford than we did against Clare. Our workrate was huge and I admired the players in so many ways for it. We had twenty-six scoring chances to their twenty-five. Some of those numbers don't include serious goalscoring chances. We had an opportunity to go 1-4 to 0-1 up but Alan McCrabbe's shot hit Shane Fives' leg and Stephen O'Keeffe wouldn't have seen it. We dropped four balls into the keeper's hand. We killed ourselves with unnecessary frees – six needless, five borderline and one reckless. And yet we still kept fighting. If Keaney's goal had come five minutes earlier, I reckon we'd have got a draw.

I wasn't just dressing up the stats for the sake of being upbeat. To me, the performance was positive, and I wanted a similar attitude and display against Kilkenny. We desperately needed to win, but we didn't hype up the game. We knew them well enough by now. We knew exactly what to expect. 'Them at their best and us at their best, we are better,' I said to the players in Bray the Thursday night before the game. 'I heard Joe Schmidt talk recently about eighty one-minute battles. Saturday night is about seventy-four one-minute battles. Let's see if they can match our workrate. Let's see if they can out-battle us.'

In the end, they couldn't. Eight minutes into the second half, our lads had their backs pressed tightly against the wall. A ten-point half-time lead had been shaved down to three. Kilkenny had a strong breeze and a tornado of momentum behind them. They attempted to ram this increasing momentum down our throat by springing Henry Shefflin at the end of an unanswered 2-1 scoring sequence but we never panicked. We dug in for a battle and ground out a three-point win.

They hauled most of their big guns off the bench but our key players had a far greater influence on the result. Our half-back line was outstanding. So was Peter Kelly. Ryan O'Dwyer won a world of dirty ball in the second half while Danny Sutcliffe bestrode the match like a giant. He ran riot on Tommy Walsh in the first half and ended the match with 1-5 from play. Tommy was gone by half-time and the hair from his scalp was sticking out of Danny's back pocket.

When I read the match report in the *Sunday Independent* the following morning, I wrote down the headline in my copybook and inserted it into my black folder: 'Sutcliffe inspires Dublin to defiant mauling of Cats'.

Fact.

Tuesday, 18 March 2014

The previous evening, I sent director of the Irish Institute of Sport Gary Keegan an email and asked him if he'd be free to take a call. I rang him at an arranged time because I wanted to go over a couple of things ahead of our final game against Tipperary on Sunday. He got straight to the point, speaking about half commitments and how badly guys wanted it. 'Ye are not a Division Four team,' he said. 'Ye are nearly at the top of the mountain. So it's all about taking on a little bit more responsibility now.'

When I dropped the phone, I wrote down the three key points I wanted to impart after our session in Clontarf that night.

1. Squad performance
2. Play with confidence
3. Backing yourself

I also planned to do a group exercise where I would ask them a number of questions, then record the feedback. Something came into my head, so I dialled Gary's number back again. 'I'm going to ask them, "What is expected of me on Sunday?"'

'Oh Jesus, no,' said Gary. 'It's not what is expected at all. It's what is *required*. There's a major difference.'

That got me thinking further. 'Rather than have them all in one large group, should I break them up into groups of six?'

'Absolutely,' said Keegan. 'Otherwise you will have the usual talkers saying everything.'

I left for Dublin earlier than normal because I was heading for Mick Bohan's wake in Clontarf – Fr Harry's brother. Harry was his typical effusive self. 'You think I'm mad,' he said to me when I offered him my condolences, before breaking into a long chat. 'I was nothing compared to that lunatic lying inside in that box.'

The air was raw and cold but it was still a perfect evening for training. The ground was in great shape and Ross Dunphy ran a top-class session. When we broke into a game centred on puckouts and puckout strategy, Shane Martin took the overflow of players to the bottom goal and worked on goal shooting.

It was a long session, over an hour and a half. When the lads had showered, they had food in the two ante-rooms adjacent to the dressing-rooms. It was a boiling dish of noodles, chicken and roast vegetables, with forests of fruit lined up on another table. There was only space for about eight seats in the back-room where the food was being served so Richie and I joined a host of players in the adjoining dressing-room. I like that atmosphere and set-up – guys sitting around, plates on their laps, everyone munching and talking together, not in some hotel where you only chat to the lads at the same table.

The only downside was the place was too small for our exercise, so Hedgo had organized a room in the Clontarf club-house, about a mile down the road. I hadn't a clue where to go and Hedgo's directions weren't much help. I took the second left and ended up along the coast road. When I drove back down the block and circled back to the pitch, I pulled up alongside Shane Durkin's car, with Conal Keaney in the passenger seat. 'Do ye know where this place is? Or do ye Boden boys get lost once ye cross the M50 toll?'

It was like the blind leading the blind. Durkin made a couple of wrong turns before doing a U-turn at a traffic lights and parking down a lane outside St John the Baptist Junior Boys' School. 'Typical,' I said to them once I got out of the car. 'Ye haven't a clue where yere going once ye go to the north-side.'

We strolled up the road and went in through the clubhouse, taking a right past Clontarf Crèche and Montessori school before climbing a huge marble staircase and entering a room on the left with a high ceiling and three huge bay windows.

'Yere all clever boys now,' I said to the group as I stood at the top of the room. 'Ye know the score, ye know the table, the scoring differences. Look, let's play this game on our merits. Two or three years ago, we would have lost that game on Saturday night. There is a new ownership of this team now from ye, but we are going to do a little exercise for fifteen minutes where I am going to ask ye one question, just one question – what is required of you on Sunday?'

'Remember, lads, what is required. Not expected. Not what we hope or wish for. What is *required* of you personally? Men needed now.'

Then Richie cut in to develop the point. 'I don't want to hear that you are going to be committed. *How* are you going to be committed?'

The chairs were positioned around the room in a large square but we broke up into pockets of six. Every group had a pen and a pad and were given six minutes to come back with their responses.

'And we are going to do it as well,' I had said of the management. 'What is required of us too on Sunday?' We had our details documented in four minutes: we would have our two gameplans refined and polished; we planned a conference call for the next day; the team and subs would be named on Thursday night; our logistics would be perfect.

When everyone had finished the exercise, Richie read out the feedback from our group first. Every group raised different points but many of the same themes kept coming up, particularly the one which Niall Corcoran had aired after the Galway game. 'We're going to get our heads right between now and Thursday,' said Ryan O'Dwyer, who was speaking for his group. 'For the moment, Thursday is more important than Sunday. Let's make Thursday a great session before we start thinking about Sunday.'

After David Treacy, Paul Ryan and Rushey fed back the detail from their groups, I went through the three points I had scribbled on my notepad after talking to Gary Keegan.

'The first time I really heard the subs this year was last Saturday night. I heard ye roaring encouragement at the lads on the field the whole way through the game. Look, I know it's tough for lads who are not playing, but that's the unity we need. You heard Paul Ryan there. He said that if he's not starting on Sunday, he's going to be completely tuned in to what's happening, watching where the puckouts are dropping, seeing if he can see any areas he can exploit in the Tipp full-back line, so he is absolutely ready if he comes on.'

Before I touched on the second and third points, I read out the headline from the *Sunday Independent* match report: 'Sutcliffe inspires Dublin to defiant mauling of Cats'.

'My main phrase for all of last year was that we hurl with "fearless defiance". We were fearless and defiant the other night. I thought ye were fantastic, but I want to see that more and more. We got that into our game last year and that's why we became successful.

'We are fearless and defiant when we play with confidence. We prepare our minds just like we said we would so we never turn up half baked again like what happened in Salthill.

We showed defiance against Waterford when we scored 1-1 in the final few minutes. How important could those two scores now be on Sunday if this comes down to scoring difference?'

Then I unfolded a copy of the sports section of Monday's *Irish Examiner*, opening up pages eight and nine of a spread. Titled 'Goodbye to a Genius', the piece focused on Brian O'Driscoll who had just played his final Six Nations match for Ireland and contained vox-pop interviews with thirteen Irish sportspeople ranging from Pádraig Harrington, Ruby Walsh and Sonia O'Sullivan to Rory McIlroy, Sean Kelly and Katie Taylor. 'I don't know how in the name of God Larry Corbett is in there,' I commented. The room erupted in laughter. Lar was well entitled to be there but I just wanted to draw a response with Tipp looming on the horizon.

Each one of them offered their own glowing tribute to Drico, but I focused on Keith Wood's contribution. 'I played Youth soccer with Woodie many moons ago, in 1988, Clare against North Tipp. Now he's a little fat baldy fella like myself.'

I had fourteen lines underlined in green marker, and I read them out. 'What separated Brian from his peers? Well, one of the first things that struck me about him was that I felt he didn't have great eyesight. He used to wear these huge glasses, lenses didn't suit him, and it was only in the last few years that he got laser treatment. So he always had to have great faith in himself. He trusted in himself, and he never, ever second-guessed himself. He backed himself every single time.'

That last line was my selling point. 'What I saw last Saturday night,' I continued, pointing at Danny Sutcliffe, 'was you taking on probably the greatest wing-back of all time, and you backed yourself totally.' I switched my gaze to Peter Kelly. 'I saw you, you mad lunatic, taking off on a solo run up the field like

Forrest Gump.' I had to stop there because lads were falling off chairs laughing. 'But hang on, Hedgo, can I say this? A Dublin full-back four or five years ago would have driven that ball into the stand, am I right?'

'Absolutely.'

'You backed yourself, Kelly. That's what I want to see. Guys backing themselves. We all back ourselves now on Sunday and we bring fucking war into Thurles. I won't forget how Johnny McCaffrey told me that one of their main guys shouted at one stage of last year's league semi-final, "Let's bury this crowd once and for all." On the sideline, they were completely arrogant, nearly making us feel we had no right to be there. Maybe that was my fault, having come from 1B, where we had put everything into getting promoted and had treated the semi-final as a bonus. That's not my or yere attitude now. On Sunday, we bring war down to that place. If we lose, we lose. But we still bring fucking war into Thurles. We are just relentless.'

Fearless. Defiant. And relentless.

On Sunday, Tipp warmed up at the top end of Dr Morris Park, while we went through our routine at the bottom end. We were still going through our drills when they marched down past us, arms all linked tightly together. Before they walked out the gate, they assembled in a huddle, well within earshot of our lads. You knew how united they were. You could hear it in the tone of their conversation. So I started dialling up our audio.

'There will be no lying down today. We'll timber the shite out of 'em if we have to.'

Deep in injury-time, we were three points down. Shane Durkin received a pass from Danny Sutcliffe and smuggled it forward to Ryan O'Dwyer. I could hear Shane roaring to

O'Dwyer, 'A point, get a point!' O'Dwyer couldn't manufacture a shooting chance so he passed the ball back to Shane who played it across the field to Niall McMorrow. Niall was inside the 45-metre line, well within scoring range and with the luxury of time and space. He was clearly thinking of the result, not the mathematical equations that would balance the outcome. He dropped the ball into the square, the Tipp defence got it clear, and the referee immediately blew the final whistle. A two-point defeat would have kept us out of a relegation play-off. A three-point loss landed us slap bang in the middle of it.

I take my share of responsibility for not making Niall aware of the permutations. I still feel that there is responsibility on every player to be aware of scoring differences on the last day of such a tightly contested division, but we made a conscious decision to focus on winning the game as opposed to telling guys they could lose by two points. In hindsight, we still should have touched on it because not everyone was fully clear on how scoring differences are totted up.

Gary Maguire certainly wasn't. He had a go at me at the dinner table for not making lads fully aware. 'I thought we were six points ahead of them on scoring difference, Dalo,' he said.

'Yeah, Gary, we lost by three, they won by three. Three and three is six.'

A big laugh erupted around the table.

'G'way, Dalo,' he said, and raised his eyes to heaven. A smile flashed across his face, but Gary always has to have the last word: 'It was totally unprofessional from the management anyway.'

I didn't know whether he was serious or pulling the piss, but I wasn't entertaining him. I wasn't passing off the criticism, but it just carried echoes of the on-field leadership we were desperately trying to create within the squad.

It's not up to me or Richie or Hedgo or Shane to explain everything. The team has to govern itself, and I think having that on-field leadership is the final piece we need to find to complete the puzzle. There is no doubt that we have made huge progress in that area, having that level of control on the field, knowing what is happening. At that level, everyone has to know the story off the field as well. Richie was adamant that the lads should have been told about scoring permutations that day, but we had targeted a huge performance. Our whole philosophy is based on performance before result, so how do you marry that ambition with talk of being able to lose by two points?

Even though we didn't win, I really did feel a little excited afterwards. We went down to Thurles for the league semi-final last year and got hockeyed by Tipp. Here we were, less than twelve months on, when they were under huge pressure to win, and we were able to out-hurl them for long stages. When we were 0-8 to 0-2 up in the first half, we had them in all sorts of bother. Ryan O'Dwyer had a goal chance but he got blown for over-carrying on a tight call. A goal at that stage would have finished the game. We had a twenty-metre free saved in the second half when we probably should have tapped it over. We over-elaborated in possession a couple of times and got turned over for scores, but I genuinely felt we played well. I wasn't that disappointed with the result, but my thought process was probably directed by the knowledge of where I was heading immediately after the match.

I travelled down with the lads on the bus while Eilís and Orlaith drove down from Clare. When we met up afterwards in the car park, I pointed the car in the same direction as the bus, back towards Dublin, en route to the Children's University Hospital in Temple Street.

For the past three years now, Orlaith has been suffering from temporal lobe epilepsy, a chronic neurological condition characterized by recurrent seizures which originate in the temporal lobe of the brain. An MRI scan in Limerick Regional Hospital initially showed a cyst behind her ear pushing up against the part of her brain which affects memory. The consultant, Dr Liz O'Mahoney, decided against brain surgery on a thirteen-year-old, opting instead to try and control the condition through intense medication.

The medicine has limited the rate of the seizures, but the overall impact has been counter-balanced and reduced by the side-effects. Some days Orlaith cannot get out of bed in the morning. And of course she has still been having seizures. For a sixteen-year old ingesting a small hospital of pills every day, it has been no way to live her young life. It hasn't been easy for us as a family either. We're well used to watching her become paralysed but it's not a nice sight to witness your daughter in distress, her eyes rolling, her lips smacking, her legs heaving, until a hit of medication eventually returns her to some form of normality.

Orlaith is starting to go to discos and learn about the ways of the world, but her condition has had a huge effect on her life. She is studying for the Junior Cert this year and there are challenges everywhere she turns. She has missed huge volumes of school hours. She suffers from some memory loss. She could do a French class and have absolutely no recall of what she learned an hour later. She plays the concertina and has lately been forgetting tunes.

The matter came to a head early in 2014 when a change of medication flattened her. The seizures were easier to handle than seeing her wiped out every day so we and Dr O'Mahoney sought a second opinion. She pointed us towards Temple

Street, which has a specialized neurological unit that can treat sick kids with Orlaith's condition.

She was booked to undergo a series of tests that Sunday night to see if she was operable. She had two MRI scans on Monday. Her medication was reduced to a small dosage before an attempt to bring on a seizure that night through a full night of sleep deprivation. With ten monitor wires glued on to her head, all linked to a camera and computer screen, they can neuro-logically examine the electric currents in her brain during a seizure, and what effect it is having on her brain activity during that time.

Nothing happened. I stayed with Orlaith on Tuesday night, then Eilís came back and stayed with her on Wednesday for another hellish slog without sleep. I got a good night's sleep in the Croke Park Hotel, but when I returned on Thursday morn-ing, the torturous process still hadn't triggered a seizure and the doctors were no wiser.

Keyhole surgery had been provisionally planned for Thursday to drain the cyst but the surgeons decided against that plan of action. I was slightly disappointed because we were still in the same position we'd been in the week before and you just want your child to get better. Yet it is brain surgery, and when you spend time in Temple Street you appreciate every-thing you have. We have a fine healthy daughter who is getting big and tall and strong. She has this cross she has to bear but it's not life-threatening and we won't have to experience the sort of suffering and death that is rampant in this place every day. Orlaith was in a four-bedroom ward. Here, as soon as one bed empties, it is filled again in the time it takes to change the sheets.

On Tuesday evening I headed out to the Spar to get a cup of coffee. The ward across from Orlaith's catered for extremely sick kids, and as I passed the nurses' station on the way back in, five of them, along with two parents, were crying, broken by the horror and terror of the death, or impending death, of a child. It would break your own heart.

We lost a game last Sunday. We'd get over it. In Temple Street, people are losing everything they have, almost every day of the week, every week of the year.

9

Glory at Last

On the way home from the Munster final in 1995, the bus stopped somewhere on the old Limerick–Dublin road, on the western side of Nenagh. We had been as dehydrated as camels in a desert after playing a championship match on one of the warmest days of a melting summer but we loaded so much drink into our bodies immediately after the game that we needed to relieve ourselves before our kidneys burst.

Before we left the Anner Hotel in Thurles, I had gone to Loughnane, bold as brass, and asked him if he could get us some beer for the trip home. He sent county board chairman Robert Frost into the bar and he arrived back with two slabs, forty-eight cans. 'Where the hell is he going with that amount of drink?' I said to Loughnane. 'We'll have that sank before we're out of Thurles.' So Loughnane hunted him back in and Frost arrived out with eight more crates of liquor.

When we were halfway home, the drink was coming out through us. The nearest ditch somewhere close to the Limerick–Tipperary border was the most accessible toilet. I was well merry and laughing away to myself as a couple of cows stared back at me over this thick hedge. I was nearly about to get into a bovine conversation with the herd when I heard Loughnane's booming voice. 'They must be Tipperary cows anyway, Dalo,' he said. 'You'd know by the big fat heads on them.'

If I had not been in the process of relieving myself, I would have pissed in my pants.

Loughnane was always capable of saying anything, but he could have come out with anything by that stage. It was like Our Lord had come down off the cross. He was the Messiah.

When he told us in the dressing-room after the league final hammering to Kilkenny a couple of months earlier that we would win the Munster title, I honestly don't know if anyone really believed him. Loughnane no sooner had the words out of his mouth than I caught Sparrow's eye across the room. He just threw his eyes up to heaven. When we got back to the car afterwards, Sparrow said to me, 'Do you hear what your man is after coming out with? I won't be putting any money on us anyway.'

That day against Limerick, he had us in the palm of his hand. There was an air of defiance about us. It was Loughnane's show. In his eyes, we had surrendered in the 1993 and 1994 Munster finals and had also raised the white flag early in the league final. We had our legs blown off us coming back from those wars but we were coming back from this battle on our shields. 'No fucking surrender,' were Loughnane's last words to us as we left that dressing-room.

Those words had a direct connection to a night we had spent in Killarney three months earlier. We were there on a two-day training camp and Loughnane allowed us to go for a few drinks on the Saturday night. We found a small pub and claimed it as our own for the handful of hours we were there. A sing-song started up and we asked Loughnane to give us a tune. He sang 'And The Band Played Waltzing Matilda'.

The song, written by Eric Bogle, is an account of a young Australian soldier who is maimed at the Battle of Gallipoli during the First World War. The soldier loses his legs and the lyrics evoke the imagery of the savagery of Gallipoli.

When he came to the line about the ship pulling into the quay, and the soldier thanks Christ that there was no one there to greet him, Loughnane stopped deliberately to emphasize a point. I knew the song, and I knew exactly what he was referring to. It was an extremely powerful moment. Loughnane had gone off and learned that song for a reason. When we asked him for a tune, he knew exactly what he was doing. I even remember explaining the background to Loughnane's subtle intentions to a few lads the following day.

I wouldn't dare attempt to compare war to hurling in a real sense, but those lines about being thankful that there was nobody on that quay to grieve and mourn and pity the soldier reminded me of coming home to Clarecastle after the 1993 and 1994 Munster finals. There were people there to meet us but they may as well have been ghosts. When we walked into the Coach House Inn, the conversation instantly died. It was pure pity.

You'd try and numb the pain and the embarrassment with a river full of drink, but when does that river stop flowing? Hiding was nearly the first instinct, but mostly you wanted to get out of Clarecastle. The day after the 1993 Munster final, I was being presented with an award in Dublin for my performance in the semi-final against Cork. I wasn't in bed long when my brother Martin dragged me out of it and said we were hitting for Dublin. His boss, Michael Slattery, had laid on two return flights for us.

We were in Dublin early so we went for an early drink. The lunch in Jurys in Ballsbridge wasn't until midday and when we arrived we met the Republic of Ireland defender Paul McGrath, who had flown over from Birmingham to collect his award. He didn't know who we were until my brother introduced us. 'Ah hurling,' said McGrath. 'Mad stuff.'

On Tuesday we went back to the Willie Clancy music festival in Miltown Malbay. We were going for one night but we stayed for two. After we ran out of money, I went to Tom McNamara in the bank in Miltown Malbay and got him to cash a cheque I wrote for £125. Tuts wanted £50 out of it but we split it between four of us to keep us going.

At one stage, we ended up in the company of Paul Hill – one of the Guilford Four. We had just walked into the Ocean View Bar and the guy behind the counter knew us from Flannan's.

'Hurleys for sale,' he said.

'Just keep filling the pints,' I replied.

Tuts bought this bodhrán, spilled porter over it before getting some dirt from outside the door and rubbing it across the base. He went over to Paul Hill and Courtney Kennedy and asked them to sign this famous bodhrán which, he boldly claimed, had seen fifty fleadhs and which he'd been playing on tour over the previous seven years. It was chaos.

A few days earlier we'd gone into a Munster final full of hope and ambition, but you could still only dream of what it would be like to actually win something, to return to Clarecastle after a Munster final with our heads high, not buried inside in our shoes. When we did, it was a surreal experience. On the night of the Munster final in 1995, nobody had prepared for a celebration. I was hoisted up on a bus shelter which acted as a makeshift stage. I knew it was a special night because my mother hadn't gone to bingo. She was staring up at me.

It was an epic night, loaded with so much symbolism that I couldn't shake it from my system. I thought back to how they had all turned their faces away after we'd come home from the two previous Munster finals. When the Clarecastle players walked into the Coach House Inn in the village after the 1994 final, my sister-in-law Anne, Martin's wife, started clapping in a genuine show of affection and appreciation. Nobody joined her. They were looking at her as if to say, 'What are you applauding those chokers for? They're after shitting themselves again.' They were only thinking what everyone else was saying behind our backs. It was that kind of sombre mood that prompted the late Michael 'Nuggy' Nihill, who was a great Clare supporter, to ask on Clare FM the Monday after that 1994 final, 'When are Clare going to stop ruining the Munster final?'

Sixty-three long years of hurt and pain and disappointment drained out of Clare people that memorable day, but for those of us who had played in 1993 and 1994 the feeling was one of ultimate liberation. Some of our people felt we had denigrated the entire history and culture of Clare hurling. Those defeats were our Gallipoli. We'd had our legs blown off. We were scorned and pitied but it didn't dull our passion or dilute the fight in our heart. The wounds were deep but the scars healed. We fought on.

We matured, but if anything, we just had to go through that difficult learning process that most young, inexperienced and unsuccessful teams have to endure. In 1993, we just weren't ready. Myself, Sparrow, Tuts and Alan Neville went golfing in Lahinch three weeks before the final. Sparrow paid the green fees, and as we were making our way to the first tee a voice piped up over the tannoy and requested Sparrow's presence back in the clubhouse. Someone had recognized us, and they handed Sparrow back the money. 'These are the perks, boys,' said Tuts. 'These are the perks.'

We had won nothing but we lost the run of ourselves. I

ordered so many tickets that I was trying to get rid of them over the counter in work on the Thursday and Friday before the game. On the Sunday, we met in the Greenhills Hotel before the game and walked in through the Clare throng on the way to a meeting room. Our pre-match meal was a cup of tea, brown bread and jam – our standard fare at the time. On the way out of the hotel, this chancer came up and asked me if I had any tickets. Then we made the twenty-minute walk to the ground, swept along in the mainstream of the crowd.

We just weren't tuned in for the game. Even the parade was a big deal. Tipp just trampled all over us. It was a total nightmare, but it made us realize the level we had to reach if we were ever going to win anything.

I had a lot to learn. Before the game started, Aidan Ryan stood in front of me. He just stared at me for about ten seconds before ambling off into his corner. I met him at the All-Stars later in the year and asked him what he was at. 'There was all this talk about you before the game because you played well against Cork,' he said. 'I'd never heard of you so I wanted to take a good look at you.' It just reaffirmed how tuned out I was. I should have planted him. When we met Tipp in the Munster quarter-final the following year, I was ready to rip the head off him. When Ryan stretched out his hand before the game, I caught it and pulled him out the field a few yards. The message was clear: you'll know all about me after today. We were all pumped up, especially Lohan, who belted the shite out of anyone who came near him.

We were on a crusade for more reasons than just atonement for 1993. John Moroney, who played corner-back, was killed in a car-crash that winter. John was a great guy. He was a few years older than us but myself and Tuts often enjoyed his company over a quiet pint. He had pulled out of the panel for a few years but he was really enjoying his hurling and the buzz the young lads had brought to the panel. It was a desperate shock. His girl-friend was pregnant with their son. I often see him around now, a lovely lad with a shock of blond hair. On the day John was buried, his clubmate and close friend Cyril Lyons spoke eloquently in Dysart church. Cyril read out a poem he had written, about how John loved music, especially Tom Petty. When we played Tipp in May, I tried to transport the lads back mentally to that cold December day in Dysart when our hearts and spirit were almost broken.

We had let the whole county down the previous year. That day took our names, and now we had to reclaim them. John, though, hadn't that opportunity. We all might have more oppor-tunities against Tipp, but that day was all about John Moroney. We were so charged up on raw emotion that Tipp never saw the uppercut coming. They hit the canvas like a stone.

Len Gaynor came to me at the final whistle and swallowed me up in his arms. Then this big ape from Tipperary arrived at his shoulder. 'Gaynor, you're a fucking traitor,' he said. Gaynor turned and flattened him with a belt of a fist.

I cried and cried and cried inside in the dressing-room. I was just overcome. We had avenged 1993, but we had done it for John Moroney. It was one of the most special days of my career.

Limerick beat us well in the Munster final, and it was devastation again. We had shit ourselves once more. I played well, but that doesn't ease the pain when you dream of winning Munster titles. You don't want to meet anyone outside your small circle. You hide again. You wonder again if it will ever happen. After successive Munster final defeats, you doubt it ever will.

By the time Ger Loughnane, Mike Mac and Tony Considine were appointed in September 1994, we were getting ready for a county final against St Joseph's Doora-Barefield. The first trial had taken place the Tuesday after the 1994 All-Ireland. We knew Mac was a brute and the word coming back to us was that the training was absolutely animal, that you wouldn't put a dog through it.

We beat St Joseph's in the county final and we went out to their place in Roslevan, the Grove Bar, with the cup the following week. I got talking to Seánie McMahon, who had gone back that Thursday night, and he said that it was chronic shit altogether. We were playing Toomevara in the Munster club semi-final two weeks later and the incentive to win was nearly more to delay Mac's brutality for as long as we could.

As soon as we went back, Mac was in our ears about losing to Toomevara. That the game was there for the taking but that we hadn't the balls to grab it. As he ran us around the place like husky dogs, lashing us with the whip of his tongue, he roared a couple of standard lines to all of us that he used throughout that winter – that we were basically a crowd of soft cissies who had disgraced the Clare jersey in the previous two Munster finals.

Mac didn't give a damn about anyone. He flogged us. For the warm-up, he had us doing more press-ups and sit-ups than Rocky Balboa did before he fought Ivan Drago in *Rocky IV*. All we were missing were the beards. All Mac was missing was the snow and the mountains. He got the snow one night and he drove us through it. And that was before he led us to the mother of all torture chambers.

There is a hill in Shannon just behind the Lohans' house in Tullyglass. It kind of slopes off to one side at the back, but Mac used to drive us straight up the incline, all the way to the top, like a lunatic. We'd meet in either De Beers' social centre or the hall in Wolfe Tones' ground to do some beastly concoction of a warm-up. You'd be wrecked afterwards. Then Mac would say,

'Right, lads, we'll go to the hill now, we'll run it thirty-five times tonight,' using the casual tone a hangman would to a convicted criminal bound for the gallows.

You'd do it in groups of seven and the priority was to grab someone who would be doing it at the same pace as yourself. If you saw Jamesie O'Connor coming near you, you'd treat him like he had the plague.

Sparrow never worried too much about what group he was in. He would do as many as he could in the first sequence of runs before disappearing behind the mature trees and heavy under-growth along the footpath halfway up the hill. You could be on run number twenty and next thing the fucker would leap out of the trees like Batman – after sitting out the previous five – and bomb ahead of you. Jamesie was leading this group one night when Sparrow appeared out of the dark and let out a roar that frightened the shit out of the boys. When he got to the top first, Mac shouted, 'Great fucking running, Sparrow, that's how you do it!'

Sparrow had every trick in the book. When we started doing some weights training in the West County Hotel gym, Sparrow would head straight for the jacuzzi. Mac never showed us how to lift weights so we had to police ourselves, and Sparrow was lethal with liberties. When the weights got more serious a couple of years later, Sparrow would justify his absence from the gym by doing extra work in the pool. There was an asterisk beside this aquatic dispensation, as he justified it, though: Sparrow never went near the deep end, which meant he swam widths, not lengths. He was absolutely fearless on the field but he hated deep water.

There was one night when Lohan, Hego and Mike 'Holly' O'Halloran were doing bench presses together in a group, with two acting as spotters while the other was underneath the bar.

They were lifting animal weights. The gym in the West County looks out on the pool area, and after Lohan finished one round of reps, chewing nails from trying to get the better of the stack of kilos on the bar, he spotted Sparrow exiting the pool with this stupid swimming hat on. 'You only need strength in your wrists, Brian,' he said to Lohan.

Sparrow still had to do some of the dogging in 1995, and we all had to make our own readjustments. I got an All-Star at corner-back in 1994. I thought that's where I would stay, but Loughnane threw me out on the wing for the first few league games. It took me a while to settle. I had problems with my lower back too during that spring, which didn't make the transition any easier. The training was just killing me. I was having constant physio. I even went down to Dr Con Murphy in Cork for a consultation not long before we played Cork in the championship.

I had a poor league. I wasn't right for the final against Kilkenny. I was marking Adrian Ronan and he gave me the runaround. I was a disgrace. I couldn't get to the pitch of the game. I had people in my ear all spring telling me that I wasn't suited to wing-back. After having such a good year in the corner in 1994, I was giving those voices more airtime than I should have allowed.

I was in the horrors after that game. Considine had a right go at me for declaring myself fit when I clearly wasn't. About a week later, I went down to the river bank in Clarecastle to do some fishing and clear my head. Hanly was there before me sitting on the rocks, his line already cast into the water in search of trout. 'Loughnane has made a balls of you,' he told me. 'You need to go to him and tell him to put you back into the corner. Sure, weren't you the best corner-back in the country last year? You were always a corner-back, just like your father before you.'

I knew there was no going back to Loughnane. Jesus, he'd ate you alive. I just had to try and cope. Even as I went on to settle into the position, I was never much good in the air. Whether I was a bit shy or windy in the air, it was something I never really had to worry about in the corner. My game was all about reading the play, sweeping up; get to the ball ahead of your man, first touch and bang, clear your lines. My head was in the clouds. I needed to come back down.

Loughnane dragged me down straight away without a parachute. He dogged the hell out of me before we played Cork. You could even see there was a different intensity about him. He raised it about 15 per cent. The sweat would be dripping off him, and him roaring at you as if he was demented. When I was in the middle for first-touch drills, he used to stand over me like a shadow. 'Too slow, too fucking slow, that won't work in the championship.' Unknown to me, I was speeding up my striking and first touch.

It was obvious that we were improving but I was still racked by doubt. I just wasn't happy at wing-back. I felt under pressure to hold on to my place. I wasn't even comfortable being captain at that stage. I felt I had no right to be speaking after my performance in the league final. After we beat Cork, I wasn't much better. Mark Mullins had beaten me comprehensively in the air.

There was something different about us in how we had managed to dig out the result, but I still couldn't shake the insecurities from my system. We were superbly prepared. We had young players with no fear. We were ready to win, but serial disappointment plays funny tricks with your head. The gremlins were rattling my skull like a flock of woodpeckers, chipping away at whatever positive thoughts I was trying to visualize.

That feeling was also triggered by naked fear. I was just dreading losing another Munster final. I wasn't the only one.

After training one night, I was sitting beside P. J. 'Fingers' O'Connell. 'If we lose this one again, I am walking away anyway,' he said. 'I won't be coming back for this torture again next year. Lose, and I am out that door.' Fingers will always say it straight, but it was as if his comments graphically outlined what was at stake for all of us. I didn't say that I was definitely hightailing out of town along with him if we lost, and how many other lads might have been thinking like Fingers? We had got up again on the horse after the two previous Munster final defeats, but could we really take a third one?

A light went on in my head. I remember going out to Sparrow's car and being very clear in my thinking. 'It's time to make a stand now. Don't do what you did for the league final. Don't do what you did for the 1993 final. Don't get caught up in the circus like you have in the past. Have a go at these fuckers.'

Loughnane settled me down further after training about a week before the game. He was great at one-to-ones when he wanted to be and he gave me the reassurance I needed. 'I know you might feel more comfortable in the corner but we have no doubts about you. Look at the shape you're in. You're some athlete now. You are ready. We all are.'

We were.

We based ourselves in Cashel before the game. On the bus journey into Thurles, we turned into a sea of Limerick supporters as we crawled towards the back of the Kinnane Stand. The Limerick hordes were banging the side of the bus, rattling their flags off the windows, telling us to clear off home and not be wasting our time again in another Munster final.

Mick Malone from Clarecastle was driving the bus, and I roared to him, 'Put the fucking boot down, Mick. Mow the fuckers down.'

That was my dominant feeling. Nothing was going to stand in

our way. I couldn't stomach another defeat. I couldn't face going to the Willie Clancy festival again and being almost forced to keep my head down in shame. We were all going to tear into Limerick. No regrets.

Of all the hurling games I ever played, I was never as tense again afterwards as I was that day. I wasn't tense in the sense of being afraid. It was more a feeling of just being ready to explode and hardly being able to wait for the spark to ignite and the imminent blast from the detonation.

Seánie McMahon had broken his collarbone against Cork, and when Gary Kirby went for him early on with a shoulder to test it out, I went bald-headed for Kirby. I didn't strike him with a hurley or my fist, I just bulldozed into him and drove him back a couple of feet. Frankie Carroll came in to Kirby's aid and Liam Doyle gave him a couple of clips. I think Ollie Baker levelled someone else. It was obvious that there was something different about us than what we had shown in the first halves of the two previous Munster finals.

We were leading by one point at the break, but gremlins know their way around the caverns of minds where they have been tenants for so long. For some reason I started thinking about the 1977 and 1978 Munster finals, when Clare were in solid positions at half-time against Cork and still lost. I was a nine-year-old at the 1978 final and could vividly recall the anticipation. Clare were level at the break and had a strong breeze at their backs for the second half. The Clare crowd were almost drunk with delirium and I was half intoxicated from the optimism on their breath. And then Clare bombed in the second half.

We railroaded through Limerick in the second half but it still took me until the game was almost over to finally evict those gremlins from my head. I wound up marking Mike Galligan, and he turned to me after Fergal Hegarty landed our last score and said, 'Well done, boy. Ye deserve it after how long ye have waited.'

I told him to get lost, but I didn't mean it in those terms. I had become so conditioned to losing that I still couldn't fully believe it. I remember Jamesie saying one time in a documentary that he was afraid the game would be abandoned when the Clare crowd invaded the field after one of our late scores. I had the same fear.

I was never as emotional again as I was after that final. I met my best friend Paraic Russell on the pitch and we both broke down. I nearly collapsed into an emotional wreck when my brother Martin swallowed me up in a bear-hug. Martin had brought me to matches all his life. That love of hurling we all had, that longing we'd always had in Clare to win a Munster title, had welled up inside us all. The dam had finally burst.

10

Putting on the War Paint

When Johnny Ryan blew the half-time whistle in the 2014 league relegation final, the four members of the Waterford management surrounded him as effectively as the Tyrone or Armagh blanket defences in the middle of the last decade would have gobbled up a Kerry forward. Johnny had sent off Shane O'Sullivan on 26 minutes and the Waterford boys arrived with the intent of a crew looking to rattle the referee. I wanted to have my say too. Richie tried to pull me back but Tommy Dunne encouraged me to keep going. So I did. Moonlighting as Johnny's best friend, I basically told the Waterford boys to fuck off and leave him alone. They told me to shut my mouth and clear off back to Clare while I was at it, and Dan Shanahan kept up the tirade as we continued walking towards the tunnel.

'Keep it up now and you'll get what you got in 1998,' I said to him.

'Go way there, boy,' replied Dan. 'I put you on your hole that day.'

'You did, yeah, with a sneaky trip from behind. You hit no wallops but you'll get one in a minute if you want it.'

There hadn't been a word between Shanahan and myself in that year's Munster final until he scored his third point off me in the drawn game. 'You're not marking Seánie McGrath now, boy,' he said in his heavy Waterford accent.

'You're definitely bigger anyway,' I replied. 'And a good bit uglier.'

Shanahan was referring to the ongoing carnival between myself and Seánie McGrath in the semi-final against Cork, which the TV cameras had picked up on. Seánie scored a couple of points off me but we still knocked some craic out of it all.

'Right, we'll do a wager, Seánie,' I said to him. 'You don't get more than two points, you're buying the pints.'

'That'll do,' he replied, me thinking that it would put him off his game. It didn't, but we kept up the chat.

'If I get a point, you're back to zero,' I said. 'I'm way back here so that will be worth two of your points.'

Billy Connolly couldn't have made it up.

I've always had a name for mouthing and jawing and getting involved with fellas, and a lot of people don't like me for it. I was never shy, or afraid to stand up for myself, or to express my opinion, but that doesn't categorize me as a trash-talker or someone with a runny mouth, with bile and venom spilling out the side of it. At the core of my being is a savage instinct to compete and to win. If lads felt there was poison or badness in the verbal arrows I was firing in the crossfire of a heated exchange, it was never intended. Maybe it was me being a smartarse, but I justified my actions through my belief that I was only defending myself or my team-mates.

One of my first games for Clare was against Tipperary in some tournament in 1988. Cormac Bonnar was full-forward and was throwing his weight around. They didn't call him 'The

Viking' for nothing. He had more hair on his face than his head, was missing his two front teeth and was one of the first players to wear one of those old Mycro helmets that looked more suited to an astronaut than a hurler.

I was only a young lad but I wasn't prepared to put up with any of Bonnar's messing. After he hit a slap on John Moroney, it ignited a row and I waded in.

'G'way, you big ugly bollix!'

'What are you talking about, young lad?' he replied. 'You're no oil painting yourself.'

'You're probably right,' I said to him, smiling.

And that was the end of it.

I was just mad to make a stand against Tipp because losing stuck in my throat. When I first established myself on the Clare team in 1990, we played a league quarter-final against Wexford in Thurles and I was marking Tom Dempsey. Tom was a really classy player and after getting one sweet point over his shoulder, I nudged him in the back. He didn't like it.

'Ah, a Clare man getting brave,' he said to me. 'Where are yere All-Irelands?'

I knew Tom had played in an All-Ireland Colleges final with St Peter's but I couldn't remember whether he had won his medal. I expected to hear that kind of guff from a Cork or Tipp fella but I had no interest in listening to it from someone down that neck of the woods.

'What would ye know about All-Irelands?' I asked Dempsey.

He recoiled and looked at me in near exasperation, almost more in respect than anger. 'You're a saucy little fucker anyway.'

The two of us have often laughed about it since. Tom took me for three points but I still felt that I'd played well. What's more, I sensed the advantages I'd accrued for standing up for myself. I wasn't going to roll over because he had a reputation and I was a rookie. I fronted up to him and I knew I got inside his head.

This was serious stuff. I wanted more of it. I wanted to be taken seriously. I wanted Clare to be taken seriously, but too many of our lads didn't view our worth in that manner. When I made my championship debut a couple of months later against Limerick, I was determined not to be shown up. I was psyched up big-time. I was marking Leo O'Connor and I wired into him. One of the girls I worked with in the bank knew Leo and said to me a couple of days later that I gave him an awful blackguarding. 'Jeez, that was terrible what you did to young O'Connor,' she said, and Leo a couple of years older than me.

This was the championship, dog-eat-dog stuff. I was the first of my direct family to play for Clare so of course I was pumped up. I stood in front of Leo, walked down on top of his toes and tried to annoy him into distraction. That was the worst of it.

I might have lit the verbal fuse through physical intimidation but I never started verbally abusing some fella for nothing. I'll be honest, I was as good as any of them to give it. But on my father's grave, I never started it. People might think differently of me but, as they say in west Clare, if you have a name for getting up early, you can stay in bed all day.

Coaches, managers and players have a greater personal responsibility now to uphold integrity and dignity within matches. Sport, and the GAA, has serious questions to answer regarding sledging and showing proper respect to your opponents, but I honestly never felt I had to reconcile any of those issues in my head.

When I played my second championship match for Clare against Limerick in 1991, I was marking Pat 'Beefy' Heffernan, who I had been very friendly with in Flannan's. I didn't even shake hands with him before the game. I barely even squeezed the words 'good luck' out the side of my mouth. At one stage he asked me to call Willie Walsh, one of our selectors whom we had both played under in Flannan's.

'Jeez, I'm gasping, Dalo,' he said. 'Call Willie there for an auld sip of water.'

'Shut up now, Beef,' I replied.

I knew there was no way I was going to win that battle if I got involved in a conversation with Beefy. He'd be chatting away about Flannan's and trying to put you off your game. 'Ara Jaysus, Dalo, what's it all about?' he'd say, and he could have a ball stuck in the roof of the net a minute later. Then he'd probably arrive out and apologize. Beefy's tongue was hanging out but I couldn't have cared less if we were in the Sahara desert.

When I was younger, I would have done anything to win. I was more ruthless. I've mellowed as the years have passed but I've never lost that determination to get an edge. I was always looking for it, always scraping around for that extra yard of rope that could get us up the mountain. We played Limerick in the 1996 Munster championship and I was marking Shane O'Neill from Na Piarsaigh, who was making his championship debut. He was six foot four and standing in front of me during the national anthem so I told him to 'get out of my fucking light, young lad'. He took a step to the right. I knew that I already had him in my pocket. I'd four balls cleared before he realized the game was even on. Shane might have thought I was a mouth-piece, but is that sledging? I honestly don't think so.

Everyone has his own parameters, and while I felt I never went over the line, I always went close to it. When we played Tipp in the league in 1995, we were top of the table and spoiling for a scrap and a scalp to confirm the progress we felt we were making. Loughnane had stirred it up all week. He kept reminding us how Tipp were coming to make a holy show of us after beating them in the championship the previous year. Myself and Seánie McMahon spoke before we left the West County Hotel about laying down the law in our town. We had to make a stand. Tipp had rolled out their big guns but we returned fire with every opportunity.

At one stage in the second half I heard this commotion behind me. Bang, bang, bang, like somebody kicking in a door. I turned around and McMahon and Declan Ryan were going at it like two stags in a glen, belting the living shite out of each other, wearing hurleys off their bodies like matchsticks against foam.

In the scuffle that followed, John Leahy and myself got stuck into each other. He told me that I had got the handiest All-Star ever given to anyone the previous year, which teed up my response perfectly. Leahy had also got an All-Star but it was on the back of a superb performance in the league final against Galway. He was injured when we beat them in the championship. 'At least I played in the championship anyway,' I said to Leahy. 'They gave you one for sitting on your hole.'

We were gone to skin and bone by then from Mike Mac's brutality, and I called Leahy a fat fucker. 'Have you had your Mars bars, Johnny?' I enquired.

Not long afterwards, there was a dispute on the far sideline and Baker kicked Leahy up the arse. We were all in the frenzy. So were the crowd.

Tipp had a late chance of a goal to save the game, and when it went wide, I let out a roar at Nicky English and Pat Fox: 'Hang up yere boots, yere finished.' Nicky commented in his autobiography that if the teams met in the Munster final later that year, I was going to get a hiding. I couldn't have cared less that day because we had made a stand. Loughnane always refers to it as the starting point of our journey to All-Ireland success, but the verbal wars and belts and battles that got us there never hitched too much collateral damage to our wagon along the way. I'm still good friends with Nicky and Pat. When we meet for a drink now, their opinion of me hasn't been formed from those seventy minutes in Ennis when I was a young lad desperate to beat them. Myself and Tommy Dunne marked each other around ten times and there was never a word exchanged between us. We hammered the shite out of each other but Tommy wouldn't be my coach now if there wasn't such mutual respect between us.

Leahy didn't take too kindly to being accused of buying boxes of Mars bars, though, and he was invariably looking to have his say any time we met afterwards.

When we did meet again, in 1999, myself and Doyler were goading Leahy at every opportunity, trying to get a hop out of him. Nicky English had him completely focused but I had an angle for the replay. After the drawn game, some Tipp supporters had set fire to curtains in one of the carriages on the train back to Clonmel. When a shemozzle kicked off early in the game and Leahy was stuck in the middle of it with Doyler, I let him have it.

'I see ye got the train home the last day.'

Leahy started roaring laughing. So did Tommy Dunne and Brian O'Meara. I got a fit then. As the shemozzle was breaking up, four or five lads were pissing themselves in front of nearly fifty thousand people.

The comments might often have been laced with razor blades but they were never intended to cut deep and most lads took it in the right spirit. Kilkenny's Adrian Ronan was another one of those fellas like Cork's Seánie McGrath, a great character, someone you could have a bit of craic with on the pitch. He cleaned me out in the 1995 league final. He was wearing a strapping for his hamstring and after he got his second point I gave him a dig to see if I could knock him off his stride. He started laughing at me. 'Where are you going with those fucking tights?' I asked him. Ronny just started laughing louder.

I wouldn't have it in me to start abusing lads about their mother or sister. You hear about extreme cases of abuse and vulgarity where nasty societal trends are often transmitted through players on the field, but that stuff was always alien to me. Certain GAA players view verbal abuse as simply a means to an end but I would have no interest in reaching that end through those means.

There is no honour or respect in it, and I know how low it can make you feel. In the 1998 drawn Munster final, one Waterford player called me 'a wife-beater'. The only thing worse you could be called in life is a paedophile. It was like a knife being twisted into my ribcage, but that slur was the high-water mark of a vortex of rumours that were swirling around me at the time. I haven't a clue where it all came from. Obviously some malicious bastard had said that I was beating up Eilís and it took off like wildfire.

The Irish are often described as a fair people because they never speak well of each other. That's not a fully accurate depiction, but a lot of them think what they want to think about you, even if it isn't true. That is the toll you must often pay for success and you just have to man up and find another layer for your skin.

After 1995 I became very conscious of what people thought, about the perception they had of me. Fellas would come up to me and say, 'Did you hear the latest joke about yourself? What's the difference between God and Anthony Daly? God doesn't think he's Anthony Daly.' Those comments don't leave any scars but you still feel the nick from the arrows.

Above: Haulie, Helen, Mam, Granny Daly and Dad, *circa* 1970.

Left: Always was a bit of a cosy arse.

Below: In the Brennans' garden. Their place was like a second home to me.

First Communion – 'Pay Day' – with my grandmother 'Cuckoo', Mam and Dad.

All together once: Patricia and Colman's wedding. (L–R) Michael, Paschal, Lucia, Mam, Trish, Coley, Pat Joe, Marian, Martin. In front, Steph and the lad in the red onesie. Who called that one? Jesus, Johnny Leahy wouldn't have feared that lad.

Dean Ryan Final, St Flannan's, 1985: A skin and bone corner-forward, I'm at the back on the right. Davy Fitz in goal.

Harty Cup final, 1987: stronger and more ready. The faces say it all. Corner-back this time (front row, far right).

Above: Clarecastle, Munster Club champions, 1997: our best ever squad? Great thanks to Rodgie, Oliver, Ger and massive captain Sheedo.

Left: The 'Well' were tough. I should have got to a few balls before Barry Foley the previous summer.

Below: Munster champions: Kenny Morrissey, Tuts and the bould Paraic Russell lapping it up.

Left: Orlaith Daly, a magpie for a day, at the County final in 2003. (Although she's now a Shannon Gaels woman.)

Middle: The only sensible man in this picture is Griff wearing 11 for Ballyea. Leave the high ones to Stephen.

Bottom left: One last time to hold the 'Cannon' in the village.

Bottom right: Munster Club quarter-final, 2003, and my last day in black and white. Sad to be beaten, but honoured to have had the chance.

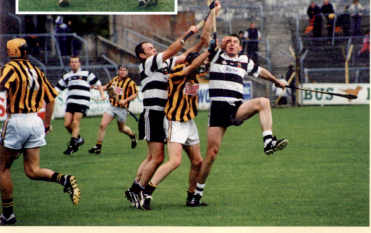

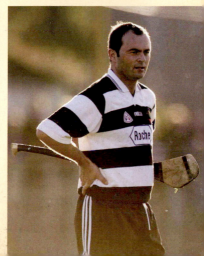

Clare County Council civic reception for the gang. (*L–R*) Myself with Howardi, Gerry, George Snr and Michael Daly, the man who accepts all the trophies.

A nostalgic night outside Navin's pub, in the little fishing village. Danno, Locky, Cock and Patsy (Sparrow's dad). Pat Joe 'Cock' McMahon went to his eternal rest the following day.

Abbeyfeale in the snow at Corn Na Féile, December 2001. Savage day. That red jacket was lucky that season.

Six creamy pints came out on a tray! Clarecastle Snooker Society presentation to myself and Sparrow getting married. (*L–R*) Myself with Russ, Leonard, Fergie, Sparrow and Tadg.

Magic week, magic end to the week, 20 September 1997. I'm glad Jim McInerney was behind me at that stage.

Orlaith's Confirmation with the new Bishop of Killaloe, May 2011. Time flies.

You learn to laugh at that sort of stuff after a while, but the price is far higher when sickening rumours about your marriage begin to spread. I can only put it down to jealousy, a small-minded mentality, a begrudgery that knows no bounds or limits. I often heard, 'Who does that fella think he is opening up a sports shop and a pub? He came out of Madden's Terrace. They survived on a widow's pension.' Their mindset is almost, 'He has no right to have a decent lifestyle.' Some people just want to drag you down, but you learn to accept that the wider GAA community has the dynamic of a village and that bad minds will have their say. And like bad weather, it will pass.

I've fallen out with plenty of people over the years but I'm still slow to make enemies of anyone. I never want to hold grudges. I was in a lift with Eilís once in a hotel in Dublin when the Waterford player who called me a wife-beater walked into it. I chatted away to him no problem. I know he was hugely embarrassed and felt far worse about the episode than I did.

But there are times when it's too much to hold your tongue. The week after the 1994 Munster final, Clarecastle were play-ing Whitegate in the senior championship in Tulla on the same evening my aunt Mary was being waked. I asked Michael if he thought I should play the match and he looked at me as if I'd two heads. 'Of course you'll play the game,' he said. 'All your aunts and uncles and cousins are home from England and they'll be going to the game. Go out and play well, and make sure you play well.'

Limerick had trimmed us the previous week and even our own people were still on our backs. At one stage in the second half, when we were ten points up, I was out near the sideline on the hill side when one of the Whitegate supporters decided to have his say.

'Ah g'way, Daly, ye shit yereselves again last week.'

I was in no form to take that guff off anyone, especially one of our own people. 'Jeez, ye've awful big mouths,' I said in front of the whole sideline in Tulla. 'It's an awful pity ye haven't a couple of hurlers.'

You can imagine what the whole of Whitegate thought of me but I didn't feel the need to take that crap off them at the time. I couldn't identify the one mouthy hoor who was having his say but I wasn't prepared to accept it. I had nothing against Whitegate but Clarecastle had six on the panel and Whitegate were contributing zero to that Clare team.

Obviously you are far more of a target as a manager. Some lads can blot out all that verbal stuff from the crowd but I can't. The abuse and the shouting matters as much as you let it matter, but I won't let anybody within close earshot insult or verbally abuse me and let them think I haven't heard it.

During the closing stages of the 2013 Leinster final, some of the Galway crowd in the front seats of the Hogan Stand began to get antsy. Dublin had been inflicting wounds on their hurlers all afternoon and the pus began leaking out of the sores.

'G'way, Daly, you're only a fucking tinker from Clare,' one big brave boy decided to roar.

His big mouth gave away his position and I turned round and spotted him.

'Come out here and say it to me,' I said to him.

Guys are always far braver five or six rows back. He never budged. He was nicely nestled in between a couple of big fellas in Galway jerseys. I'd have had to do a Trevor Brennan on it if I wanted to get at him, jumping into the crowd and fighting all around me. Jeez, I'm bad enough. I wouldn't bring that grief upon myself.

There was one occasion when I nearly turned into Trevor Brennan. The only difference was I didn't have to jump into the crowd. We lost to Kilkenny in the league in 2012 in an absolute dinger of a match. At the final whistle, this big ape came in over the wire, jumped up on my back and gave me a dunt. 'Ahhhh, Daly, shove it up your hole!'

In a split second I went from shock to temper and I took a run at your man. I was going to bate him up and down Nowlan Park but Vinny Teehan levelled him and then Johnny McEvoy waded in. The place was gone nuts. When I saw Michael Carruth arrive, I said to myself, 'We're safe now anyway.'

A cop came and dragged your man away.

'What the hell happened there?' Cody asked me.

'Ah some ape, Brian. Sure you know yourself, they're everywhere.'

Then Ned Quinn, the Kilkenny county board chairman, arrived over. I didn't want to make any issue of it, but he did. 'We might give ye a couple of clips on the field,' he said. 'Yourself and Cody can have it whatever way ye like, but that won't go on here.' He barred your man out of Nowlan Park. I got a follow-up call from a cop about making a statement but I had no interest in nailing your man.

We all make mistakes at times when emotion gets a hold of us, but the only time I was ever red-carded was in the 1990 U–21A final against Wolfe Tones. We had lost the three previous finals and were on the way to losing a fourth when I was overcome with frustration. I hit Pat O'Rourke a slap off the ball. Pat, who I had played alongside with the Clare minors and U–21s, gave me one back just as hard and it triggered an unmerciful brawl. All hell broke loose and I got the head kicked off me on the ground as there were boots flying everywhere.

Myself and Pat would have been entitled to take hit-man contracts out on each other afterwards but we remained good friends. I never wanted to fall out with anyone over hurling. It's not in my nature. If a guy had a few pints in him and had a go at me in the pub, and I took offence and returned fire with a couple of verbal hand-grenades, I'd be on the phone to him first thing the following morning to apologize for the fallout. I never wanted any enemies. I'd fire lads out of my way on the pitch, tell them to get out of my patch, or that they wouldn't hurl snow off a rope, but when the final whistle blew I always made a point of shaking hands with them and apologizing if they felt my actions were over the top.

I never felt they were because there's always something tribal about going out on the field and going to war for your own people. There's a great story told in Clarecastle about a county final against Newmarket in the early 1970s. Before the ball was thrown in, Tom Slattery hit some Newmarket fella down on top of the head.

'Jesus Christ,' the poor old cratur from Newmarket said to Tom as he lay dazed on the ground, 'the match hasn't even started.'

'The match started when I got the [Clare] *Champion* on Thursday,' said Tom.

While I wouldn't be in Tom's league when it came to the passion and aggression for the game, I always got myself wired for matches. I often had a go at the Dubs about being properly tuned in to the right frequency. The boys were in shock with Galway's approach in February 2014. David Treacy walked up to Iarla Tannian before the game and extended his hand. Tannian caught it and threw him back three yards. Tray was in shock. He was probably thinking, 'First round of the league, we'll hurl away here.' Galway came ready to wage destruction and we weren't ready for it. That's why I keep telling our lads that they must get themselves mentally ready for these games. Put on the war paint. And then go to war.

*

On the Friday night before we travelled to Walsh Park for the 2014 league relegation decider with Waterford, I bounded on to the pitch like an energizer bunny, wound up and pumped up. I wanted to transmit a positive message after the defeat to Tipp and I clapped my hands together as I pulled the lads in around me. 'Less than forty-eight hours to go, get yereselves ready now. We'll bring fucking war down to Walsh Park.'

I knew we were relaxed. By Sunday morning, it appeared as if we were too relaxed. We had arranged to stop in the Springhill Court Hotel in Kilkenny for our pre-match meal and team meeting and I drove from Clare to meet the bus below. I had just gone through Ballyragget when I rang Hedgo.

'Everything OK, Hedge?'

'Yeah, everything OK, Dalo, bar Mr Rushe. He couldn't get out of bed so I left him there.'

'Wha— Is he coming?'

'He is, but he's making his own way down now.'

Although Hedgo had left five reminders on our Facebook page on Saturday, along with sending out two texts that the clocks were going forward, our Liam still managed to sleep it out. 'Will I go through him or leave him off?' I asked myself as I drove into Kilkenny. I went on my instinct and decided to leave him be. That's just Rushey.

He caught the first two Waterford puckouts and had a stormer.

What pleased me most about the five-point win was the maturity we showed. Against Tipperary, we showboated a little when we were ahead, while we played panicky enough hurling at times in the second half. We were 0-5 to 0-0 down after ten minutes against Waterford but there was no evidence of panic or anxiety in our play. We battled our way through every match

141

since the Galway fiasco, which highlighted the incremental maturity and progress we showed throughout the league. We took a lot of positives from the spring, and retaining our Division 1A status meant a lot to all of us.

And I bookended the campaign by hugging Big Dan at the final whistle.

When we returned to the Springhill, there were about ten lads inside at the bar before we went in for the meal. I bought every one of them a pint. Ryan O'Dwyer said he'd have a bottle of Clonmel champagne – in other words a Bulmers.

'When was the last time a drop of alcohol passed your lips?' I asked him. 'You can tell me now, because I know you've had a few things on.'

'The twenty-eighth of December, Dalo.'

'Well, you're entitled to a few drinks tonight, kid. Enjoy them.'

After we got back to Dublin, we arranged to meet in the Palace Bar near Temple Bar. The lads left around midnight for Copper's or God only knows where else. I didn't ask any questions, I just let them off. Feel-good nights are an important part of the team-bonding process and they were deserving of a blowout. There won't be any messing on Monday because we have a gym session tomorrow night and lads know they won't get away with it.

Shane Martin and myself left the Palace after one a.m. and I drove home the following day in great form. Even though Mrs Navin is dead about ten years, I called in to her place in the early afternoon. The usual crew were there.

'Ye stayed up the skin of yere teeth,' was the first greeting I got from the president of the coursing club. 'Ye were poxed lucky.'

He shouldn't have opened fire because I was loaded with

more ammo than Arnold Schwarzenegger in *Commando*. His son was walking his greyhound around our pitches recently when he let him off the lead. He is a good dog who won a trial stake in Clarecastle last year but injury ruled him out of Clonmel. The dog had no muzzle on and he went wild when he spotted a poodle above on a wall. The emergency vet was called but the poodle had to be put down.

A lot of trainers only start training their dogs in late July for Liscannor, which is the first coursing meeting of the year. They had begun the process in March. 'Ye'll be good and ready for Liscannor this year anyway,' I said. 'Ye'll have an awful advantage.'

Only in Clarecastle.

11

Men Needed Now

From the moment I met Eilís Murphy to the moment I married her four years later, you could say that Tipperary was a constant theme running through our relationship. We first got together the week after the 1993 Munster final and were married the week after the 1997 All-Ireland final. And that game very nearly ended in a draw. Holy Jesus.

I'd had my eye on Eilís for a while. We didn't start going out properly until the end of 1993 but Eilís knew the story from day one. Her brothers hurled with Kilmaley and it didn't take her long to discover how much of a fanatic I was. The draw for the 1994 championship was made at the end of the year and the date for our first-round fixture against Tipp – 29 May – was tattooed on my brain from that moment. We'd often go back to west Clare for a spin and a drink and Eilís would say to me, 'Are you having another one?' And I'd say, 'No – May twenty-ninth.' She thought she was going out with a fruitcake.

We poured everything we had into that match. John Moroney had suffered with us in 1993 before he died that winter. Our fondness for John was more coal on a fire which was blazing like a furnace by the time 29 May finally rolled around.

The mistakes we'd made in 1993 had also shaped our outlook and changed our approach for ever more. Our match-day routine had been completely amateurish, but the biggest sin of all was how much we had stood off Tipp. In 1994, there was a fair bit of scutching. People gave out about our manner and the edge in our play but we either had to do it at the time or stay the way we were – being nice and losing. We had to up the ante if we were to have any hope, and our spiky league meeting with Tipp in March 1995 was really the starting point on our journey to glory. When Tipp returned to Cusack Park again in 1997, it was absolutely vicious. Loughnane described it in his book as 'the toughest match' he ever saw. He wasn't far wrong. There was no ball being played, by both sides. Frank Lohan got sent off but two or three more of our lads could have walked. We kinda bullied Tipp and got away with it.

Tipp always brought out a different side to Loughnane. Nicky English's smile to a team-mate late in the 1993 Munster final became a hackneyed image in the iconography of the Clare–Tipp rivalry but Loughnane was still using its power in 1999, in Nicky's first year as manager. Loughnane drained every last granule from the image. 'Do ye want him laughing at ye again?' he repeatedly asked us in 1999. 'Do ye want to crawl home again?' And he'd be looking over at me and Lohan, deliberately. 'I'll never forget it,' he'd say, 'sitting up in the stand in Limerick.'

Before the drawn game against Tipp in 1999, Loughnane was as hyped as we'd ever seen him. When we pulled into Páirc Uí Chaoimh, the Tipp bus was parked in front of the entrance to the dressing-rooms. Mel Keating used to drive our bus in those years and Loughnane got up from his seat and let out this roar: 'Get that tinkers' caravan out of here!' Poor Mel didn't know what to do or where to look because Loughnane was more or less suggesting that he ram the Tipp bus and start the mayhem there and then.

The reality was somewhat different, but in the imagination of the hurling public during the latter part of the 1990s, 'Clare and Tipp' became a byword for murder and mayhem.

When I was in St Flannan's a lot of the Tipp students were salt-of-the-earth lads, but more of them walked around like they owned the place, looking down on Clare lads with their strut and inflated sense of worth. Some of them threw their weight around too because they felt they could. They thought Clare lads were inferior to them. They were happy to win their Harty and All-Ireland medals in Clare but they were never slow to assert their heritage of supremacy because they thought that Clare would never amount to anything more than 'whipping boys'.

Most Tipp people are decent and sound, but while they might not have intended to disregard us, that's how they felt deep in their gut. In their hearts, beating Clare was never a surprise.

When we met Tipp in the 1997 Munster final, Loughnane drove us on like a madman in training. He dredged up how they had laughed at us in 1993 and that this was now payback. 'This is the day,' he would repeatedly say. 'This is the day we are going to bury them. We're going to show the whole world that we're here to stay.'

I was doped up with the narcotics of Loughnane's emotion and years of pent-up frustration but I didn't go out to have a direct swipe at Tipp after the 1997 Munster final. I hadn't any pre-prepared speech, but those memories from Flannan's and how Tipp had always perceived us came into my head when I was on the podium. I told the crowd we would 'no longer be the whipping boys of Munster'.

That line was an irrelevance to me until I went to watch Clare and Cork in the Munster U-21 semi-final ten days later in Thurles. Liz Howard, then Munster Council PRO, had a right cut at me in an article in the programme. My comments had clearly touched a raw nerve in Tipp. I was wearing a baseball cap and I pulled it down over my eyes in case some local nut-job came after me.

I said it to Loughnane the next night we went back training. 'Leave it with me,' he said, 'I'll sort it out.' He went on the rampage. In an open letter to the *Clare Champion*, he scorched and burned all around him like napalm. He cut the ground from under Liz Howard. Len Gaynor also got nicked by some of his bullets. After charring Tipp, he turned the flamethrower on Wexford before their All-Ireland semi-final against Tipp. After he accused them of adopting 'rough-house tactics', Wexford effectively blamed Loughnane for losing the All-Ireland semi-final.

Loughnane didn't care what anyone thought at that time. The week before we played Kilkenny in the All-Ireland semi-final, he stirred it up down there as well. Before they got off the bus in Croke Park, their manager Nickey Brennan played a recording of a radio interview Loughnane had done on RTE. Then he reportedly asked the players, 'What do ye think of that?'

'He's dead right,' replied Eddie O'Connor.

We were better than Kilkenny, but opening fire on Tipp and Wexford was far riskier. Maybe it was part of Loughnane's great master plan in that he wanted to meet Tipp, but I would certainly have preferred Wexford in the final. Tipp had radically reconstructed their team from the Munster final and were a better outfit. We had only beaten them by three points in the Munster final and I had a complete nightmare the same day.

It was the nearest I ever came in a match to asking to be taken off. I just couldn't catch my breath. I felt weak and couldn't seem to generate any oxygen in my lungs. There was a huge atmosphere in Páirc Uí Chaoimh and the air was sticky and humid. At half-time, lads were opening windows and waving the bathroom door like a fan.

Kevin Tucker cleaned me out. He was a tricky player but I was at nothing and he had a free rein. Even the lads around me knew I was in trouble. My knees were wobbling. I was gasping so much that I was wondering if I was an asthmatic. I glanced over at the sideline on more than a few occasions because I was sure management would haul me off at any moment. I finally got my second wind for the last ten minutes.

The final whistle was absolute relief, but the build-up to the All-Ireland final was a complete nightmare. I was just riddled with fear. It wasn't a fear that John Leahy would break three of my fingers on the first ball, it was that trepidation that I might be the one to let the team and the county down again, and that this time the price to pay would be too much to bear.

The difference in my demeanour and attitude from the 1995 final was marked, the polar opposite, because I just had this sense of dread. The county was full of confidence. There was a jingoistic vibe in the air, with all this talk of locking the back-door, which Tipp had come through. Kieran McDermott, the musician and song-writer, brought out a song and one of the lines stuck in my head: 'We'll have to stop off in Nenagh, to really rub it in.'

I remember thinking, 'Will ye all shut up. If Tipp beat us now, they'll redden our holes.'

They had nothing to lose. If Tipp won, I knew their supporters were going to invade the pitch and that guys would be jumping up on my back, whipping me for my whipping boys comment.

When Leahy got the ball in the last minute for his goal chance, my life flashed in front of me. When he had been presented with another goal chance to draw the Munster final, and had missed it, I bellowed in his ear as I passed him that he had shit himself. I could just picture him running across the pitch to me at the final whistle and telling me to shove it all up my hole.

A couple of days later, a group of us were watching the video of the game in Clarecastle when I spotted Baker grabbing Leahy by the scruff of the neck at the final whistle. I nearly spluttered into my pint. 'Come here,' I said to Ollie, 'did someone not tell you that the final whistle had just blown and that we were All-Ireland champions again?'

Holy Jesus, I was just trying to picture myself in the same position if Tipp had won.

The week before Dublin played Tipp in the league in March 2014, Tommy Dunne was walking behind me when I drew a kick on a bag of sliotars and sent them spinning like ten-pin bowls. 'Argh, let's bate this crowd on Sunday,' I said.

I was only trying to wind up Tommy but he wasn't taking the bait. 'Go way, you clown,' he said to me on his way to setting up another drill.

There are plenty of times when I'll dial up the ante, but I never felt the need in Dublin to transform myself into one of those Pat Shortt characters and start ranting and raving like a lunatic. I don't want us to hate Tipp or anyone else. I just want us to embrace the challenge that is in front of us, no matter who or what it is.

The psychological approach is vastly different now, but what we were reared on in Clare is the complete opposite to what the Dubs were brought up on. Before the 1997 All-Ireland final, Loughnane drove our fear and anxiety of defeat through the roof. 'Everything will count for nothing,' he told us over and over. It was nearly a paradoxical statement but he kept hammering it into our subconscious.

Lohan was brilliant at half-time in that final. We were four points down and he was asking questions of fellas' manhood. 'Now is the time,' he said. 'It's easy to do it when you're four points up. Can we do it now when we're four down?'

Before we went back out, Loughnane stood at the door and stopped me from getting past him. 'Men needed now,' he bellowed. Loughnane's war-cry was still ringing in my head as we burst out that door. 'Everything we have done will go down the fucking drain!'

Every sports psychologist now would tell you to focus on the exact opposite, but it still depends on the individuals and the group you have because that was the best thirty-five minutes of hurling we ever played. We needed that fear. We fed on that stuff. It was what Lynch, Baker, Lohan, Seánie and I got off on. Jamesie, Frank, Hego and Tuts would have benefited more from the modern approach, but our fear of the apocalypse in 1997 drove us all on to ensure we didn't see the four horsemen coming over the hill.

We also had the major disappointments from 1993, 1994 and the league final in 1995 to draw on. We knew what it felt like to be trampled on, and Loughnane knew how to exploit those fears. It is easy to generalize and say that it was Loughnane's way anyway but he was fully aware of the type of guys he was dealing with. He knew that he simply had to tell Lohan that 'they're only laughing at you' to draw down the red mist from beneath the red helmet.

It's the same with some of the Dublin guys, especially Conal Keaney, Joey Boland and Peter Kelly. 'Are ye going to be bullied like you were last week?' I'd often ask them. You knew damn well that they wouldn't be. You learn to read guys. You goad the beast. And then you unleash it.

The 1997 All-Ireland was the ultimate victory, but the Munster final was Loughnane's greatest satisfaction. The atmosphere inside the dressing-room afterwards was one of total and absolute contentment. 'We're not supposed to feel it in this life-time,' Loughnane once said. 'The downside was that you knew that there was never going to be a day like that again, but it is a feeling that will last for ever.'

I suppose my own performance subtracted some of my emotion from that day, but the feeling really was that good. Len Gaynor was Tipp manager by then and I have a great picture in the pub of Gaynor speaking in our dressing-room after that Munster final. Loughnane has just come out of the shower, he is bare-chested and has a towel around his waist, but you can see the absolute respect in his face as he listens attentively to Gaynor's words.

We all had unbelievable respect for Gaynor because he played such a huge role in our success, especially mine. When we were marching around in the parade before the All-Ireland final, Gaynor was facing me in a yellow 'Finches' polo shirt. I stared at him and he eyeballed me back. I don't know what was going through his head but I knew exactly what was running through mine. 'By God, you made me but I just have to take you down today. And I'm going to bate you today.'

In an interview beforehand, I was asked about my relation-ship with Gaynor. I hadn't met him since 1995. He wasn't around Clare any more. I was busy. So was Len. So the basis of my answer was that we had more or less 'lost contact'. When we met in the Burlington Hotel the day after the final, he came to me and was mildly annoyed by what I had said. 'Feck you with your comment about losing contact,' he said. 'Who lost contact? I didn't see you calling in to me in Kilruane for a cup of tea. You're passing me as often as I'm passing Ennis.'

I hadn't meant it to come out the way Len interpreted it but I remember saying to Eilís afterwards that he was dead right. I wouldn't be someone for calling to people's houses for cups of tea but Gaynor had been such a positive influence and role model that I should have kept in touch. The time and effort he put into Clare went above and beyond his call of duty. He is a super individual. The way in which he called around to players' houses before games showed how he was man-managing long before any of us knew what the term meant.

I was a little disappointed in myself that I had let Len down, but I had enough on my plate that week with the wedding on the Saturday. The afterglow of the All-Ireland and the anticipation of the wedding turned it into one of the best weeks of my life. Rakes of relations had come home from England for the match and they returned on the Wednesday evening for the wedding. I went back to Powers after the annual 'Goal' challenge and the drink was flowing. The hours passed in a happy blur.

When Eilís rang the house the following day around noon, I was still welded to the bed. She left a stern message with my mother, who delivered it to me verbatim: 'Tell him if he doesn't cop himself on, I won't be there in Connolly church on Saturday.'

I was just losing myself in such an epic week but I had to straighten myself out. I had to be fair to Eilís too because she had to sacrifice as much as anyone with the hurling. We had planned to go to Paris for a weekend in March the previous year but I was skank bad in a league game against Galway the week beforehand. As I was walking out the door, Loughnane roared over to me, 'Fucking cancel Paris!'

I copped myself on for those few days before the wedding. I went back down to Powers on the Thursday night but I was only sipping 7-Up. On the Friday night I ordered in a Chinese and washed it down with a few glasses of wine to help me sleep.

Eilís turned up on Saturday and we had the day of our lives. Being All-Ireland champions added to the glow. The Liam MacCarthy was sitting at the top table but Leahy crept into my mind at one stage of the evening when I glanced at the cup. What if Fitzy hadn't made that brilliant late save and Leahy had rifled that ball into the net?

Holy Jesus.

12

The Fierce Summer

The morning after Cork beat Clare in the 1998 league semi-final, Loughnane rang the house for a chat. Cork had trimmed us. We were struggling for form but I had no interest in getting into the minutiae of the performance. 'Ger,' I said, 'get me a few quid and a bus because we're going back to west Clare for a few drinks.'

'What the—'

'Ger, just get me a few pounds and a minibus and I'll have the lads right for seven weeks. We'll head back to west Clare this evening, there will be no hangers-on, just ourselves. And I'll get every man to swear that nobody will have a drink again until we avenge yesterday.'

Loughnane agreed.

It was the Bank Holiday Monday in May. Word went out that we were meeting in Woodys pub in Ennis but we just assembled there before taking off back to Liscannor and ending up in Doolin. Even Jamesie, Davy Fitz and Colin Lynch, who don't drink, drove back together.

Late in the evening, we got everyone around a table and I took to the floor. 'Lads, I like a drink as much as anyone, but we make a vow here and now that not a drop of alcohol passes our lips until we beat those boys again in seven weeks. They shit down on top of us yesterday but we'll show them who the bosses are in June.'

We felt aggrieved. We had a point to prove. And that mentality set the tone for our summer.

Cork had to play Limerick in the quarter-final but we knew we'd be meeting Cork. We trained like savages in the lead-up to that game. At one stage we did twenty nights out of twenty-two. When we met Cork again in the championship, we were like wild animals. As I was leading the lads out the tunnel, I nearly mowed down Jimmy Barry-Murphy and Dr Con Murphy. 'Get out of my fucking way,' I roared at them. They did. So did Cork.

At one stage of the game, the TV cameras caught me hissing in the face of Fergal McCormack. In his *Sunday Independent* column the following week, Kevin Cashman, the old Cork hurling writer, went to town on us. On how Clare had come to wage war and destruction on all good hurling folk, how my snarling face was enough to turn the stomachs of all those good hurling people.

It was a charge we seemed to be fighting all summer because we found a battle everywhere we turned. When we went back to Killaloe after the drawn Munster final against Waterford, I asked Loughnane if I could speak to the players before he did. We were in Syl Addley's hotel and I took the lads out to the conservatory, which was baking hot like a sauna.

There had been rumours going around about me for over a year, about how my marriage was over, how I'd gone off the rails. But being called a 'wife-beater' was a new low. The comment had shaken me to my core. It was like poison on the tip of a blade twisted hard into my gut. Did people really think that badly of me? Were those the kind of low-life tales doing the rounds about me now? Despite all the battles we'd had with other counties, no player had ever debased himself by delivering that kind of a rapier thrust.

Loughnane never asked me what I said to the players but I told him anyway the following night at training. He didn't need that comment to stoke the fire burning inside him because he was like a volcano about to erupt with a vengeance of more than just lava and black ash. All it did for Loughnane was reaffirm how we, both the players and management, had been bullied all day by Waterford. He was like a nutcase.

As a form of punishment beating on that Monday night, Mike Mac walloped us with hard running. On Wednesday, we played a forty-minute match in training that was absolutely filthy. There were fights breaking out all over the field. 'Now we're ready for these bastards,' Loughnane roared.

On the Friday night, he brought us in to the goal at the bottom of Cusack Park and had us in the palm of his hand. We were mesmerized, almost hypnotized by the craze in Loughnane's eyes. We were never going to be bullied again. We were never going to dishonour Clare again. Loughnane had everybody wound up, especially Colin Lynch, whom he had been picking on and goading all week long.

On the Sunday, both sides went at it like pitched warfare, but we were like men possessed. Waterford hadn't a chance.

Loughnane had loads of piseogs. One of them was to tog out beside me any time we played in Thurles. When I returned to my place in the dressing-room after the game, he hugged me. I could feel the raw emotion coming off him like kinetic energy.

Back then, journalists were allowed to come into the dressing-room after matches. The press pack had assembled about a metre from Loughnane, waiting for the cue to approach him and open their line of questioning. Loughnane was fully aware of their presence but he acted as if they were invisible.

'We showed them, Dalo,' he said to me, the delight and disdain in his voice clearly audible. 'We gave it to them. We showed them who is boss around here.'

I was nearly pretending not to hear him, half hoping that the pack of journalists would think Loughnane was just rambling away to himself.

A couple of minutes later, after I'd emerged from the showers, with a towel around me, the press pack made their way over to me. I knew from the first question that they weren't impressed with our performance and attitude. I was diplomatic, saying that Waterford had come at us with physicality and aggression in the drawn game and it was just our intent to match it in the replay. One fella asked if I thought we went over the top. Before I could answer him, I could hear Loughnane in a fit of laughing in the background, with only his underpants on. 'Ha-ha hahaha, wait 'til you see *The Sunday Game* tonight, Dalo.'

Holy Jesus. When the journalists eventually built up the courage to approach Loughnane, he went off on a rant about fellas ringing up Dessie Cahill's radio show the following evening. He laughed off any accusations of over-the-top-tactics. His attitude was just 'Bring them on'.

And on they came. You couldn't have made up what happened next. Lynch's suspension on hearsay evidence that wouldn't have stood up in a kangaroo court. Loughnane going after Marty Morrissey after he stated on live TV that Lynch's grandmother was dead when she was still alive. Robert Frost overhearing three priests, who Loughnane said had called him and the Clare team a crowd of tramps that had it coming to them. We were supposedly all on drugs. All of it led to

Loughnane's state-of-the-nation address, when the whole of Clare stopped like they did on 9/11, and Loughnane stirred the Clare public into a frenzy.

Mike Mac spoke after training one night and said that he didn't care what the whole country thought about us as long as there was a Clare flag flying out of every window in the county. We all thought the same.

We believed exactly what we heard and what Loughnane believed we needed to hear. So did the Clare people at that time. When I look back now at some of the stuff that went on in 1998, I do cringe. But in the moment, I thought it was totally logical to assume that the world and its mother wanted to do us down, that certain officials in power were conniving and planning to burn us and the whole county in a blaze of controversy.

I fully believed Loughnane because I trusted him. I respected his judgement. Anyway, when your back is pressed tightly against the wall, you can find an angle wherever you turn. Tipp were getting fed up of us because we'd sickened them twice in 1997. Limerick were bitter because we had won two All-Irelands while they had blown the two finals they appeared in. We had beaten Cork in three successive championship meetings and Cork couldn't stomach ritual beatings from us any longer.

Jamesie said a few years later that he found the whole circus that trailed us through the summer of '98 a distraction, but it didn't bother me. Loughnane was leading the show and we just followed him. He told me about his intentions but he made all the calls and I just let him off. If anything, I felt his actions were going to galvanize us even more and that we were definitely going to win the All-Ireland.

We would have if 'Babs' Keating had kept his mouth shut and hadn't labelled his Offaly players a pack of sheep in a heap. They wanted to shove Babs' comments up his hole. Spite was the poison in their bite and the fuel in their tank for the rest of the summer.

Even at that, there was still anarchy in their camp. In the first replay of that semi-final, the players were making all the switches on the pitch. Brian Whelehan moved himself into the forwards. Michael Bond had reorganized them and rejuvenated their waning spirit but they were still a law unto themselves.

We should have buried them in that first replay. We still beat them, but then Jimmy Cooney blew up two minutes early and all hell broke loose. I often felt partly responsible for Jimmy's decision. A couple of minutes before he prematurely ended the game, I ran up alongside him: 'The time is up, Jimmy, blow it up.'

'Two minutes, Anthony,' Jimmy replied.

When the game did end early, I didn't take a blind bit of notice. I swapped jerseys with Gary Hanniffy and headed for the dressing-rooms. Brian Whelehan came running after me, desperately trying to get my attention. 'Dalo, it's not over, it's not over.'

I didn't entertain him for a second. The Offaly jersey on my back provided my answer. 'What do you want me to do, Brian, play the rest of the match for ye? Sorry, but I'll see you around.'

As soon as I entered the dressing-room, I let out a roar: 'Revenge for '48!' Only Sparrow, the late Fr McNamara and Robert Frost had any clue what I was talking about. My father had played in the 1948 county final – known in Clare as 'the Long Whistle final' – which Ruan won after a fifty-three-minute second half, due to the referee's watch stopping. A replay was subsequently ordered by the Munster Council, which Clarecastle lost.

By the time we'd reconvened in the players' lounge upstairs, we looked down and saw a sea of Offaly supporters swaying on the pitch. Johnny Pilkington was observing the brewing storm as he sipped a pint on his own. I strolled over.

'What do you make of that craic?' I asked.

'Would you think they'd just fuck off home?' the bould Johnny replied. 'Have they nowhere to go?'

Even though there was no smoking allowed in the players' lounge, Johnny was dragging the last ounce of tar out of the cigarette he was chewing on.

'What the hell are you doing here anyway?' he asked me. 'If I was after reaching an All-Ireland final, I'd be up the town having a cold one.'

The two of us had downed a couple of pints together when this announcement came over the PA: 'Tá an bar dúnta.' Johnny skipped up to the bar. When he arrived back, Michael Bond came over and half scolded him. 'Go handy on those,' he said. 'We could be out again next week.'

'We were beaten fair and square, Mike,' he said to Bond. 'We'll take our beating now.'

Bond reiterated his words of caution, even to me. I laughed at him. 'Sure, look, Mikey, we might see you again next year.'

We were after bursting ourselves in a replayed match which had just made the GAA a mint of cash. A crowd of thuggish-looking bouncers had escorted Jimmy Cooney off the pitch as soon as he blew the final whistle. Those guys were never seen before or since in Croke Park, but that whole day was surreal, and the mood was encapsulated by that PA announcement: 'Tá an bar dúnta.'

The bar is now closed . . . though those words could just as easily have translated to 'Nobody really cares about ye so just clear off'.

When Loughnane arrived back to the Burlington at ten p.m.,

he said that he had to go to a meeting in the morning and that we could be facing a replay. Every Clare supporter I met that evening said that the GAA could stick any notion of a replay up their hole, that the referee's decision was final. Yet when Loughnane asked me what I thought, I was emphatic. 'If we have to play it, we'll play it. I'd rather risk it than win an All-Ireland and have them saying we didn't do it honestly. And anyway, we'll beat them next week.'

Whatever the outcome of the meeting, we were told to assemble in the hotel lobby at ten in the morning. I was crippled and had no intention of training. Neither had Baker. If anything, we should have been heading to a pool for a recovery session, but Mike Mac dragged us out to Belfield and proceeded to murder lads.

Myself and Baker were throwing a rugby ball around the place. Mac was throwing dagger looks in our direction, totally disgusted with our no-show. He just unleashed his venom on everyone else. 'How fucking dare ye throw away an eleven-point lead. Ye haven't trained hard enough when you throw away an eleven-point lead.' I said to Baker, 'We only threw away eight points of that lead. Jimmy Cooney took care of the rest.'

When Loughnane appeared from Croke Park and said that a second replay had been fixed for Saturday, I tore into him about giving Mac the licence to flog guys. Loughnane said he knew nothing about the nature of the session. Mac was thick with me and I was bull thick with him. The mood had clearly been contaminated. The sombre silence on the bus journey home confirmed as much.

There was very little spark in training that week. By Saturday the fire had reignited, but it never had the same heat which had burned so many other teams over the previous two years. After a summer of madness, the fire finally went out.

The dressing-room was probably the saddest I ever experienced as a Clare player. I had a towel over my head, but it was no camouflage. I was in bits by the time we got on to the bus, around forty-five minutes after the match had ended.

Loughnane's speech added to the sadness of the mood. In his opinion, we had done the right thing by agreeing to a second replay. We had kept our dignity and our honour. 'Keep your heads up walking out of here,' he said to us. 'Keep your heads up for the rest of the year and for the rest of yere lives with that gesture ye made by playing today. Other teams would not have played. Their county board officers would have found some loophole, but we did the honourable thing because we always did the honourable thing.'

One of my overriding feelings from that summer was how sorry I felt for Colin Lynch. He was publicly excoriated like a criminal. But what bugged me more than anything about that second game was why the referee did not see fit to send off Michael Duignan when he struck David Forde with a hurley, because with Offaly reduced to fourteen men at that point, there would have been no controversy as we'd have been out of sight at the end.

You could tangle yourself up in regret and recrimination, and there was enough of that to wrap yourself up like a mummy. Kilkenny weren't up to much and we would have taken them in the final. Lifting the Liam MacCarthy for a third time would have equalled a feat last set by Christy Ring. It would have conferred huge status. But when I think of 1998 now, I don't think of it as a lost opportunity. I think of it as the year I lost my big brother.

The day of the All-Ireland final, a few of the lads from the club called to the house to offer their condolences. In the chat that followed, they suggested that joining them in Powers to watch the game might do me some good, just to get out of the house and leave the pain behind for a short time. I decided I would, but as soon as I walked in the door, I felt I had no right to be there. I drank two pints and was gone ten minutes into the match.

Loughnane once asked me what I would have done if we had been in the final. Would I have played? Would I have suppressed the grief for those few hours and let the emotion and adrenalin drive me on? Not a hope. I had nothing in me. I was grieving intensely for my brother.

As Offaly were in the process of winning an All-Ireland that should have been ours, I was walking up through Clarecastle village, streets deserted, the Limerick road barely humming with the sound of passing traffic. I wasn't thinking of missed opportunities, fallen glory or what could have been.

I was only thinking of Paschal.

13

The Greatest Honour

The week before Clare played Waterford in the 1992 championship, Tommy Guilfoyle had a run-in with a lawnmower. I don't know if Tommy thought he was Robocop with metal hands, or whether the lawnmower wouldn't do what Tommy wanted it to. Either way, there was only one outcome: Tommy nearly lost a couple of fingers, which meant he couldn't lead the team out the following week. Len Gaynor offered the captaincy to John Russell. Rooskey wasn't interested. 'Give it to one of the young fellas,' he said. Five days before the match, Gaynor came to me.

I was in shock. The feeling was like being told when you're a young fella that some young wan fancies you. You'd be delighted and keen to have a go but slightly nervous too. More than anything, though, it was a massive honour. Especially for my family.

I didn't see it coming. I was only twenty-two but I was really driving myself hard to make myself a better player, to become more of a forceful figure on the team. That winter and spring, myself and Davy Fitz had gone on a craze in the handball alleys in St Flannan's. Fitzy had a car and he'd call for me every

Saturday morning. We'd beat balls off the wall until our hands were blistered. There would be blood draining on to the handle of the hurley. I'd be crying for respite. Fitzy would be craving the pain. 'Ah no, Dalo man, we'll do another half an hour.'

It was only my third year on the team but I wanted to be more assertive in the dressing-room. Gaynor had this policy of having regular team meetings after training, where everyone would be invited to have their say. Some nights the meetings might only last ten minutes, other nights they could go on for over half an hour.

One evening in the spring of 1992, I cut loose when I had the floor. 'Some fellas here are deadly serious about trying to get to the top of this thing. But there are a lot of lads who are only wasting their time. They turn up here on Tuesday, Thursday and Sunday and that's all they do. I know there are some lads doing extra training after work, during their lunch breaks, extra stuff with the club, down taking frees at the local pitch. But there are only a handful of those guys. Are we fanatics or not? Are we, lads?'

It must have left an impression on Gaynor because he could have gone to plenty of other lads after Rooskey turned it down – Cyril Lyons, Jim McInerney, Sparrow, John Moroney. In the early days, all those guys were massive pillars of support. Russell was a serious warrior. Jim Mac was a huge leader. So was Cyril in a quieter manner.

Gradually I grew into the captaincy and became very comfortable in the role. I decided to step out of myself more. Good young lads were coming. They were bold and ambitious and I thought, 'I'll drive these guys on now.' I felt I had to up my game and show more leadership.

In 1993, I felt I was the proper captain. We had just been relegated in the league and Limerick were convinced we were only dead men walking and they were going to bury us in a shallow grave in that year's championship. Jim McInerney gave a great speech on the Friday night, focusing on the importance of not losing to them again in front of our own people and how we were going to 'bate them back to the bridge in Limerick'.

I was hyped up big-time myself. John Hanly once told me about words old Tom McNamara from Crusheen often used to deliver before matches. It was so old school it was 1950s speak, but I invoked a similar message. 'Cut the heads off a couple of chickens, lads, and get the taste of blood in yere mouths.' Mikey McNamara, a good friend of mine, often said that Tom used to tell the Crusheen lads to 'put your head on Sunday where you wouldn't put a crowbar on Monday'. I delivered that line as well. The core message was that we more or less had to turn into a kamikaze unit prepared 'to die to win this match'.

Myself and John Russell had it planned beforehand that we were going to level one of them before the game began. Just after we broke from the parade, I decked Mike Reale with a sneaky shoulder into the chest. I just kept going because I didn't want to get booked but Russell knew it was coming and he got down over Reale and wouldn't let him up off the ground. I met a man afterwards who told me that while he was watching this developing, he said to himself, 'Jeez, we have a few boys who are finally going to stand up to this crowd.' Sparrow and Stephen Sheedy were brilliant the same day. Limerick weren't ready for us and our level of aggression and we won a championship match for the first time in five years.

As the team grew, more and more leaders grew in tandem with the team's development. The first time Seánie ever spoke in 1994, before we played Tipp, it was as if he stripped back his skin and displayed the steel underneath. The passion and determination and love for the Clare jersey which oozed out of him that night encapsulated how Loughnane referred to him in his book – if he was in the Mafia, he'd be their main assassin.

Jamesie was a lot like Cyril. He was a real leader but it was more in a practical and articulate sense. He would often speak about the type of ball we needed to play or give instructions on how he felt we needed to adjust our tactics. Doyler wouldn't be a man for talking. Mike O'Halloran was. He'd often more than likely say 'Give it to them' – as in timber the living shit out of the opposition. Davy Fitz was always very vocal. Lohan wouldn't say much, and then when he did, everyone shut up, even Loughnane. Tuts would say something if he felt the need to say it. If things were going wrong, that's when you'd hear Baker. That kind of summed him up. He could be shocking in league games but he always stepped up on the big day. Baker was very confident in himself. He never had any fear of anyone, no matter where they were from. You never expected Fingers to be a big orator but he made his own contribution in a more subtle way. He could be one of the three or four of us who might get together in the team hotel on the morning of a game to discuss tactics.

Lads on the periphery of the panel made big contributions at different times. They could speak about a hurt and a longing and an appreciation that maybe we took for granted. Tommy Corbett from Éire Óg captained St Flannan's to an All-Ireland Colleges title in 1991 and was a super underage player. He never made it at senior level but he was on the extended panel in 1997. The weekend before we played Tipp in the 1997 Munster semi-final, he made a massive speech down in Cork. Something as basic as Tommy talking about how privileged we should feel – the panel of twenty-four – were the perfect words for us to hear at that point.

As time went by, the team became comfortable in its own

skin. Certainly into 1998 and 1999, there was a very easy understanding within the squad. Anybody was free to talk if they wanted to, but it wasn't like a club dressing-room where you sometimes had lads yapping for the sake of talking. It just became easy after a while. And it worked.

Loughnane would often run stuff by me. The Friday night before we played Limerick in 1996, he said that he planned to speak about how Tom Ryan had dishonoured the Clare jersey with comments he had made that week. Loughnane wanted the last word that day and I had no issue with it. 'Bang on,' I'd say to him.

You would be trying to come up with something fresh, but Loughnane always had an angle on everything. We were nearly mad for every game. We always had a grudge to settle. Invariably you'd try and take an angle off Loughnane's angle. We often had more angles than a trigonometry textbook.

He always had his antennae out for comments made by other managers. Johnny Clifford from Cork was over the Munster Railway Cup team in 1994 and he called Jamesie 'the little boy of the O'Connors'. It was a harmless, almost affectionate term for Jamesie, but Loughnane doused it in kerosene and lit the match. Johnny wouldn't say boo to a goose, but before we took on his Cork team in 1995 Loughnane had us believing his words were a cruel sneer.

Even during training, Loughnane looked like a man possessed. His T-shirt would be drenched in sweat from just roaring. I asked him once how he had any voice at all and he said his remedy was loads of honey and water. He must have had his head in the honeypot as often as Winnie the Pooh because he never shut up once training started.

The training games reflected his persona on the pitch. They were pure savagery. You could do what you liked. It was often a free-for-all. Lohan and Conor Clancy would be belting each other to such an extent that if they did it on the street they'd have been locked up.

Loughnane liked the defenders to rough up the forwards, and the forwards didn't always stand for it. One evening in 1996, Jim McInerney called them into a huddle before the game began. He said that they were sick of taking our shit and they openly declared war on us from the first ball. Jim himself was going around like a Grim Reaper in a bad mood, cleaving anything that moved. It was a total butchering match. There was only a handful of ground-rules observed by the players, which was basically no slapping down on the hands and breaking fingers.

By 1997, fellas were getting a bit rattier and were losing the rag more often, but Loughnane always dialled it up. Even when we'd play two in-house games on training weekends the week before big games, he'd always somehow have the score level on the Friday night, with the second forty minutes to be played at seven a.m. the following morning. 'We'll see who has the balls for it in the morning,' Loughnane would say.

We played so many big games in Cork over the years that we seemed to have shares in Páirc Uí Chaoimh. After one Friday-night training session, Loughnane asked the groundsman if he could be there for 6.30 a.m. on Saturday to let us in. Loughnane slipped him £50. Your man grabbed it and said, 'Ah sure, look, we're all GAA.' I heard him and so did Tony Considine. 'Did you hear your man,' said Considine, 'and he after stuffing the fifty quid into his pocket?' The following Sunday we were going in under to the tunnel to the dressing-room. I was psyched up like a lunatic. The groundsman was hanging around and Considine hit me a puck into the back. 'We're all GAA, boy.' I nearly pissed myself. Considine was a great man for breaking the tension.

Loughnane always understood the importance of the group dynamic and not stretching it beyond breaking point. When we would go on those training weekends, he always allowed Baker and myself to head off and have three pints. We'd plant ourselves in the quiet corner of some pub and shoot the breeze for a couple of hours before heading back. We never had more than three pints because we didn't want to abuse Loughnane's trust.

It was a ritual I started coming up to big games in 1995. I didn't want to go behind Loughnane's back so I was upfront about it. Throughout 1996 and 1997 I would go to an Italian restaurant in Parnell Street in Ennis on the Sunday before a big game, load up on carbohydrates with pasta and wash it down with a couple of glasses of wine. I felt that was my chill-out time before I'd start building myself up for the game from Monday morning.

We celebrated hard after the matches. Loughnane encouraged it because he felt it strengthened the bond we had. He'd be asking me who was out. Then when we'd come back on the Thursday night, he'd snarl at us in disgust. 'Look at the fucking state of ye.' I used always to say to the lads, 'The [*Clare*] *Champion* is out, it's time to straighten up.'

The only time there was hassle with drink was after the drawn game with Tipp in 1999. Myself, Baker, Tuts and Sparrow and our four women stayed in Jurys in Cork that night. We didn't expect the game to end in a draw so we had made our own plans and didn't intend on changing them. I got Eilís to buy a bottle of Radox in a supermarket and I sat in a warm bath for an hour. It was better than sitting on a bus for nearly four hours, which is what happened anyway.

After dinner, I had four pints of Guinness. Baker only had three before heading for bed at 11.30. I was gone fifteen minutes later. Seán Stack was a selector with us that year and he was also in the hotel with his wife. We were all in the bar that evening but we stayed together in a corner. Maybe I should have invited them over, but Stack never came near us.

When we went to Cusack Park for a recovery session at two p.m. the following day, management were waiting for us. Stack told them that we had been drinking and Loughnane was bull thick with the replay fixed for Saturday. When I got into the dressing-room, Baker told me that they had already savaged him.

They were in the other dressing-room so I marched straight in to face the inquisition. I was primed like a top defence lawyer.

'Have ye a problem with four of us staying in Cork last night?'

'There is, Dalo,' replied Loughnane. 'Were ye drinking?'

'Yeah, I had a couple of pints.'

'What's a couple of pints?'

'Four pints of Guinness with my dinner. What's wrong with that?'

'There's a lot wrong with that,' said Loughnane. 'Especially when Tommy Dunne got three points off you yesterday. I don't think Tommy Dunne was drinking pints last night.'

'I can't account for Tommy Dunne's movements last night. For all I know, he could have had ten pints last night.'

I knew Tommy no more drank ten pints than Daniel O'Donnell did but it was descending into a back-answering bitching match. Then Considine intervened and took control.

'What time were ye in bed, Dalo?'

'I was gone at a quarter to twelve, Tony. Sure ask Seán, he'll tell you that.'

'How many pints did Baker have?' Considine asked.

'Three. Maybe he had more but I can't confirm that.'

'What time did the other two lads go to bed?'

'How the hell do I know? I didn't ask them this morning but they looked OK to me.'

'Fine so,' said Loughnane. 'That's the end of it.'

It wasn't really. It was the end of Sparrow. The recovery session involved Mike Mac running the shite out of all of us. Halfway through the torture, Sparrow just jogged into the dressing-room, togged off and never came back. He had been an unused sub the previous day. He knew the end was coming so he finally cut the cord. He wouldn't give Loughnane the satisfaction of having the last word. Typical Sparrow.

There were plenty of times when it was easier for Loughnane to have a go at substitutes or peripheral players than established ones, but in fairness to him, he always took my word. We didn't blackguard him. We hadn't gone overboard that night, but you dare not push it either. He savaged me one night after the 1995 Munster final, a couple of weeks before we played Galway in the All-Ireland semi-final. He said our carry-on since the Munster final had been a total joke and I was the clown leading the circus. The same night, Stephen McNamara wasn't training because he was sick. Loughnane hit him a belt into the stomach with his fist. 'Sick,' he said, 'is coming out of Croke Park after being beaten by Galway.' If Loughnane was in that kind of a mood, Mike Mac would then be invariably rolled out to administer serious punishment with a heap of runs that would murder Mo Farah.

Loughnane could be vicious during training games. He'd be half commentating while the play was developing, which added extra spice to the matches. He used to insult certain players to get the best out of them, but he would insult everyone else because he felt like it. 'You were a fucking disgrace in the league last Sunday. You were cleaned out. They were laughing at you above in the stand.'

Loughnane cut loose on Hego one night in 1997. Hego wasn't going great and Loughnane roared at him, telling him that he was in a trance. Hego went nuts. He thought Loughnane called him a tramp. He said to me coming off the pitch, 'I'm not taking that shit.' I tried to calm him down: 'Sure I've been called a lot worse, take no notice of him.' When we were in the showers, Hego was reeling off all the abuse Loughnane had given him over the years and concluded that this was a new low. The lads knew what Loughnane had said but they didn't let on anything. I had to pull the towel up over my face in case he'd see me laughing. Hego was so incensed that we thought he was going to grab Loughnane by the throat, but not even Johnny 'Mad Dog' Adair would have the balls for that. We knocked some mileage out of that for a couple of weeks. We were all going around to Hego telling him he was 'in a trance'.

Being the captain, I was invariably the intermediary between players and management. The week of the 1997 All-Ireland final, Hego was named on the starting team but everyone knew that Niall Gilligan would be starting in his place. Hego was told by management on Monday but he called in to the shop to me the following day to tell me he wasn't happy. He had an uncle flying home from the US for the game and he wasn't allowed to tell anyone he wasn't starting.

I rang Loughnane to relay his disappointment, and Loughnane cut me in two. 'If Hego isn't happy with the situation, tell him to stay at home on Sunday. And if you aren't happy, you can stay at home with him.'

If Hego thought getting dropped was disappointing, he had twice as much to chew on after the match: he was brought on and taken off again. Hego was a great player for us in those years. He was really underrated and was our best player against Limerick in 1996. He was also a great character, a sound bloke with a brilliant sense of humour. He was just really disappointed at being dropped for the final in 1997, but you were wasting your time trying to reason with Loughnane.

The only one who wouldn't take Loughnane's lip was Sparrow. Coming up to the Cork game in 1995, there was debate about whether or not Sparrow would start. I mentioned it to him going to training one night and Sparrow just brushed it aside with the palm of his hand. 'If Loughnane wants to pick me,' he said, 'he can pick me because he knows how good I am. I regularly cleaned him out.' Sparrow had that brazen attitude towards Loughnane because he had played with him in 1986 and 1987. In all the training games we played, I never once heard Loughnane give out to Sparrow. If he was shouting abuse in Sparrow's general direction, Sparrow would just shout back.

At the end of the 1998 season, Loughnane rang me up out of the blue one day. 'Dalo, go up to one of the travel agents there in town and book a holiday.'

Booking holidays had never been part of my captain's brief so I more or less asked him if he was raving.

'Go up and book a holiday,' he repeated. 'Nothing fancy, the Canaries or somewhere handy. There's a good few quid in the holiday fund. The lads deserve a break after the year we put down.'

I booked a week in Gran Canaria plus three nights in London. When I rang Loughnane back with the details, he never even queried it. 'Spot on, spot on.'

It was one of the best holidays I was ever on. Loughnane had to come home early because his father John James passed away a couple of days before we were due to fly home. We were back in time for the funeral, but Loughnane gave me a few cheques to settle the hotel bill and pay for dinners, along with an explicit warning that there was to be no pay-per-view TV.

We were staying in this palatial hotel in Kensington. There was this huge fountain just inside the door, with all these tropical fish swimming around in tanks at its base. There were more fish there than in an aquarium. I remember looking at it when I was checking in and saying to myself, 'Holy Jesus, this could go any way.'

On the morning we were leaving, the phone rang at nine a.m. It was the hotel manager, a Mr Charlemagne, who was of Asian descent.

'Mr Daly, would you please come to my office.'

I knew exactly where this was going. 'I'll be down in a few minutes, bud. Is there anything wrong?'

'Yes. They try to kill fish.'

I arrived downstairs in an auld tracksuit and pair of sandals and announced myself to Mr Charlemagne as Mr Daly.

'Come, I show you,' he says, leading me over to the scene of the crime.

He outlined how some of the lads had tried to assassinate Flipper junior and his army of small friends. They'd used heavy bundles of Sunday newspapers as depth charges. Some of the papers were so thick they'd have taken out a salmon. They could have been scraping exotic fish off the bottom of the tank all morning.

In my own mind, I identified the main suspects immediately. They denied it. 'I had nothing to do with it,' one of them insisted.

'I bet you suggested it though.'

'Well, I'll show you what they were at,' he responded, which was a total admittance of guilt. They were more or less teasing each other. 'I bet you won't get the big lad there with the fancy pink spots.'

I just signed the cheque and ran.

It was inevitable that I was always Loughnane's first port of call when it came to liaising with the players, gauging the mood within the camp or making plans for the next battle. The morning after we lost the 1999 Munster final to Cork, Loughnane called to the house.

'Now, Dalo, we have to resurrect this from somewhere. We're down but we're not out. We'll have Jamesie back for the Galway game and they won't be ready for what we'll bring. And if we get another shot at Cork, we'll definitely beat them. We'll have that badness again inside ourselves.'

I was low, but it sounded an attractive proposition. We thought we'd beat Cork. We were slightly complacent and got caught. In the parade beforehand, Donal Óg Cusack was roaring, 'We're Cork, we're Cork, boy! We have twenty-seven All-Irelands. Ye have two.'

I was nearly half tempted to correct him. We had three All-Irelands. He must have forgotten about 1914. I was only laughing across at him. 'Go way, young lad, you fucking eejit.' In reality, I was taken aback by his comments, which was a clear sign that I wasn't fully tuned in. The same day, Timmy McCarthy roasted me.

Loughnane's initial plan of action was to send the players off on a bonding weekend to Finnstown House Hotel in Lucan. We could also take in the Leinster final between Offaly and Kilkenny. 'A few pints, some craic, and we'll get the spirit going again. And I'll leave you in charge.'

'Good man, Ger,' I said to myself.

We played golf in Finnstown on the Saturday before going into the city centre that evening. I was coming home in a taxi with John Reddan when I saw one of the subs chasing a peacock around Finnstown House with a five-iron. Another player was tearing after him on a golf buggy.

'Holy mother of Jesus, stop the car,' I said to the taxi driver.

I jumped out and asked them what the hell was going on.

'We're bringing the peacock home with us when we catch him,' they said. 'And then we're going to stuff him.'

Jesus wept.

My own standards slipped that summer. We drew with Galway and I went to the Galway Races the following day. The replay was fixed for the Bank Holiday Monday and I took serious liberty with the extra day's grace. I had two glasses of red wine at the racecourse and the buzz coursed through my system like a narcotic. When we went back to Tony Nugent's pub in Clarecastle, I drank a few pints.

I held Alan Kerins scoreless in the replay but Brian McEvoy took me for four points in the All-Ireland semi-final against Kilkenny. That night I was racked with guilt over how I'd behaved at the Galway Races. I felt I had let myself and the team down. I had dropped my discipline. I'd carried half a stone on my hips into the summer and never really shed it. My lifestyle and eating patterns weren't what they needed to be. I drank more than I should have. I wasn't proud of some of my actions in 1999 but I remember talking to Brian Lohan after that season and he said it was a general malaise in the group. The previous year had mentally drained us, but that wasn't a good enough reason either for the slackness in attitude.

The edge was just gone from us.

When we played Waterford in the championship replay in 1992, the game was tied at 0–14 each when we conceded a late free near the touchline, sixty yards out. My man Kieran Delahunty took it and drove it over the bar.

When he arrived back into the corner, Delahunty turned to me and said that we should stick to our traditional music. For his cheek, I sunk the hurley into his ribcage, but a minute later he landed another free and the match was sealed. That jibe, though, remained in my head. When I started my speech on the Hogan Stand after the 1995 All-Ireland, it came back to me. 'Down through the years, we've listened to many jibes. We were told to stick to our traditional music. In Clare, we love our traditional music. But we love our hurling as well.'

I wonder if Delahunty ever knew where that line really came from.

The issue of captaincy was never aired at the outset of any year. It just rolled on from one year to the next for eight seasons. I never asked any questions. The first time it was raised was during the league in April 2000. After one of our early games in Miltown–Malbay, Loughnane and I discussed it. At the end of our chat over a meal in the Armada Hotel in Spanish Point, Loughnane said we would leave things as they were for the league. A few weeks later he called me down the line in Cusack Park and said that he was changing the captaincy. I had struggled for form that spring and Loughnane's reasoning was that he wanted to allow me to focus fully on my hurling.

I was taken aback. I couldn't say much, but I'd have preferred it if he had made the change in February. I had been captain for so long that losing the honour was like hitting a trip-switch in my head. All the other switches flicked off in my brain as I was driving home after training that evening. Were my legs gone? Was my message gone stale? Is this Loughnane's way of dropping me?

There had been obvious slippage in my form in 1999. I knew my playing days were numbered but I would still have loved to finish up as captain. It cut the ribbons in my heart because I didn't want to relinquish such a massive honour; but my biggest fear that evening was losing my place. Playing was far more important than being captain. Maybe Loughnane was right. Maybe it was the spark I needed to reignite my form because I never put in more effort than I did in the two months prior to the 2000 championship. I lost so much weight I was gone gaunt. Outside training, I was living in the Clare Inn gym, and walking the roads as much as Rob Heffernan. I was never more ready for a championship game.

On the night Loughnane announced the changing of the guard, he had barely started this paean to my eight years of captaincy when I cut him off. 'Ah, save it for the book, Ger.' The dressing-room erupted in laughter. One chapter was closed. Another was opening.

Lohan was always a massive leader for us. Pound for pound, he was the best player I ever played with. Any time he would clear a ball, it was like another fella clearing three balls. The crowd went crazy. He had an aura about him, with the red helmet. He was quieter than me and was far more of a serious character. When I took over as manager for 2004 I made Seánie McMahon captain, but Lohan was still a natural fit to take over from me. He had a huge influence on all of us.

On my last championship game for Clare in 2000 Lohan led us out the tunnel, but I had no less influence in the dressing-room. It was one of the best games I ever played but we were flat and Tipp hammered us. They were laying down markers all over the field.

We were always comfortable with the guerrilla warfare of the championship. We got off on it. In our transformation from losers to winners, we pushed physical force to the limit of the law and beyond. We all took up arms, especially the defence, but that raw badness was non-existent that day. We needed that poison in our veins to drive the machine forward. When it was fully ramped up, we trampled over everything in our way like a

Panzer tank. Hatred was our fuel. We hated everyone. We hated referees, the Munster Council, the opposition, opposing managers. Maybe that was why I played so well that day. Deep down, I was probably still bulling with Loughnane for taking the captaincy off me.

I knew the show was over at the final whistle. I walked over to Leahy and extended my hand. 'The war is over, Johnny,' I said to him. 'You won't be seeing me any more.'

You knew by Loughnane's body language in the dressing-room that the show was over for him too. After he said what he had to say, he ambled over and shook my hand. 'Ah, Dalo,' he smiled, 'defiant to the last.'

I had my jersey off, a mat of sweat covered my body, but I stood up and hugged him tightly. It was as much to say, 'You're gone, I'm gone, and that's that.'

The embrace was an unconditional show of love for all Loughnane had done for us as a team and for Clare as a county. We were different characters, but our attitude and thinking were broadly similar. In our revulsion at losing and our rejection of Clare's history of submission, we were identical. We wanted to see better days, but we never thought we would see the days we had, those eternal summer Sundays when we felt untouchable, bulletproof.

When I started with Clare twelve years earlier, the very idea of winning Munster and All-Irelands was a distant fantasy. We made it a reality. We had the time of our lives.

14

All Over

Playing with Clare was such a passionate love affair that breaking it off was always going to be a massive wrench. So much so that the end-game amounted to a long goodbye.

I'd first contemplated retirement at the end of 1999. I felt my legs were going that summer, but at the beginning of 2000 my heart overruled every other vital organ in my body. I made a pact with myself that it would be my last year but I buckled under Cyril Lyons' entreaties and returned to the panel again in March 2001.

Coming back only three months before the championship was cutting it very fine. I knew Clare were going with younger defenders during the league but I was playing well in training. When we played Galway in a challenge game in Tubber on the eve of the championship, I was really happy with how I had played. On the car journey home, I told my clubmate Danny Scanlon that I was confident of starting.

Gerry Quinn was nailed down at number 7 so it was between myself and Dave Hoey for the other wing-back position. They went for Hozer. Dave was a great lad. He was a real character who gave me great service when I was manager. He had a fine game on his debut, but I was still annoyed that I didn't make the starting team for that Tipp match.

John Minogue was a selector and I always felt that he never fancied me from my time in Flannan's, where he was a teacher. Louis Mulqueen was the trainer and there had been a lot of tension between us when he was coaching St Joseph's Doora-Barefield. We had some savage battles with Joseph's and I wasn't sure if Louis was turning the gun on me after some of the stuff I had said to him in the heat of those battles over the years.

When I look back on their decision now in cold blood, management obviously wanted me more for my dressing-room presence and experience than my hurling ability. Some of the older lads had left, or were cut, after the previous season and there was a slight transitional feel about the panel.

In the vacuum, I couldn't help myself. Four days after we lost the league final to Tipp, less than four weeks before we were due to meet them again, I went berserk during a players' meeting in the dressing-room in Cusack Park. I felt we were comforting ourselves with the belief that we were going to be better than we'd shown in the league final. In my opinion, Tipp were going to be twice as good in June as their display in May.

We were wired to the moon when we ran into them again and I take most of the responsibility. Cyril said to me on the Friday that he wanted me to have the last word in the dressing-room. I knew I wasn't playing so I was able to focus on the message I wanted to deliver. I made the most savage speech I ever made in my life. It was so raw and full of emotion that most of the players ran out the door with tears streaming down their cheeks. It may have been over the top, but the words came from deep down in my gut. Tipp weren't just coming to Cork to bate us, they were coming to bury us.

We were all on a war-footing. Páirc Uí Chaoimh was rattling like a boiling tureen. When Tipp introduced John Leahy, it stirred the Tipp crowd into a frenzy. I left my place on the dugout and made my way up towards the Clare terrace at the city end. I raised my arms and remonstrated with the Clare crowd like an orchestrator, demanding a response, an audible counter-strike to the Tipp roar that would reach our lads' ears.

By that stage, I was like a raving lunatic. As I made my way through the chaos of the tunnel under the covered stand at half-time I spotted a high-ranking Munster Council official – a Tipperary man – walking into the referee's room. He certainly had no business in there as a Tipperary man. When I went over to investigate, I could hear him giving out hell, cursing and blinding like a sailor.

I was ready to break the door down, but a steward stopped me. When I told him I was going nowhere, he called a Garda. The cop told me I had to move away.

'Why should I be told to leave? Why has that guy been allowed in that door?'

'Leave it alone,' said the Garda. 'Just walk away.'

The game hinged on a sequence of Tipperary frees, all of which I believe were wrong calls. The referee blew Colin Lynch for over-carrying on the fifth step. Declan Ryan shouldered Lohan into the chest when he was coming out with a ball and the referee gave a free in. The most scandalous decision of all, in my view, was awarding a free against Baker for knocking the ball off Tommy Dunne's hurley with a perfectly timed flick. Tipp won by one point and went on to win the All-Ireland.

I completely lost the head at the final whistle. I headed straight for the referee's room. The door was closed but I was prepared to kick it down if I had to. I had only barely squeezed inside the room when I caught the referee's eye.

'I don't mind being beaten, but what you did out there was a disgrace,' I roared at him.

'Ah go way, Anthony, go way now,' was his tame response.

His umpires were pushing me away as I unleashed the tirade. The cop who had cleared me at half-time arrived and escorted me up the corridor to the Clare dressing-room. Hordes of Tipp supporters were milling outside their dressing-room but I was like a time-bomb waiting to go off.

In all my days as a player, I was never as mad. I was devastated by the manner in which we lost that match. Our season was over. I knew my playing career was as good as over too. I got word a few days later that a two-month suspension for verbal abuse was pending, but the referee never reported me. He probably weighed it up and decided not to highlight the issue. It was a good call. If he had, I would have publicly gone to town on him.

Eilís's uncle Jimmy Bermingham from Kilrush was a bachelor all his life. His aunt May Hennessy was married to Murty Browne and they ran a pub in Tullycrine in west Clare, just south-west of Kilmihil. They had no family so they left Jimmy the pub and the couple of acres of land beside it. Jimmy farmed the land and worked the pub before he closed it in the early 1970s. It was shut for twenty-five years, but Jimmy kept a few bottles of beer in stock to share with his neighbours and show some return which allowed him to keep the licence.

One night in 1998, I got a call from Eilís. She said she didn't know whether she had good or bad news but she had major news: Jimmy wanted to leave her the pub.

I was thrilled. It was always a dream of mine to have a pub and now we had been granted the opportunity. Jimmy had also left us a site beside the pub to build a house, so we suddenly had a massive decision to make. We were living in Ennis and weren't sure where we'd finally plant our roots and grow our family. We decided to make our home in west Clare.

The pub was in bits because it had become derelict but we knocked it into shape. Jimmy had already put a new roof on which saved us from levelling the place to the ground. That decision also preserved the character and shape of the original building, which was first constructed in the mid-1800s.

When we opened in October 1999, we got a great start. The pub had been closed for so long that it quickly became a focal point in the area. It created a whole new culture. It even spawned a new soccer team.

A friend of mine, Brian Bradley, was bringing his local pub soccer team from London over to Ireland for a five-day trip. They were going to spend a day in the pub but they were mad keen to play a match and Brian asked me if there was any chance I could round up a team. I recruited a clatter of local fellas and we loaded the pub with cans of beer and played the match in the local school field in Kilmihil. The English boys tanked us but we went back down to the pub and had a brilliant night.

In the early hours, fellas got talking. Some lads were dreaming about a franchise and a dynasty but we set down the foundation stones of a small, rural soccer club. Marty Culligan offered to be manager. Michael Dillon said that his father, Bertie, might give us one of his fields, the top meadow, for a pitch. I could organize goalposts and gear through the sports shop. We named the team Tullycrine Celtic.

We entered Division 3 of the Clare league and were runners-up to Cratloe in 2001. Our pitch became known as 'The Bertie Bowl' while we christened the field beside it 'The Bull Field'. When the Ennis teams came out to play us and the ball would be kicked into Dillon's field, they would only go as far as the gate because there was invariably a bull there. One of our lads would have to retrieve the ball because the townies were afraid that the bull would have them for breakfast.

Playing soccer that winter kept me in sufficient shape to return to the Clare panel just before the 2001 championship, but that regime wasn't going to suffice when I was called back again for 2002. I couldn't face Crusheen that January so I asked Cyril Lyons for a break until the end of the month before I threw myself back into the madness. I kept the weight in check by doing some jogging and going to the gym but even that was hard going. In my own mind, that was telling me everything I didn't want to fully admit to myself.

I soon had no choice but to accept reality. It was difficult to balance running the pub with trying to play inter-county hurling, but my body was beginning to bend under the load anyway. When I went back training, I was way off the pace.

We were training one night in Crusheen and I was in a running group with Colin Lynch. I was in serious oxygen debt and only hanging on but one of the rookies cut a corner and Lynch stopped the group, went back and caught the young fella by the lapels. 'Do you think that will win you an All-Ireland?' he said. I remember saying to myself, 'This is animal stuff.' I wouldn't have wanted it any other way but I was nowhere near that level. Pain is always part of the deal of pre-season training but my mind was processing more than just the pain I was experiencing; it was also computing the hardship to come down the road. I knew it was over.

A couple of nights later I was caught late with a rep who was showing me new stock after the shop had closed. By the time I got to Crusheen it was 7.10 and the group were just finishing the warm-up. As I did a lap of the field, I heard this unusual noise. My heart sank. I thought we were doing the bleep test. More torture.

Then I realized it was Louis Mulqueen's voice. He had a little microphone attached to his jacket, which was linked to two speakers. I joined the group and gravitated towards John Reddan and Davy Hoey, who would always be good for a bit of craic.

'What in the name of Jesus is this?' I said to the two boys.

When I look back now, I can see the absolute logic in Louis's method. My own voice would be in bits some nights after training. Louis was a teacher and he needed his vocal cords the next day far more than I ever needed my voice. But for some reason, that was the breaking point for me. 'That's it,' I said to myself. 'I just can't do this any more.'

I sat back into my little red Peugeot van afterwards and was trying to talk myself out of my decision on the road home. 'Are you basing this on poor Louis trying to do the right thing for him and the group?' But it didn't matter what defence case I was trying to construct. It was baseless and without foundation. I just didn't have the heart or stomach for it any more.

The next night at training, I arrived with an overcoat. I walked out to the middle of the field and spoke to Cyril. He didn't try to talk me out of my decision.

There was a sense of relief as I drove back home. I walked into Murty's and drank a few of my own pints.

I played sweeper for Tullycrine Celtic. I was no Franz Beckenbauer but I always felt that reading the game was a big strength of my hurling and it was far easier in soccer, especially in Division 2 of the Clare league and especially with a fully fit John Downes in front of you. I really enjoyed myself, but the games were beginning to extract a massive toll on my body. After matches, my ankles, hips and knees would swell up like balloons.

In that spring of 2002, my ankles were constantly swollen. I wear a size nine shoe but I was struggling to squeeze my feet into every runner and shoe I had. Eilís borrowed a couple of pairs of her father's slippers – size ten and a half – which I wore around the house and the pub. That offered some respite physically but it was no balm to my mind. I went to the doctor, who referred me to the arthritis unit in Merlin Hospital in Galway. I met with Professor J. J. Gilmartin who said he wanted to do a chest X-ray. Afterwards, I was sent for a breath-lung test.

When Prof Gilmartin showed me the results on screen, it was like looking at a satellite weather picture smeared with fog. The first thing that came into my head was that I had leukaemia. I had sarcoidosis. I hadn't a clue what that was but it sounded a lot better than leukaemia.

Sarcoidosis is a disease involving abnormal collections of inflammatory cells that can form as nodules in multiple organs. It is a relation of TB which can be caused by an immune reaction to an infection or some other trigger that continues even after the initial infection is cleared from the body. The consultant told me it was completely treatable for white Caucasians, but it is like a form of cancer for black Caucasians because their immune system can't cope with the attack.

I had probably picked it up from inhaling a germ, most likely in the pub because there was no smoking ban in Ireland at that time. I had never smoked but I was told I had the lung capacity of a seventy-three-year-old smoker. And me thinking I was fit, swanning around the soccer fields of Clare like Beckenbauer.

Treatment was an extremely high dosage of steroids. I also had to stay in hospital, in the leukaemia ward, for four nights to undergo a series of tests, one of which was a lung biopsy. One night I hit off across the road to throw a bet on a horse. Ladbrokes was beside Supermac's so I went in for a burger. One of the nurses noticed I was gone and she rang Eilís, who called me in a panic.

'Where the hell are you?'

'I'm here in Supermac's. I was starving.'

I said nothing about the horse, which came in at 12-1. I arrived back in the hospital and washed the burger down with a glass of water and more steroids than you'd squeeze into a box of tic-tacs.

One of the side-effects with steroids is that they blow you up. I put on a stone and a half within the first month. As I became more inflated, so did the rumour mill. I supposedly had every disease ever known to man. Then I had cancer. Some lads even had me waked and buried.

The only end-game was hurling. Tommy Howard had taken over Clarecastle in 2002 and I was really looking forward to giving him and the club everything that season. Professor Gilmartin said I could swim and walk but contact sports were a non-runner for at least a year. As a compromise, Howard asked me to train the team. It was another opportunity to cut my teeth as a coach and it provided some form of methadone for the habit I was still craving.

We lost the county final to Sixmilebridge and I was still coaching the team in 2003 when my course of steroids finished and I had a notion to go back hurling again. I got myself re-graded to play Intermediate and ended up just fighting with team-mates I was good friends with. I was mad for road and was never interested in just playing hurling for the craic. That was what soccer was for. The Clarecastle Intermediate team was stocked with former Clare minors and good players but their ambition stretched as far as the commitment they were willing to give. That was completely understandable and acceptable for them, but I couldn't get my head around that lukewarm attitude.

At half-time in a league game against Clonlara, I wound up having a stand-up row with John Pyne and Eoin Vaughan, two guys I have massive time for. The two boys told me to piss off, which more or less translated into the words, 'If you want to go back playing senior, go back. And leave us alone.'

The seniors got to the county quarter-final and Howardy asked me to slip on the number 26 jersey. We were in trouble with fifteen minutes remaining and he threw me in at corner-forward. I won three balls, scored one point and made another. Jeez, like Lazarus, I was back.

I started the semi-final against Wolfe Tones and was taken off with twenty minutes to go. I was absolutely bulling with Howard. He handed me a water bottle and I caught it and fired it against the dugout. 'If you can't accept that decision,' Howard said to me, 'it's not my problem.'

My ego had got in my way. In my own mind, the whole of Cusack Park was laughing at me. I was raging with myself for coming back and putting myself in this position. I spent five minutes stewing in my own brew, then Alan O'Loughlin went down with a knee injury.

'If you're that thick,' Howard said to me, 'will you go back on?'

'Put me back in corner-back,' I replied.

In the last quarter, I must have cleared eight balls. I stopped a certain goal with a flick. Howard was declared a genius around Clarecastle that evening. I am better at other things in life than accepting that I'm wrong but I will always hold my hands up when I have to. 'It worked out for both of us,' I said to Howard afterwards.

We beat Ballyea in the county final, and walking down the

village that evening with my fifth county title was as satisfying as any of those previous victory journeys. After we lost to Patrickswell in the Munster club quarter-final later that month, I went to the club chairman Martin Reynolds.

'Is there any way I could have that jersey, Martin?' I asked. 'I'll pay for it if I have to.'

'Does that mean what I think it means, Dalo?' he replied.

It did.

My playing days were finally over.

We have a small cross to bear now with Orlaith's condition but she still lives the most vibrant life she can. We are just thankful for the daughter we have and the beautiful young lady she is becoming. We've become conditioned to watching her being paralysed and left helpless with epileptic fits and learned to cope with the process and getting her through it. Anyway, as a family we've had our share of health scares and the anxiety and worry that comes with them.

Eilís and I were at Claire Kelly's wedding in 2007 in the Falls Hotel in Ennistymon and were just sitting down to the meal when Eilís's phone rang. She had undergone tests the previous week and her doctor wanted her to come immediately to Limerick. That was an obvious red flag. I wanted to go with Eilís but she insisted on my staying. Like myself, she was trying to suspend any thoughts of potential bad news.

Over an hour later, Eilís rang, crying. The only word I heard was 'cancer'. I was in shock. I was raging with myself for not having gone with her but my mind was scrambling for normality and reason. I told her to go to my mother's house in Clarecastle and we'd meet there.

When you hear the C word, it's a natural reflex to think and fear the worst. Eilís had been diagnosed with ovarian cancer.

When we met with Dr Kevin Hickey, probably the most impressive doctor I ever came across, he outlined the route Eilís had to take. Maybe chemotherapy, possibly surgery, but definitely hardship. The prognosis was good, though, because it had been caught early. It hadn't spread, and Dr Hickey felt he could remove the cancer in one fell swoop with surgery. Within three weeks, Eilís had had a hysterectomy.

On the evening of the operation, I went to a local restaurant up the road from the Limerick Regional Hospital and bumped into Ciarán Carey, the former Limerick hurler. We'd had several chats over the years over a pint. Carey could arrive in Clarecastle or I might meet him in Sixmilebridge after a Clare game. But we just made this perfect connection that evening. We spoke for over an hour. I told him the whole story. He told me about the demons he had faced in his life. 'It's never easy,' he said. 'Something will always come after you.' I went back to the hospital in a far better place than when I'd left it.

Eilís made a great recovery. She spent a week in her mother's house and I stayed at home with the kids. It was hard going at times trying to explain why Mammy wasn't coming home but our lives soon returned to normality. The terror which has wrecked so many homes had visited our door but it didn't come inside.

When Eilís went back for her initial check-up, there was no need for radium treatment. Dr Hickey had cleaned out all the cancerous cells. The follow-up scan confirmed as much. Her one-year clearance soon melted into further positive check-up results, and she got her five-year all-clear in August 2013.

We're just thankful that Eilís was diagnosed in time because we've seen the devastation and destruction that disease and death can bring. We've all lost members of our extended families, but watching my young cousin David being claimed by leukaemia exacted a huge toll on us all. It was almost unbearable.

You never want to think about the horror that death could wreak if it arrived on your doorstep and barged its way in, but our family's history of heart disease sometimes gains tenancy in my mind. You never know when it could strike you down, because the first time that worry intruded into my life I had never been as fit.

Before we played Tipperary in 2000, my sisters had been on to Eilís about getting myself screened. The memory of Paschal passing away so young had been on their minds. Michael and Martin had gone for check-ups and they saw no reason why I shouldn't do the same. We had trained like animals and I was jumping out of my skin but I went to the cardiac unit in the County Hospital in Ennis for peace of mind, for both myself and my family, just ten days before the game.

The following Monday, Dr Terry Hennessy rang and said he wasn't that happy with the readings from the stress test I'd done on the treadmill. The results were irregular and he wanted to do an angiogram. So six days before I was due to chase Tommy Dunne and Johnny Leahy around Páirc Uí Chaoimh like a greyhound, this was landed on my plate.

I rang Loughnane and asked him if he thought I should have it done. If I was to proceed, I wouldn't be able to train for a week. 'Jesus Christ, of course you'll have it done,' said Loughnane, half laughing, half serious. 'I won't be responsible for you dropping dead below in Páirc Uí Chaoimh.'

On the Tuesday, I had a tube inserted into my groin, which peered into the arteries around my heart. It was a daytime procedure and I sat out training that night under the camouflage of a groin strain. If it got out that there was something wrong with my heart, half the county might have thought Loughnane had literally flogged me to near-death.

The boys went hard that Tuesday night but I had my feet up

in the stand. I got the all-clear the following day and just went for a few handy pucks on the Friday evening. When we lost to Tipp on the Sunday, I had one of my best ever games for Clare. The boys were flat but I was fizzing.

You could drive yourself mad worrying about what could happen to you with a family history of heart disease, but I got a desperate scare in April 2013. We went to Bere Island for a beastly training camp the week before the league semi-final but I never made it. I drove from Clare but I wasn't feeling great on the road down. I thought it might be indigestion. I had gone through Cork city and was somewhere near Inniscarra when I got this tightness across my chest. I was struggling to catch my breath. Beads of cold sweat started running down my forehead. 'I'm on the way out here,' I said to myself.

I rang Eilís in a panic. She told me to turn back. I called Richie Stakelum and he issued me with the same instruction. Eilís made a few calls and I wound up in an emergency VHI clinic in Cork city. They got oxygen into me as soon as I landed and it was like a baby getting its mother's milk. The nurse on duty was from Kilkenny and she recognized me.

'This management craic isn't easy,' she said.

I had an electrocardiography (ECG) done immediately and everything showed up fine. I more than likely had a palpitation and an anxiety attack. I knew the weekend was going to be savage, that the army lads were going to make the players' lives a misery for two days. I had planned to suck up some of that hardship with them by doing some of the running. Maybe that thought, of a furry old sheepdog with plenty of layers around its waist trying to hold on to its pride when pitted against greyhounds, brought on the attack. I don't know.

From the first time I met the Dubs, I told them to fake it until you make it. At least appear like you're boxing clever, even if you're getting smacked around the ring. I always abided by that principle because I was never as confident as I often portrayed myself.

When I was in St Flannan's, I always had plenty to say, sometimes to teachers. But I got lost in that world because I loved it so much and I felt so comfortable there. It was only when I started having success with Clare that I had to deal with anxiety. A couple of weeks after I won my first All-Star in 1994 I was asked to present medals at the Ogonnelloe social. A few minutes before I was due to speak, this wave of anxiety coursed through my body. I barely made it through the evening. I have lived with sporadic forms of anxiety ever since.

I enjoyed Brent Pope talking about his anxiety issues in his book because I could completely relate to them. I can stand up in front of anyone and deliver a speech. I could talk the hind leg off a dog or charm the birds out of the trees. I have always been optimistic and positive, but there are still times when I have to check myself. I might be talking at a corporate gig, relating my management experiences to highly qualified business people, and I might suddenly ask myself, 'What the hell am I doing here? I might make a holy show of myself.' I know I won't, but that anxiety often sneaks into my subconscious.

I know I'll always be fine when I prepare well, and that frames everything I do now. I am always very conscious of trying to be absolutely professional in all I do. When I missed a few Dublin sessions earlier in the season through illness or because Orlaith wasn't well, it really bothered me. I felt I was letting the lads down. Deep in my gut I knew I wasn't, but that is just the way I'm built.

Managing the Dublin hurlers could be a highly pressurized position at times but I absolutely loved it. I've been involved in management now for over ten years. But another part of me thinks I should still be playing. I'd be confident of lining out with the Clarecastle Junior Bs if I made a real burst for a month.

We were training in Clontarf one day and I stepped into a drill where one group was short a body. I'd normally be patrolling the pitch like a sentry, so Hedgo came over and asked if I wanted him to step in instead. I ran him. 'Go way from me, Hedgo, I need this.'

I was bulling with myself a minute later when I put one ball out over Cian O'Callaghan's head. The lads in the group were going like blue-arse flies but I'd like to think that they knocked a bit of craic out of me doing it with them as well.

When Joe Kernan stepped down as Galway manager in 2010, Gilly said that big Joe was an awful loss to me. He reckoned I'd now have the biggest belly of inter-county managers patrolling the inter-county sidelines. I was carrying extra weight at the time and I had another screening done at the Hermitage Clinic in 2010. Thankfully, I got the all-clear again.

I could do with another check-up again soon because you can never be safe enough with our family history. On the other hand, I'm nearly as bald as any of the Keanes – my mother's family – and they're nearly all in great health. My mother is still flying around the place. My uncle Mickey is eighty-five and he runs around like a March hare.

I don't know if I'll make it that far. But then I dive into the Pollock holes in Kilkee, which is as cold as the waters in the Antarctic. Every part of your body is shaking when you emerge, and I just say to myself, 'I'll be here for another while anyway.'

15

Stepping Up

When we met up in St Vincents before the league final in 2011, there was too much tension and anxiety hanging in the air. I even overcooked my speech. I returned to how much it would mean to win, focusing more on outcome than the process, when Gary Keegan had been wiring the exact opposite message into my hard-drive.

On the bus journey into Croke Park, I felt I needed to do something to puncture the pressure. Before we got into the dressing-rooms, I said to myself, 'I'm going to lighten the mood.' I always have swimming goggles and blue shorts in my bag because I often go for a swim when I stay over. So while Martin Kennedy was getting the warm-up area ready and the players were loosening out before the warm-up began, I began stripping off. I didn't go as far as the boys in *The Full Monty*. I left the shorts on, but I looked like the 'Dave' character in that film because I'd a nice fat belly on me at the time.

So in I walked with the goggles and the swimming hat and the look of someone who had just walked out of a lunatic asylum. As soon as I'd opened the door there was this exasperated look that said 'Who the Jesus is this?' I remember catching Alan

Nolan's eye and he nearly keeled over. Once I knew that the players realized it was actually me and not some poor fella who had escaped from an institution, I summoned the best Limerick accent I could manage.

'Whaare's the pooool?'

In my head, I was trying to recreate this image of a fella who had taken a wrong turn in the leisure centre of a hotel and arrived back at the lobby.

'Iz thaare no poool here at all?'

Then I turned on my heels, walked straight back out the door and put back on my tracksuit. I wasn't too sure how it had gone down but I was certain it hadn't done us any harm. When I made my way back into the dressing-room, there was a general grin. Lads were still sniggering. Kennedy was shaking his head, half exasperated with my actions.

Then I addressed the players as the Dublin hurling manager, not as some Tommy Cooper impersonator. 'Look, lads, that stunt was just to lighten the mood. Let's go out and enjoy it. I know we want success but let's just go out and play with freedom. Cut loose. Express yourself. That's when we play our best.'

And we did.

Can you imagine Cody pulling a similar stunt in the other dressing-room? I have tried to picture it. Jesus, it would be some sight.

We were having a few beers the following day and Conal Keaney said to me that the general conclusion after I walked out the door was 'Yeah, we have a complete fruitcake for a manager'.

I have been managing at inter-county level now for nine of the last eleven years and I'd like to think that I have evolved a lot during that time. Some people still accuse me of being too close to the players, but that perception stems from my time with Clare. They thought I couldn't separate the loyalty I had shown those players as team-mates from the ruthlessness I needed to show them as their manager. But that was never an issue for me.

The theory that I went into management too soon was exacerbated by the fact that I was only thirty-four when I took on the Clare job, but I knew exactly what I was doing. I still felt that we had a chance to win an All-Ireland with the players we had and that a lull was coming when most of those older guys moved on. That's exactly how it played out. After being narrowly beaten in two All-Ireland semi-finals, the senior team faded from the inter-county landscape for five years.

We got the most out of ourselves during those three seasons between 2004 and 2006 but Loughnane was still always on my case. He continually accused me of showing Lohan and Seánie too much loyalty, but those two guys were the best players in their positions in Clare at that time and there weren't any better alternatives. You do tend to reward people anyway who have served you well. That applies in every walk of life. Even Cody has been accused of being too loyal to certain players. But I'd always choose a guy with character ahead of someone unproven. That is just too often interpreted as blind loyalty and an un-willingness to change.

Everyone needs time to evolve, and it was obvious in my first season in charge in 2004 that I was only a rookie. My management style was based on what I had learned from Len Gaynor and, mostly, Loughnane. I knew no other way, and I thought his way was gospel. I'd be a great man for not second-guessing myself but I should have done my own thing from the start. It probably took me until 2005 before I started to find my rhythm and develop my own style.

I'd put a lot of work into honing that style over the winter of

2004/05. I began to read voraciously. I had always been a reader but my attention was more drawn to Paul Williams and lads killing each other on the streets than lads murdering themselves in the pursuit of sporting success. I began hoovering up sports books and searching for an edge wherever I could find it. I pored over the words of Alex Ferguson, Clive Woodward, John Wooden and any similar guru-material I could get my hands on.

I had recruited good people to my backroom team: Fr Harry Bohan, Alan Cunningham, Johnny Glynn and Liam Moggan. I began to delegate more, but Loughnane was continually cutting me down, telling me in print to 'Do it yourself, Anthony'. That day was gone. The days of me standing up roaring and shouting were over. I couldn't do the bulk of the work like he did, but Loughnane didn't realize the volume of on-field leaders he had either. He subsequently found out as much when he went up to Galway and couldn't win a game in two years.

I'm not cutting down Ger. He did it his way and it worked in Clare, but I knew we needed more than the standard stuff which had applied in the 1990s. We introduced video analysis but we were still two years behind Cork. Ger didn't do video analysis. The day after the first Offaly game in 1998, I suggested to him that maybe we should watch the game again, both the players and management. 'I saw enough yesterday,' he barked back at me. 'If you want to look at it again, you can watch it yourself.'

I knew we needed to go down that road and I just wanted to cover as many angles as I possibly could. I knew we had fellas whose heads I couldn't get inside. Harry and Liam did that job for me, which allowed me to focus on other areas of my management.

As a manager in the modern game, if you're not always learning, adapting and evolving, you're going nowhere. At the end of

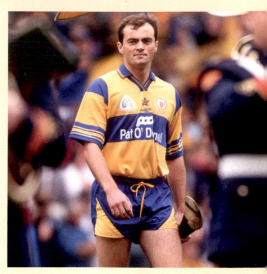

Left: Cork bate in the rain, 1993. Clare FM's Michael Gallagher enjoys the moment.

Above: Nerves, what nerves? 1995 – oh Lord!

Below: Ready! 'Our Day' – first All-Ireland win in eighty-one years.

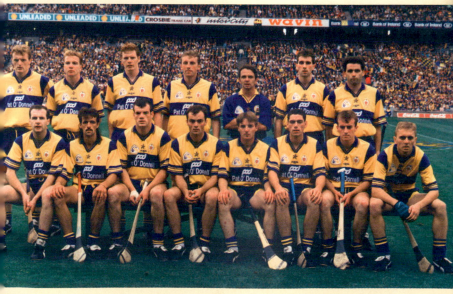

Above: 'Goodfellas': Mike, Tony and Ger.

Left: 'The Gaffer'.

Below: Five magpies, and probably the best magpie of them all, the Sparrow. (*L–R*) Sheedo, Sparrow, me, Nev, Morr and Fergie 'All Star' Tuohy, 1995.

Above: 'Fergie, can we talk about that tonight?' Meanwhile, Fingers is in the zone.

Right: At the 1997 Munster final: 'There's always the back door, Johnny.' Lynch disappearing with the ball in the background.

Below: Seánie Mac's eyes in the background tell it all. Total respect for the legend from Kilruane MacDonaghs' Len Gaynor.

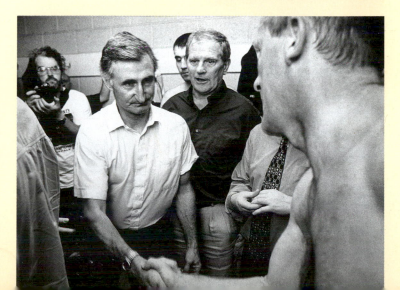

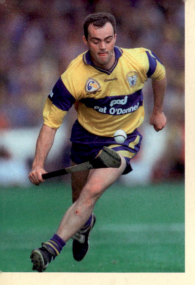

Above left: All-Ireland final, 1997. Just a total honour to wear the saffron and blue.

Above right: Celebrating 'The Double'. Liam and the Irish Press Cup coming home together, with Joe O'Meara from the minors. Are we Kilkenny in disguise?

Left: 'Have you the watch set right, Dickie?' With referee Dickie Murphy and Offaly's Hubert Rigney, the third match in 1998. An unforgettable summer.

Below: Against Kilkenny in 1999. My last day with the honour of leading the boys round. Brian Quinn is psyched.

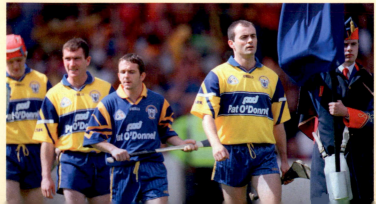

Above: Taking off one of my best friends. 'This management craic is not gonna be easy.' Ollie Baker, a Clare legend.

Above left: With Harry, Ollie and Alan at the National League, 2006. So near and yet so far.

Above right: Relentless shadow: hard to break free.

Below: Only in Dublin. A press conference to announce me as the new manager, with the men who recruited me, Gerry Harrington and John Costello.

Right: First day out. Vinny telling me who's who.

Below: 'Jesus, lads, the Hill is nearly full!'

Left: Borrisoleigh and Clarecastle united. Richie and I celebrate after winning the League.

Below: 'Did ye lose Aoife?' League final, 2011.

Above left: The most animated Maor Fóirne in the game, Hedgo. The Bainisteoir is very calm.

Above right: After beating Kilkenny in the 2013 replay: The tunnel in O'Moore Park was never as sweet. And Dotsie was a star.

Below: Finally, *finally*, I get to say 'hard luck' to the greatest!

Left: Ryan O'Dwyer at his best. Leinster champions at last, 2013.

Middle: 'Danny, you beauty.' Danny Sutcliffe: an All Star at twenty-one years old.

Bottom: Here come the girls! Magic moment after Johnny had lifted the Bob O'Keeffe Cup, 2013.

the 2012 season, when Dublin bombed out of the champion-ship, the players came back to us with a document that assessed all aspects of our season, including the management. One of the points raised was that performance was not being fully rewarded, that we had been too loyal to certain players who had played well in 2011. When we subsequently took ourselves apart on that accusation, we had to hold our hands up and accept that we should have been more ruthless.

When that point briefly raised its head again in February 2014, when we took off David Treacy ahead of Conal Keaney at half-time against Galway, I regretted it immediately. I knew I and the management had not been true to our principles, and that was the last time it happened. You live and learn, and you move on armed with those lessons.

After the 2003 season, there was a general feeling around the county that the players wanted a change. I knew managing Clare might appeal to me down the line, but at that time I had plenty of items on my 'to-do' list before I could begin considering that option. Seánie McMahon was the first to ring. Then Lohan and Fitzy called. Colin Lynch dropped in at the shop to make his request in person. The general gist from all these entreaties was 'We think there's another All-Ireland in us and that you're the man to get it out of us'. My reaction basically was 'Holy Jesus'.

I wasn't sure if Cyril Lyons had been keen to stay on, but after he departed, Loughnane wrote a column in the *Star* where he lambasted the players for pushing Cyril out in a heave of player power. I didn't know where Loughnane was coming from because he was the first person I contacted for advice after the players had approached me. 'Go for it, Dalo,' he said. 'Jesus, if anyone can get a year out of them, it is you. Go absolutely gung-ho at it but only do it for one year.'

Loughnane effectively made up my mind for me. Pat Fitzgerald, the county secretary, rang and said I was the guy both the players and the board were after. That was a huge start, but I still rang Cyril for advice and a list of questions as long as your arm. The call may have seemed strange from Cyril's point of view but I never felt bothered by ringing him. He was withdrawn when he initially answered the phone but he soon loosened up and doled out as much advice as I requested. He knew that if the boys were after pushing him out, I had nothing to do with it.

At that stage, the biggest drawback was naturally my closeness to so many players who I had soldiered alongside throughout my career. Only eighteen months separated my final training sessions as a player and my accession to the managerial job. That played on my mind a lot before I took over, but as soon as I did, I crossed that threshold and swore there was no going back. At my first night meeting the players, I gave it holly. I told them I was here to win an All-Ireland in the short-term, in 2004, but that whatever history, or perceived history, I had with a lot of the group, it meant nothing from that moment on. The line was firmly drawn.

The last thing I could bring to the job was gratitude for the support of the older players for my appointment. I had to reach an accommodation because there was no point in me changing my personality completely, to become a dictator who wouldn't talk to them. It would have been ridiculous for me to turn into something I'm not. If they wanted me as manager it wasn't for me to become someone else when I became manager. It was to appeal to them to give it everything themselves.

I appointed Seánie captain straight away. McMahon is like myself, he's a good man to winter well. He wouldn't be out drinking porter, he'd be sitting on the couch, drinking pots of tea and eating plenty. Seánie was always a savage man to eat. In other years we always accepted Seánie would be right for the championship, but I told him that I needed him right for the stamina runs in deep winter, like a beacon at the top of the group leading the younger lads through the darkness. During the three winters I ended up spending as manager, McMahon was like a lighthouse in an angry storm. We used to do these brutal one-mile runs around the pitches in St Flannan's and there wasn't one night when McMahon wasn't in the top five. He retired at the end of 2006 but he cemented his reputation as probably the greatest hurling centre-back during those final three seasons.

Those older guys went beyond the call of duty for me, but they gave the service I expected of them. They were super men, but I still never found the occasional need to goad them that difficult because I knew the response I would get. One night after training in 2004 I absolutely savaged Seánie, Jamesie and the two Lohans. 'Where are the men that I once knew gone? Yere gone soft and we'll win nothing until ye harden up. Ye can go for coffee with lads all ye want when yere packed up. Ye can go to lads' funerals and send them mass cards for their dead mothers and fathers all ye want, but we're at fucking war now with these lads and we need ye to turn into killers again.' The next night at training, I called Seánie to one side and asked him if he thought I had gone over the top. 'You were one hundred per cent right,' he said. That pack of assassins polished up their rifles and sharpened their spears and went back to the frontline.

When hard calls came my way, I made them. Out of loyalty to myself, Baker agreed to give inter-county hurling one more year in 2004. He burst himself to get fit and made the championship team for our opening game against Waterford, but I took him off after fifteen minutes. He was bulling, looking at me while coming off and shaking his head, but within twenty minutes he was up with a bottle of water on the sideline. It left no stain on our friendship. The possibility never entered my judgement.

I got the response I was looking for from everybody after we went off the cliff-edge on my first day when Waterford annihilated us by nineteen points. To this day, I still can't put a finger on what went wrong. We were stuck to the ground. I was hoping an earthquake would hit Thurles and a giant hole would swallow me up. Nothing went right. Jamesie didn't start because of a hamstring injury; we brought him on and had to take him off again minutes later. When Jamesie was coming off, Tony Browne roared out at me, 'Bring 'em all on, bring 'em all on, we're fucking ready for all of them!' I stared back at Browne but I hadn't even the heart to answer him.

We were sliced, diced and wiped out. Seeing the crowds streaming out with fifteen minutes to go was heartbreaking, absolutely devastating. I struggled to compute the ramifications in my head because I felt I was letting the whole county down. I wasn't on the field but I had to take responsibility for the performance and I really struggled to come to terms with it.

I was never as low after a match. I was shell-shocked, completely numb. When I got home, I collapsed in a heap. Eilís and the kids were gone to bed and I was still sitting motionless in the dark when she came down looking for me in the early hours.

I didn't know where to turn. I swallowed a sleeping tablet and just wanted the world to go away. I woke up at eleven a.m. the following day and went downstairs for a glass of 7-Up. I heard a rapping on the patio door. I didn't want to know about it but it was as if somebody was trying to break the door down with a sledgehammer. It was Tommy Howard and the two Sheedys outside.

'Come on,' they said, 'let's go.'

'Get the hell out of here,' I replied. 'I'm going nowhere.'

I tried a second time to run them but they weren't going any-where. 'Come on,' said Stephen Sheedy, 'get the keys of the pub, we're going over.'

The three lads were a huge support to me that day. We drank very little, just chatted it out. I felt much better about myself afterwards. Later that evening I sent a group text to the whole squad – 'It's fight or flight now.'

The whole day against Waterford reminded me of a let-down world heavyweight title fight. You had the weigh-in, the sparring session for the media, the press conferences and all the hype that goes with a big event. But once we got into the ring and Waterford put up the gloves, we ran. We never ran again. We didn't win anything but we always fought.

We battled our way through the rest of that summer of 2004 and forged a pathway through to an All-Ireland quarter-final showdown with Kilkenny. We came up with the idea of playing Alan Markham as a sweeper to silence their guns and we drew with Kilkenny in Croke Park. We went with the same tactic for the replay in Thurles and restricted them to just 1-11, but that gameplan was only effective to a point because it diluted our own scoring power. Kilkenny won by five points.

Johnny Glynn had been a huge hit with the players as fitness coach in that first season but he wanted to develop the strength and conditioning culture in 2005 so we set up a gym in the old squash courts in St Flannan's for individual and group sessions. We got fitter and stronger and more comfortable with our whole system. Kilkenny beat us in a league final and we went one step further in the championship by reaching an All-Ireland semi-final.

On the night before that game, the lads did a super group session with Liam Moggan. As a reference point, Liam focused on Muhammad Ali and the famous 'Rumble in the Jungle' when he outwitted George Foreman with his 'rope-a-dope' tactics. Lohan and Colin Lynch initially never bought into that kind of stuff but they soon did, like everyone else. We were never as ready for a game as we were against Cork. We were savagely mentally alert and we nearly pulled it off. We were six points up entering the last quarter but once the Cork tide turned, we couldn't stem it. I was never as proud of a group of players as I was that day, but pride didn't do much to siphon off the hurt we all felt after that defeat. That was our best chance to win an All-Ireland. Galway took Kilkenny out in the other semi-final and we all felt we would have had Galway's number in the final.

I was ready to walk away, but the lads asked me to give it one final shot. Bar we won an All-Ireland and I was given another term to build a new team, I was definitely going at the end of 2006. We kept searching for that edge that would take us over the line. I consulted a lot more with Liam Moggan. I delegated more. I handed over more responsibility to the players.

We tried completely different methods. On the Thursday night before we played Cork in 2006, we herded the players into a bus with the windows blacked out and drove to Dromore Woods in Ruan. Three army rangers, who were already there before us, handed the players tents, ground-sheets, a few crackers and a bottle of water each. They were looking at us like we'd gone completely mad as the management hopped back on to the bus. 'All the best, lads,' I said to the group, 'We'll see ye in the morning.'

It was only a smokescreen. They knew it was ludicrous preparation three days before we were due to take on the All-Ireland champions. Still, when we returned an hour later, most of them had their tents up and were bracing themselves for a night's hardship. We loaded them back into the bus and treated them to a big feed in the Sherwood Inn. 'We just wanted to see if ye were ready,' I said. 'And I know we are now.'

Cork beat us, but we made it back to another All-Ireland semi-final. The players put together their own motivational video which they screened the night before that semi against Kilkenny. We tried and tried and tried but we still came up short, going down by eight points when the scoreboard made the game look like a complete impostor.

We didn't win a Munster title or an All-Ireland but I felt we got the best out of that group of players. Fr Harry Bohan was a huge factor in that achievement. He is more known now around the county as a great humanitarian and socio-political activist, but it is easy to forget the extensive managerial experience he has. He guided Clare to two league titles in the 1970s and remained actively involved with Clare teams until the mid-1980s.

When I was first appointed Clare manager I was only just turning thirty-four. Alan Cunningham was only a few years older, so I saw Harry as the ideal father figure to benefit both the management and players. He was a good man to fight his corner on team selection but his role was more as a facilitator and counsellor, somebody who could connect with players.

Some lads would ring Harry before they'd ring me. They loved him. Some of them really bonded with him, especially Tony Griffin, Diarmuid McMahon, Tony Carmody, Andrew Quinn and Barry Nugent, guys who we extracted massive performances from in those three seasons. They might be strolling out the gate after training, Harry would be smoking a cigarette in the car, and he'd strike up a conversation. Before they knew it, they'd be pouring out their soul to him. He just got the best out of people. Harry was parish priest in Shannon when Lohan was growing up and he always said he was the only reason he went to church. 'Going to mass with that man,' Lohan used to say, 'is like therapy.'

When Harry said mass at the team hotel in Dublin on the day of a big game, it was as good as a team talk. Three or four lads never went. I never pushed it on them but all the lads who did go could never understand the guys who didn't. 'Why would you miss those masses?' Gilly would often ask. 'They're mighty.'

Gilly used to love them for more than Harry's oratory skills. Harry would invariably get him to do a reading, or act as altar boy. Harry would dole out Holy Communion – 'Body of Christ' – then Gilly would stick the paten in under your Adam's apple, half trying to choke you.

'Aaaaamen.'

Harry could have a group in the palm of his hand. Peter Garvey, who owned the Sunnybank Hotel, was a great friend of mine, but when he passed away back in December 2013, the Dubs couldn't get over Harry. He said his funeral mass and Harry was still talking an hour and fifteen minutes after mass started. 'I'm keeping ye a bit,' he said. 'But there were a lot of ye here who stayed a lot later in the Sunnybank and ye didn't mind.'

That positive vibe was reflected throughout the squad, but Ger never seemed to have any faith in us or what we were about.

After a while, it was obvious a trend had emerged. No matter who we were playing, he would tip us in his column in the *Star* on a Saturday. If he was on *The Sunday Game* he would be critical if we lost before going to absolute town on us in his Monday column, especially myself.

I was invited on a charity junket to Cyprus for ex-GAA players at the end of 2004. Loughnane and Tony Considine were on the same trip. I was spending most of my time with Michael Duignan, Stephen O'Brien and Christy Heffernan and I only really ran into Loughnane at the airport. I didn't spend any decent time in his company until one of the last nights of the trip when I had a drink with himself and Tony. I told him that I was thinking of making Tommy Howard a selector in 2005 but that I wasn't sure if the county board would agree to another Clarecastle man being part of the management. It had originally been made clear to me that I had to take geographical representation into account when assembling my backroom team. Loughnane was aghast at those restrictions. 'Forget about the board,' he said. 'Do whatever you want to do.'

Maybe Ger felt that I didn't do that enough, but he never spared me when the opportunity arose to let fly. His comments were so public and so loud that neither I nor anyone else could get away from them. He was invariably forthright in his commentary, but his observations caused increasing offence to more than just me. Some of the other players he soldiered with through the 1990s regarded his columns as excessively critical and personal. It was the kind of stuff you accepted from him behind closed doors when he was our manager, rationalizing it back then as his primary motivational tool. But reading it cold on the printed page, it had a different quality.

Naturally, Loughnane wouldn't accept the charge of disloyalty. He gave it hard to every county and he wasn't going to be seen to spare any. But he was hard, really hard, and some players suffered more than others. In 2001 he was heavily critical of Baker, who he accused of 'swanning around, living off his reputation'; he later declared that Baker was a 'spent force'. It was the kind of goading that Baker was accustomed to under Loughnane's management when they routinely insulted him to wind him up. But that was private, and for a common purpose.

In the Diamond Bar one night over Christmas in 2004, Baker and Loughnane spent the whole night eyeballing each other. Gerry Kelly, owner of the Diamond and a great supporter of us in Clare, said that the tension was unreal in the place that night.

I never got involved in any verbal altercations with Loughnane during my time as Clare manager, even though I had plenty of opportunity and reason to get stuck in. Throughout 2005, he never let up. At one stage he described me as 'indecisive, and timid, lacking the confidence and cockiness that marked him as an exceptional captain'. Worst of all, he stated, 'his [as in, mine] team reflects this'.

Every inter-county manager is intimate with pressure, but a lot of it was off the scale because Ger cut the ground from under my feet so often. In hurling commentary Loughnane's is the loudest voice, and he was roaring in my ear. There was a lot of tension, and it was a rotten time. If I'd thought it was going to go that far, I probably wouldn't have taken the job in the first place, especially when I had based my decision on Loughnane's advice.

There were times when I felt really let down. We had some hugely painful defeats where the hurt was more acute because I knew we had done everything we possibly could. I couldn't have asked any more of myself, the management or the players. But when you wanted some support and backing, Loughnane disparaged our entire preparation. When we lost to Cork in the Munster championship in 2006, bringing the squad over to Bisham Abbey for a training week was described as a 'total joke'. We were on the floor but it appeared as if Ger was tramping the dirt down on top of us, kicking it into our mouths and eyes.

I learned to deal with it, but targeting my backroom team was the worst of it. In print, Loughnane kept encouraging me to 'clear out' my backroom. Maybe he felt at the time that I should have been doing more of the training myself but I took the majority of the hurling coaching once the clocks went back, just as he had always done himself. He obviously thought otherwise because he christened Johnny Glynn the 'soccer guru'. He must have assumed Johnny was coaching us how to play tiki-taka with sliotars. Johnny's role was just a more scientific approach to what Mike Mac had done a decade earlier, and Johnny was one of the best physical trainers I ever came across. He was brilliant at his job.

Loughnane found an angle everywhere he turned. Fergie O'Loughlin was training the Miltown footballers in Rockmount woods – Cardiac Hill as they call it – the week after the Willie Clancy festival in 2005, purely to run the drink out of them. Loughnane was walking his dogs up the hill when the boys passed him. In the *Star* a couple of days later, Ger said he witnessed one of my 'sidekicks' purging a hurling team on one of the warmest days of the year. He had no clue of the context but the last line in the column was, 'Wouldn't it make you sick.'

My sidekicks and backroom team were obviously grating on Ger, but the dye was cast. Ger never let up. The relationship we had enjoyed when I was captain and he was manager appeared to be in tatters. He had drifted away from all of us and the distance looked like a gulf.

Two months after we lost to Kilkenny, I was walking through the market in Ennis on the day of a funeral when I spotted Loughnane and his wife Mary coming against me. 'Ah Jesus,' I said to myself, 'look who's coming.' About ten yards before we came against each other, he started smiling. 'Weeeelll, Dalo.' We stopped up, and it was just like old times again. Even though I had that residual anger inside me over his comments, I didn't want to start shooting back. It wasn't the time or the place, and

I had no interest in falling out with him either. I just settled the account in my own head, wrote it off on the spot like a bad debt. We were still shooting the breeze twenty minutes later when Mary had to pull him away to make the funeral in time.

There was never a night over the following couple of years when we met or spoke about that time. We just weren't moving in the same circles. We never had a cross word between us, though I had a swipe at him on *The Sunday Game* the night after Cork beat Galway with fourteen men in 2008. 'Maybe Ger is realizing now,' I said, 'that the players had something to do with our two wins in the 1990s.'

Loughnane sent me a nice text when I got the Dublin job and he has given me the support in print ever since that he never seemed able to summon when I was with Clare. Even when we lost to Clare in 2012, he suggested that it might be time for me to move on but he still wrote later that I had 'crucially' got the support of the county board.

It is strange, but we began to get close again after Ger was diagnosed with leukaemia in 2011. Close is probably too strong a word to use, but the odd time we do meet now we talk like it was the old days again.

It was a shock when he got sick. We all thought he was indestructible. I sent him a text as soon as I received the news, which summed up how all his former players felt. 'You're the best man to bate it,' were the words I scribbled on the screen. 'Nothing ever bate you yet.'

My cousin David was in St James's Hospital with the same disease around the same time as Ger, in 2011. Ger had actually taught David in school and he was very cut up when the illness claimed David the following year. Ger battled his way through, just as we all hoped and knew he would.

The week after I heard he'd been diagnosed, I got a card and left it in the shop and all the lads came in to sign it. On the morning of the 2011 Leinster final, I tried to get in to see him. One of the nurses came out and told me that he knew I was there but she couldn't let me in for fear of him picking up an infection. I left her the card to pass on to him and he sent me a lovely text a couple of hours later.

We were going to war with Kilkenny but he was waging his own war, fighting to stay alive, battling a disease that isn't selective in terms of who it claims. We spend our lives squabbling and fighting about hurling. We routinely ask ourselves to die for the cause, continually getting mired in the agony of defeat and unfulfilled ambition, but people like Ger Loughnane are fighting every day to win the ultimate battle. All the battles he won as a player and a manager, all those crusades and conquests pale into insignificance when placed against this greatest victory – staying alive.

16

On the Wall at Last

Every time I used to go upstairs in Parnell Park, I would tip the photograph of the 1961 Leinster title-winning team and say to anyone alongside me or within earshot: 'We'll be there, we'll be the next crowd beside them.' We are up on the wall now.

The satisfaction after the 2013 Leinster final win was incredible. I knew how much it meant to Dublin but it was vindication for myself too. I was emotional because the journey had been dotted with so many days when I doubted myself, so many dog-days when everything collapsed around me, so many questions. How can I not get it right? Why am I not connecting with the boys? Am I too nice? Am I not enough of a mean, bad bastard? Looking for the answers tore me apart.

I couldn't hold back the tears because it hadn't been just the five years of emotion with Dublin which were welling up, there were three years with Clare too. I was finally able to say to myself, 'I can do this. I am able for this thing.'

The worst days leave scars that are never easy to conceal, but those wounds are your roadmap in trying to avoid similar pitfalls in the future as you keep trying to get up that mountain.

In 2010, when I thought we had got the foothold we needed and that lads would drive up the rest of the mountain themselves, I still didn't understand the whole animal that is Dublin GAA – the media, the attitude that we are Dublin and that we almost expect to win. I didn't notice it at the time but there was a drop-off in intensity in training and we fell off the mountain and landed in an unmerciful heap.

Kilkenny hockeyed us. We regrouped, beat Clare in the qualifiers, won the Leinster U-21 title the following Wednesday night and went into our next qualifier against Antrim looking and thinking that we were in good order. The game was as good as over when we led by six points with fifteen minutes remaining. We took off Rushey, who had played in the U-21 final, and Antrim got a run on us. We started doing crazy things with the ball, went into a fatal tailspin and got caught.

It was our final game of the season and there was a sort of doomed feeling afterwards. It was the worst dressing-room I was ever in. We were all numb and shocked. I don't remember walking back to the car. I was like a fella who was concussed from getting a belt to the head.

Eilís rang and I didn't want to talk to her. Úna, who was seven at the time, was upset in the background. Orlaith was eleven and I knew her first question when I got home would be, 'Why did ye lose, Daddy?' I couldn't face home so I took the M4 turn-off on the M50 and drove to Galway. With a baseball cap pulled right down over my eyes, I booked into a hotel, paid cash at the desk and stole away to the bedroom like a convict on the run. I didn't drink. I could have taken the sting out of the pain with a bottle of wine but I didn't even want to. I spent the night looking up at the ceiling.

I sat in the car early the following morning and started driving. I hadn't eaten since the pre-match meal the previous day but I hadn't the stomach for breakfast. I headed home on the N17 but I turned right at Kilcolgan, headed for Kinvarra and burrowed my way deep into the Burren in north Clare. I eventually stopped in Fanore. I went into a coffee shop and bought a sandwich and a coffee. I left the sandwich after me and picked up a slice of fruitcake on the way out the door. 'I'd say you need the coffee this morning,' the young fella behind the counter said to me. I thought I was still in Galway but I'd crossed into Clare.

I drove down the coast road and stopped off after a couple of miles. I got out, sat on some rocks around Black Head, sipped my coffee and ate my fruitcake as I tried to make sense of it all. I couldn't. I was tempted to drive down to the safe-house of Murty McMahon's in Ennistymon but I couldn't even face that sanctuary.

As I stared out at the Atlantic Ocean, I was taking myself apart. Why am I in this position? What did I do wrong? Did I take my eye off the ball? Why did I let this happen? I was playing the blame game in my head to try and deflect some of the heat but I knew that wouldn't provide much cover from the snipers out there looking to pick me off.

I knew there would be some hard questions asked, especially about taking off Rushey. When you are a player, there is always some sanctuary from being part of a group. You can have your few drinks, hide, nod away and, in the darkest part of your soul, agree that the manager messed up. When you are the manager, there are no hiding places.

That Antrim defeat was the trigger point for a whole other series of bad memories. I had never won a first-round game with Clare in Munster. We had lost two All-Ireland semi-finals in games both of which we could have won. We were also six points ahead in the 2005 semi-final against Cork and we couldn't close out the game. Why didn't I think of some move to take the sting out of Antrim's momentum? Had I learned nothing from that Cork defeat?

Even though you know you love the job, and you feel you have something to offer, you rip yourself to shreds. I felt I wasn't cut out for management. You get the odd snide text. 'Great players don't always make great managers.' They may be sent in jest but they cut you deep because you are afraid to admit that they may be true in relation to you. On that day, sitting on those rocks, I said to myself, 'I am just not good enough.'

I was set to walk away because I was in a total mess. The shop, too, was approaching a crisis point. Debts were mounting. The Sheriff was looking for money and post-dated cheques. I was wondering if the Dublin job was a hindrance to what should have been more of a priority. The economic downturn was killing small businesses like ours, especially with online sales, but I was wondering if I could be doing more. 'Walk away from this, go back and run your shop and pub, you eejit.' But even that wasn't straightforward.

In 1995, winning the All-Ireland changed all of our lives. It opened up doors and opportunities for most of us. As I was captain, the TSB decided that I was a wasted asset serving behind their counter so they gave me a job on the road selling pensions and fitted me with a company car. My first car.

It was a nice change, but it wasn't me. Materially, there were gains to be made from Clare's success if you had the guts to take a risk, so I did: in the summer of 1996 I took a leave of absence and opened up a sports shop in Ennis. I left the bank in April and didn't intend hanging around, but the renovation of the building was so extensive that the actual open date was pushed back to August.

Hordes of people were saying that I was a cocky boyo planning the opening before another All-Ireland final. The easy assumption to make was that I expected us to be in the final so I could hoover up money and cream on jersey sales. The reality was that I was haemorrhaging cash. The roof was leaking. The walls were rotten. I was helping the builders throughout the summer while we were getting ready to open.

Winning the All-Ireland in 1997 was a huge boost to the business. We had a few good years afterwards, but you always knew there was a limit to how much you could grow, how successful you could really be. In the retail trade in this country, there is very little incentive. Even in the boom years, every time you had a good month, you had a bigger VAT bill. You think, 'Jeez, that was a great Christmas,' but then the VAT man has a bigger cut off you and you're back on the limit of the overdraft again by the end of January.

Being in business is a big commitment, especially when you spread your wings that bit further. When we opened the pub in 1999, I was still trying to play for Clare and run the shop. Eilís left her job in late 2000 to take over the shop so I could concentrate on the pub. We were only passing each other at the door. She would be in the shop from nine to six while I'd be in the pub, on my feet from five until closing.

When the shop eventually closed, lots of people said, 'Sure, he was never there.' That does wreck your head. Deep in the recesses of my mind I know that is true, but I made life choices as well. Apart from my family, hurling is my absolute passion in life. I was never afraid of hard work – I worked on the roads for the council for two summers when I was a student – but when I was playing for Clare, I didn't want to be on my feet every day in the shop during the summer. When I took over the team, I wanted to get the absolute most out of myself as a manager. If that meant staying in the Temple Gate Hotel until 2.30 in the morning with Harry and Alan Cunningham, trying to find another inch that would get us closer to the top, I was prepared to do it.

In that context, I just couldn't be in the shop every day, especially when I was running the pub as well. When we leased out the pub and I became Dublin manager, I still spent every day in the shop. When we were training, I would be in the shop until 2pm. But even if I had been there every hour from day one, even if I had put my absolute heart and soul into the place, it might have sustained us for another year. We might still be open but we would only be surviving.

For a finish, you couldn't pull a wage from the business. That is the honest to God truth. Rent was a killer. Rates would crucify you. So would insurance, light, heat. There were overheads and expenses everywhere you turned, down to paying for your own parking spot for the day.

People didn't have the money any more. Ennis as a trading town was dying on its feet. You would walk up O'Connell Street some days and all that was missing was the tumbleweed blowing down against you from the Daniel O'Connell monument. Those who did have money could get their merchandise cheaper in the bigger outlet stores or else online. Some people would come into the shop, try on a pair of runners or boots for size and fitting, walk out and order them off a laptop or phone.

O'Neills eventually saw the wood from the trees with all their small independent retail customers. O'Neills were virtually like an overdraft facility because they would grant you a €20,000 limit. As they gradually sensed the potential pain coming over the horizon, they sliced that limit in half.

The end-game was inevitable. From the first day of November 2011 right up to Christmas, every voucher we sold we put the money into an envelope and wrote down the phone number of the recipient on the back. We weren't announcing we were closing down but it was obvious once we started a sale the week before Christmas. Knowing we were shutting the door on 11 January 2012, we rang all those people individually who had vouchers. We received enormous goodwill from that gesture but we had no intention of being underhand. We were Clare people with a local shop and there was nowhere to hide.

Once you have a profile, though, there is literally nowhere to shelter. On the day of the liquidation meeting in Limerick, I was crossing a street when this photographer suddenly appeared in front of me. He immediately began snapping, stepping back to get a better shot like he was following a murderer coming out of the High Court. I didn't know whether to get sick, hit him or fall down on my knees with a weakness. I just felt criminalized. A journalist then appeared from the *Irish Independent* asking me if I had any comment to make. I couldn't believe it.

'Why are the *Independent* doing this to me?' I asked him. 'I could understand if it was some other paper but I have co-operated with the *Indo* for the last twenty-five years of my life. I never refused ye any cooperation but, independently, ye have gone after me.'

That was as much as I said but they already had enough angles for their front-page story. Seven creditors turned up to the meeting, two of whom were Cork hurlers, Ronan Curran who worked for Mycro and Ben O'Connor from their family business, O'Connor Hurleys. Curran texted me straight away afterwards and was very understanding and compassionate about our plight. He said some nice words in an interview and I won't forget him for it.

We never bounced or kited a cheque in our lives. We were

trying to make an honest living, like every other small business. We didn't want to have to let staff go, or have the worry and anxiety that goes hand-in-hand with plummeting sales and rising debts. We didn't want to go under. We just did.

A lot of small businesses don't make it past one year's trading but we got over fifteen years out of it. It won't be long before Orlaith turns sixteen. I can see her turning into a woman, and that is how long the business lasted. You're just happy the kids were younger at the time and they weren't coming to you asking harder questions when we did close. 'Why did this happen? What did you do wrong?'

You still do feel a failure. You feel embarrassed for the people around you. It's a horrible feeling to owe money. It feels like a stain on your character and your name. Trying to keep your head above water when you're constantly submerged with debt, it feels like you're drowning. It was a horrible, horrible time, so when it was all over it was just pure relief. I felt I could breathe again.

I often think of my brother Michael. He is an alcoholic who has turned his life around. He went through difficult times. He has relapsed on a few occasions but he always speaks about that moment of liberation when he finally put up his hand and admitted he needed help.

I never wanted to see my business fail. Even when my mother told me I was mad in 1996 to leave my good, pensionable job, I didn't care, I wanted to have my own independence. It was another life choice I made, and hurling was a central part in that decision.

When I went for a promotion in the bank in 1993, to grade 3 level, I had no bank exams on my CV, which was an obvious hindrance to my chances. When I stood in front of the interview panel and explained the reasons why I hadn't the time to go into Limerick a couple of evenings a week, how I was too

consumed with hurling because I felt Clare were going somewhere, I sensed that they smirked at me. It wasn't that I wasn't
ambitious. I was. It's just that my main ambition was to get to
the steps of the Hogan Stand. When I opened the shop, I
wanted that independence of working for myself which would
facilitate my ambition of being the best hurler I could be, and
subsequently the best manager I could be. Seeing that project
fail was like swallowing an ocean of cod liver oil.

I was really low that January. The curtains stayed closed in
the front room at home for most of that month. I was hiding.
The only time I ventured out was to head to Dublin for training. I didn't even want to go to Murty's for a pint. I didn't even
want to go to Clonmel that February. I was embarrassed and in
pain. I felt I had let my family and so many other people down.

Eilís could see the hurt in my heart and in my face and she
didn't want it to drag me down any further. 'Don't lose faith in
yourself,' she said to me one evening. 'You always believe that
things will go your way. Jeez, don't lose that.'

I didn't, but it was a slow journey back to normality. On the
road to training over the following few months, I listened to
nearly every self-help and promotional CD that was ever
burned. Some arsehole rambling on about the seven secrets to
life. Eventually I came round. 'Feel the fucking fear and drive
on,' I would say to myself. 'No matter how low you are, there's
another day coming.'

I lived by that mantra during those months. When I'd be in
bed and not wanting to get up, I'd kick myself out through a
mental trigger. 'Get up. Get back and do the cliff walk in
Kilkee. Clear your head. Drive on.' I'll still make a balls of
myself again doing something. That's me. Whatever it is about
me, that is in my make-up. But I know if the worst comes to the
worst, even if we're on the point of losing the house, I know

that I will go into Murty's at ten in the morning and work until two a.m. No matter what it takes to educate my three girls Orlaith, Úna and Aoife, I'll do it.

You just have to feel the fear and drive on because you are often a target when you have a profile. When a list of insolvent companies in liquidation from January and February 2012 was released in a report from the Office of the Director of Corporate Enforcement (ODCE) at the end of that February, we were one of 153. All small companies gone to the wall. We owed thousands. Others owed millions, but they weren't on the front page of the *Irish Independent*.

The story just wouldn't go away. The week after the 2013 Leinster final, a local journalist rang me. The figures from my final liquidation meeting the previous year had been made public and he wanted a reaction. In all my time dealing with the media, that shocked me more than anything.

'Are you for real?' I asked him. 'Why is this coming up now? Is it because we're after winning the Leinster title?'

'No, it's a matter of public interest,' he said.

'The country is rife with scandal,' I told him. 'Bankers are after wrecking people's lives and you're coming after me? Lookit, my mother is over eighty and is still alive. Eilís's parents are still alive. They don't need to read or hear about this. I have a young family who are old enough to know the story now and they don't need this thrown in their faces. We're trying to get on with our lives. But if you want to make your few bob from a story like this, off you go and do whatever you want.'

He never ran with the story. But talk about sticking a pin in my bubble the week we were Leinster champions.

I always hoped we would win a Leinster title but I knew it would take time. I knew that from my experience with Clare.

Things don't just happen unless you try and make them happen. We had taken our beatings in Clare but we had reached Munster finals. We had made Leinster finals with Dublin and, similar to Clare, we were all evolving and developing and becoming mentally stronger as we went.

After our setback in 2010, I was willing to try anything. We had lost Jim Kilty as our physical trainer but I felt the training had gone soft anyway and I wanted us to become meaner. I knew Paul Grimley, the former Armagh player and coach, was at a loose end so I took a notion to ring him. I didn't want him taking hurling sessions – Jeez, can you imagine that one – I just wanted to see if he might be able to unleash the animal within the lads. I wanted him to harden us up, and he had that reputation. I met Grimley above in the Carrickdale Hotel outside Newry and we had a great chat for over two hours. He was interested but he went with Monaghan instead that year.

Denise Martin put me in the direction of Martin Kennedy, who brought that approach to our play with a lot more science. He certainly changed my thinking. I was always of the opinion that you work on ball drills to improve your touch and focus on tackling and contact work in practice matches, but Kennedy married together and refined all those disciplines to make us more competitive and combative for the demands of the modern game which Kilkenny had patented.

That whole culture change gave us huge momentum in 2011. We won the league for the first time in seventy-two years. We beat Galway in the Leinster semi-final in what I would regard as our first big championship scalp. When we were stuck in traffic afterwards, we were looking out the bus windows at hordes of young Dublin kids who had left their cars, pucking along the side of the road or on grass verges. Dublin jerseys were everywhere. It was magical. 'This is something else,' I said to Richie. 'We are finally beginning to see the light.'

We still weren't ready to take that next step, though. We got too uptight for the Leinster final. Kilkenny were coming for retribution after the league final and we bought into it; we saw the impending backlash, the snarling teeth, Cody like a lunatic. 'The you you will be is the you you see,' is one of Declan Coyle's great phrases. That's what we became. When we met on the Tuesday afterwards, we had a very honest and frank discussion. Some lads admitted that they were beaten in the parade. Some of the questions asked were almost embarrassing. 'Why are we shitting ourselves again?'

We changed our whole attitude and mindset for the rest of the year. We became what we saw. Declan Coyle and Gary Keegan had a big impact in that transition but we just became looser and more relaxed. I could identify with that myself from the 1995 All-Ireland final. My attitude was 'Let's go up and have a go at this thing'. We beat Limerick and narrowly lost to Tipp in an All-Ireland semi-final.

Gary had always challenged us that we were making this too much about Kilkenny and that this was all about ourselves. That we were so caught up with how well they were doing that we weren't performing ourselves. We knew it, and we continually addressed the theme, but it was just so hard to overcome that mental block.

I really like Dotsy. He just has this way about him. He is not called the Dalai Lama for nothing by some of the boys. When I sat in beside him after Kilkenny had wiped the floor with us in 2012, I was just exasperated. I asked him what it was about us, why had we fallen so hard again? Why did we do this to ourselves again?

'It's just them, Dalo,' Dotsy said to me. 'Whatever it is about them, we just can't cope with them. Whatever is in our heads about Kilkenny, we can't get it out of our heads.'

I could smell the fear off him and everyone else around me. I can't understand that fear but Dotsy's words were in my head when I did a TV interview a few minutes later. I was asked to account for the performance and I couldn't. I said that if we had rounded fifteen lads up at the Red Cow roundabout that morning, we'd have done a better job. I got hammered by some people for disparaging the team but I wasn't exactly exaggerating. I probably should have protected the players more but I was just concussed from the disappointment and the paucity of the performance.

Friday, 4 April 2014

Michael Carton had a super game against Kilkenny in March 2014. Yet when Jenny Coady did a stats analysis wrap-up presentation at the end of the league, she was able to show Mikey that with seventeen of his nineteen possessions he faded to go right and turned back on his left. If the opposition are studying us as closely as we are analysing them, that is a trend in Mikey's game that will be targeted.

I'm big into that stuff, but I'm always conscious of overdoing analysis. It can force guys to go off-track. If our lads think they have it all worked out, they don't perform. That can stem from a deficit in on-field leadership intertwined with getting carried away with the 10 per cent zone.

Our nutritionist, Crionna Tobin, is excellent at her job but I had to remind her recently that she is still operating in the 10 per cent zone. As in, there's no point her telling lads that if they eat a burger, they'll collapse. Going to the ball, being manly, being willing to put your life on the line, beating your man, that is my definition of the 90 per cent zone. Diet, nutrition, video analysis and speed-work are, in my mind, all in the 10 per cent category. You can improve your sharpness and agility, but I would still place those improvements in some grey area between 10 and 90. When the 10 starts dictating to the 90, a team is in serious trouble. In more clichéd terms, when the tail starts wagging the dog, it's only a matter of time before the dog gets run over.

When we got splattered across the road in Portlaoise and Ennis in 2012, our guts spilling out across the tarmac, the primary reason was that the 10 had dictated too much to the 90. We did more man hours that season than any other but we tried to do too much. We had to be more professional. We had to be more like Aussie Rules. We had to train in the gym in the Aviva Stadium. Guys who had to be at work for eight on a Wednesday clocked in at five a.m. for their gym sessions. I would regularly stay up on a Tuesday night, set the alarm for four, and drive down the road afterwards, having to stop four times to load up on coffee to try and keep myself awake. Madness.

We were in Bray at 5.50 a.m. for hurling training on a Thursday morning and lads who had to go back to the north-side for work were running out the door with a rasher inside in a roll for their breakfast. It was animal stuff. We thought we were working harder than anybody else but we were overworking our bodies and blunting our minds. The same intensity wasn't in the training and we all turned a blind eye.

The science took over from the rawness. We went away from process and focused on outcomes. We got relegated in the league but I still kept reiterating that our whole focus was 23 June in Portlaoise against Kilkenny. 'No matter what happens, we'll be right for June twenty-third,' I repeatedly told myself and the players. And then Kilkenny arrived down the M7 and mowed us down like we were a dumb dog running in under the wheel of an articulated lorry. I'll never make that same mistake again.

At the end of 2012, I would have walked if I'd felt the players wanted me to go. Around October, Johnny McCaffrey, Gary Maguire and Niall Corcoran sat across from myself, Richie and Hedgo during a meeting which felt like a Union debate. They had come back with their recommendations after an intense players' meeting. We took them on board and threw back some stuff at them. We all searched our souls, but once I'd agreed to go back again, preparations began for a new season.

Martin Kennedy had agreed to return until his head was turned by Jim Gavin. We interviewed three guys for his job and Ross Dunphy was the outstanding candidate. Johnny McEvoy and Vinny Teehan went their own ways as selector and coach. Johnny and Vinny were super guys who contributed so much to Dublin hurling. They were real hurling men, Johnny from Clough-Ballacolla in Laois, Vinny from Coolderry in Offaly.

Shane Martin came in and was an absolutely massive addition. Tommy Dunne came on board as coach and was another godsend. One of the reasons I love him is because he is so focused on the 90 per cent zone. A lot of his drills are basic enough but guys are always going at an unmerciful pace, pinging sliotars around like golfballs on concrete. The dog is going like 90. And you can barely even see its tail.

Fr Harry always says that humanity is like an iceberg, so much hidden underneath; so much is governed by the processes we have gone through in life. The bad days can beat you down and keep you down. There are times after those days when you wonder if the mundane is a better way of life, but this is my way of life, this is who I am. I'm happier in life when I'm stuck in hurling. As Gilly would say on nights out after a bad defeat, 'The going up is never worth the coming down.'

We kept going up but always seemed to be slipping back down. When we were coming home from the drawn Leinster quarter-final against Wexford in 2013, Shane Martin said to me that if we could win the replay we would be nicely set up for a shot at Kilkenny. I couldn't share Shane's optimism because I couldn't feel it around me. We had got out of jail but I still thought some of our lads were big-game chokers. I said it to them upstairs in Whites Hotel afterwards that thank God we had the fireman – Mikey Carton, who was savage that night – because everyone else was jumping out of the burning building.

Richie was down in Clare on holiday that weekend and I asked him to come over to the house in Tullycrine that Monday evening and we'd get Gary Keegan on a conference call. Gary reminded us how we had to respect everyone. He felt by our talk that Wexford were only a ticket to get to the big show, Kilkenny. I got great reassurance from him that night.

I felt Wexford had bullied us in the drawn game. They timbered the shite out of us, and twelve or thirteen lads took it. There were some vicious belts thrown but I said I didn't care what was thrown the next day, we would stand up to it. Wexford came out again like a cell of Grim Reapers in a bad mood but we kept our heads. They were wild, we stood. We made a stand and were finally ready for Kilkenny.

At half-time in the replay, I pointed to my head. 'This is all up here,' I said to the players. 'Now, now do ye believe me? We're every bit as good as this crowd. Now kick on and beat them.'

Finally, we were beginning to believe.

We had mentioned Bob O'Keeffe so much over the years that we stopped talking about him on the advice of Gary Keegan. Too focused on outcome, we forgot about the process. We just wanted the game to be over with the win in the bag. Gary, just as Len Gaynor had always preached, told us to go and love it, live it, enjoy the game, embrace the experience. That was our attitude in 2013. It finally took us to the top in Leinster.

When Johnny McCaffrey raised Bob over his head, I pulled the baseball cap over my eyes and dropped my head to try and hide the tears streaming down my face. Seeing Eilís, Orlaith, Úna and Aoife afterwards was magical. In different ways, they had invested as much as anyone else in Dublin hurling.

It was a great, great day for so many people. Our first stop on the bus afterwards was to Peter Garvey in the Sunnybank Hotel. He was a big man but the tears were running down his face. That was nearly the moment of the day for me because Peter had been such a huge part of my life over the last decade. Even through the bad times, he always stood by me. His great friend Fr Harry first introduced me to Peter in 2004. We shared common interests – a love of National Hunt racing, GAA, a few pints and having the craic. He was the most generous man you could ever meet. He was so worried about everyone else's health that he nearly forgot about his own. He died suddenly at the age of fifty-nine at the end of the year.

I am so glad that Peter got to see that day, but we all embraced it, loved it, lived it, enjoyed it. And finally won it. The All-Ireland is still the ultimate goal, but apart from the Galway game in Salthill, we have shown that attitude in every other game this year. Even in Thurles against Tipperary, we stayed in the battle. The league quarter-finals, semi-finals and final are all happening without us; we're out of sight and out of mind. Nobody is talking about us. Nobody is rating us.

We're under the radar, coming into the championship now like a stealth bomber. Ready, I hope, to lay waste to all before us.

17

The Engine Room

Friday, 18 April 2014

After the 2014 league campaign ended, the Dublin club championship ramped up for two weeks and I took in as many games as I could. We would all go to different matches to try and watch all the players and assess their form, but myself and Ciaran Hetherton ended up at the same double-header in Parnell Park in mid-April. Hedgo couldn't miss Craobh Chiaráin and St Vincents because he had two sons playing. On opposing teams.

Before he and Patsy got married, there was a prenuptial agreement. Hedgo is a diehard Craobh man but Patsy is an even more fanatical Vincents woman, if you can picture that level of fanaticism. So it was decided that their first-born – whether a boy or a girl – would play with Vincents and the rest of the family could play with the Craobh. The first-born just happened to be this strapping big fella, John.

I was sitting beside Hedgo but the whole family piled in around us. Hedgo's brother was home from Australia and the match was at the top of his to-do list. Patsy's brothers and sisters and father and mother were also there. After a few minutes,

Hedgo's mother Phyllis, who is eighty-three, took her seat.

There was a lot of slagging going on during the match but there was still a lovely family vibe as two sons faced off in a local derby, John for Vincents, Kevin lining out for the Craobh. The only member of the family I couldn't see was Patsy, but I eventually spotted her sitting on her own up against a wall in the shed in Parnell Park. Talk about nailing your colours to the mast. Classic stuff.

Hedgo just has to suck up Patsy's loyalty to Vincents but it's no bother to him because he is such an inherently decent and generous guy. His mother is a lady. I'd say he was well reared; played with the Craobh, plenty of timber, well able to dish it out, but absolutely solid.

A couple of hours after last year's Leinster final, Phyllis went looking for her son to celebrate with him. Hedgo was with the rest of the panel, drinking in the Grafton Lounge downtown. That's where she tracked him down. Unannounced. Uninvited. The slagging was unreal. The lads were saying to Hedgo that they'd have to put an upper age limit on the door in Copper Face Jacks to keep his mother out.

Phyllis had begun her search in the Craobh Chiaráin club-house. She is the Craobh president and they gave her a standing ovation when she walked in, primarily for the contribution Hedgo had made to Dublin hurling. He was blooded on the Dublin senior panel as an eighteen-year-old in 1984, when Dublin were the defending All-Ireland football champions and nobody thought much about hurling. Not much good came of it until Lar Foley arrived as Dublin manager. Lar had a three-year plan: promotion from Division 2 in Year One, reach a Leinster final in Year Two, win it in Year Three. All the targets were met until Kilkenny beat them by two points in the 1991 Leinster final. The next Leinster final didn't come for eighteen years.

Hedgo finished as an inter-county hurler in 1993 but he didn't go far. Kevin Heffernan was on the committee tasked to establish development squads and Heffo asked Hedgo to get involved. He started with a group of talented thirteen-year-olds and stayed the course until they reached an All-Ireland U-21 final eight years later in 2007. Dublin lost, but the barriers were gradually being torn down. It was Dublin's first Leinster U-21 title in thirty-five years.

Richie Stakelum is a different character. Absolutely first-class guy, he just comes from a different background. He grew up in a Borrisoleigh house with big connections. His uncle Pat was a great Tipp player of the fifties. Richie remembers his late father calling him down from bed one evening to meet Christy Ring who was sipping tea at the kitchen table.

Richie made his own history. In 1987, he became the face of Tipperary's escape from the badlands with his immortal words after that year's Munster final that 'the famine is over'. His speech retraced the heartbreak of a lost generation, but heartbreak defined his own career. Tipp lost that All-Ireland semi-final to Galway and Stakelum slipped to the periphery afterwards. He walked away after Tipp won the 1989 All-Ireland.

In the meantime he had moved to Dublin to work as a teacher before joining Kilmacud Crokes in 1992. Richie later moved from teaching to the pharmaceutical trade and has been very successful in his job. Hedgo is a prison officer in Mountjoy, dealing with rough and tough individuals every day of the week. Richie and Hedgo hurled against each other, and Richie always said Hedgo was a hard nail. The Craobh are a working-class club from a working-class part of town and their attitude was 'We'll give it to these posh south-side boyos'.

The three of us are all hewn from varying environments but

our backgrounds still neatly rhyme with one another. We can all identify with that want, that hunger of the underdog to bite back, that desire to prove a point. That savage ambition to win an All-Ireland.

The three of us have been together now for six years and Richie would always be the first to say that we couldn't exist without Hedgo. He is an absolute perfectionist. We were in Portugal a couple of years ago on a training camp and we did this exercise with the sports psychologist Declan Coyle on establishing your personality type. I wound up being classed as a romantic poet. It was probably accurate – fond of wine and talking shite. Richie was bracketed as a figure of authority, someone always in control. Hedgo was described as an absolute perfectionist. And that is exactly him.

Hedgo and kit man Ray Finn are almost identical in their approach to detail. I would recommend Ray for any job in the country. If I was being operated on in the morning, I'd nearly want Ray to open me up because I know he'd do everything perfectly. Everywhere we have been all over the country, groundsmen have come to me and said the lads are a credit to me, the way they leave the dressing-rooms. Pristine. Better than when we first walked into them.

Hedgo and Ray have everything laid on for the players. When Hedgo first got involved, he wanted to go down that road of supreme organization. His attitude from day one was 'Take away all the excuses from the players and just let them out and hurl'. I have often tried to rein Hedgo back in on that approach because players need to have an appreciation of how much is actually being done for them. You hear stories of Premiership players going on holiday and their agents handing them their passport, boarding pass and suitcase of designer clothes and jewellery at the airport. The same guys couldn't wipe their own arses. Our players wouldn't be anything near that level but lads need to organize themselves as much off the pitch as on it to become more rounded players and grounded people.

In Dublin, there are still strains of what I would call a 'wipe-your-arse mentality'. It initially stemmed from the development squads model and how those first recruits were so well looked after in an attempt to make Dublin hurling more attractive in the battle with football. Some lads still have that sense of entitlement and selfishness in their DNA. More of them are Celtic Tiger children, and that attitude manifests itself in different forms. It's a mindset of 'Ray will sweep the dressing-rooms', 'Ray will pick up the sliotars', 'Ray will have our gear ready', 'Hedgo will organize everything else for them', and if me or Hedgo don't do it for them, get some other guru. Ray and Hedgo want to take additional burdens off the players, but myself and Richie will always argue that point with them.

All of the players are great lads, really good people. Anything you ask them to do, they will do it. When we took them to a training camp on Bere Island last year, the army said they never saw a group like them. They would stay on the pitch for three hours every night. Their attitude is amazing in that capacity because they prosper in a structured and managed environment. But that attitude is too often divorced from reality in such a cut-throat game where chaos is often the only structure.

It's only been in the last few years that I've realized how much I come from the Loughnane school. It was a different time, and Loughnane was not your standard manager, but we did assume a lot of responsibility ourselves off the pitch and it fostered huge leadership on it. I don't want to be always telling players what to do. I don't want lads waiting for me to roar or for Hedgo to run into them with instructions. I want them to do it themselves.

In 2014 in the league against Tipp, we made bits of them at so many stages of that game but we still fell down on tiny details of on-field leadership and game-management. We have broken down many barriers in the last few years but I passionately believe that is the last hurdle we have to clear to make us into something really special. Great teams make it happen. If we want to be a great team, we have to make it happen.

Trying to foster and develop that attitude among the players is always on my mind. On the day of the 2014 relegation final against Waterford, we still had four minutes before we left the dressing-room when I walked out the door. 'I've enough said,' I told the players. 'I'm going.' The players had their say, and Michael Carruth had the last word. In February 2014, José Mourinho got masseur Billy McCulloch to give the Chelsea pre-match team talk before their 1-0 victory against Man City. I don't know who the hell Billy McCulloch is, but Michael Carruth is one of the few Olympic gold medallists we have in this country. I don't know what Carruth said but I'm sure he had more to offer than McCulloch.

When we were having a few drinks in the Palace Bar that evening of the relegation final, I had a conversation with Rushey. I had let him away with missing the bus but I couldn't let it lie. I just couldn't marry how I was pacing the front room in Tullycrine at 5.30 that morning, waiting for a chink of daylight to give me the green light to get into the car and head to Kilkenny to meet the squad, with Rushey not as wired and not able to get out of bed to be in the Louis Fitzgerald for eleven a.m. He went out and did his business but it wasn't good enough.

'What way did that look to Colm Cronin this morning?' I asked him. 'You are probably his hero, really.'

'Jeez, I wouldn't think I'm anyone's hero, Dalo.'

'Sure, you're the only Dublin hurler to win two All-Stars.

You're seen as one of the best players in the country. Cian O'Callaghan, Paul Winters, Chris Crummy, all those young guys really look up to you. Yet you failed to make the bus, even though Hedgo put five reminders on Facebook, plus a text message, that the clocks were going forward. And there am I in Clare pacing the floor, mad for road. I need you to be mad for road. That's the kind of leadership we need from you.' He had nothing to say for about thirty seconds.

Rushey is an absolutely savage player for us. He is a super fella, a real salt-of-the-earth guy. His mother is from west Clare and his father is from Galway and Liam has a lot of those laid-back west of Ireland traits. That is part of his problem, that he is sometimes too laid back. But when he goes to war, he is fearless, almost unbreakable.

We weren't talking behind his back, but when Rushey went to the toilet, myself and his girlfriend Sinéad continued the conversation.

'He can't hear enough of that off you,' she said.

'Yeah, but that's not what I'm trying to get at. I want Liam to be first to the bus. I want him to be making sure everyone else is there on time too. I want him driving this, not me. That's the little edge we're missing. That leadership might be the difference of us being as close as we were last year or not getting over the line at all.'

Wednesday, 23 April 2014

I just had war on the phone with John Costello. I asked him where we were training next Thursday night and he couldn't tell me. I asked him about the availability of Parnell Park and he ruled it out because there's still more club championship matches to be played. When he told me we were in St Paul's, I nearly jumped down the phone. 'So we're in a field with rabbit holes all over the pitch? And a soccer match on beside it? No, we're not going back there. I want one night in Parnell Park and that's it.'

I have a great relationship with Costello. He is the ultimate professional, but I was already after having it hot and heavy with him about the home-and-away agreement made with Wexford, which had only been clarified to me a couple of days earlier. If we meet Wexford, we'll have to go back down to Wexford Park, even though it will be a Leinster semi-final.

'Would it happen to the footballers, John? Have the footballers somewhere to train next week? I need Parnell, and I need the grass cut. I don't care how bad the surface is but I need the grass cut to the bone so the ball is moving.'

'Right, right, right, take that as done so. Drive on, I won't stand in yere way.'

The primary reason I rang Costello was to get his permission on an idea which we have formulated to try and create greater leadership qualities within the squad. When we had a management and squad meeting a couple of weeks back to review the league, I asked Tony Griffin a few days beforehand to come up with a concept we could develop. 'I've been racking my brains to try and come up with something,' I said to Griff. 'But I'll bow to you on this one.'

Griff proposed that the lads would mentor a group of young fifteen- and sixteen-year-olds. Then that hardened into a plan to cater for the Dublin U-15 development squad. 'That's a great idea,' said Michael Carruth. It was. As well as developing their own leadership abilities, these guys have a duty to Dublin hurling anyway, to pass the baton on, to inspire the next generation coming after them.

I'd first approached Griff about getting involved in the winter of 2012. Some hurling diehards in Clare never forgave him for cycling seven thousand kilometres across Canada to raise money for cancer, if you can somehow square that argument. They felt it prematurely ended his hurling career, but did they ever think of all the good that did outside of hurling? To me, Tony is a positive guy, and I want positive people around me and our squad.

When he accepted the request to join our set-up, Griff embedded himself within the squad, training with the players, doing the gym work, trying to get as close as he could to build their trust. His ultimate task was to strengthen their minds, but there are many approach routes to that summit and Griff didn't necessarily take the routes most travelled. At a couple of key moments in 2013 he was given free rein and he absolutely delivered.

When we were in Castlemartyr in Cork on a training weekend, he facilitated a session which turned into an emotional letting. One of the players opened up about the tragic death of a sibling. He felt it was holding him back within the group and he wanted to let it out. Lads would have died for their teammate on the spot. And maybe that level of emotional honesty and investment in each other was a reason we did so well last year.

I have always made it clear to the players that when they and Tony have their sessions, firstly, I won't know what is said by the players and, secondly, I don't want to know. Recently they did an exercise where Tony recorded them all for thirty seconds having asked them all two basic questions: Why are you here? What are you going to do between now and September? I haven't a clue what Griff and the players got from the exercise but I get the impression that it was very worthwhile. I asked Rushey that weekend and I knew by his reaction that it was positive. 'Good, yeah, good,' he said with a wry smile.

'Interesting stuff.' If he looked at you with a blank stare, you'd know well he thought it was shite.

I got up early today: by 7.15 I was walking the beach in Doughmore, just behind the golf course in Doonbeg. It was a beautiful morning. The sun was shining. The water was lapping delicately against the sand. The wind was caressing the thick thatch of grass above the sand dunes. But I wasn't just purely motivated by the scenery, the serenity of the moment and the promise of a fine day on the edge of summer. I was really trying to wipe myself out so I might sleep tonight.

Myself and Richie are meeting Ireland rugby coach Joe Schmidt tomorrow at eight a.m. in the Aviva Stadium. Richie is good mates with Robbie Kelleher, who is friendly with Mick Kearney, the Irish team manager. We asked if a meeting with Joe might be possible and it was arranged. I wasn't overawed by the prospect of meeting Joe, but if there is something important on, I can't switch off. That's why I got up so early.

But it makes no difference. I only get two hours' sleep, from four to six a.m.

Thursday, 24 April 2014

Joe is a really nice guy. Very engaging, very helpful. I find Gary Keegan a really intense influence because he works on the mind and how to get the best out of people. I was expecting Joe to be of a similar mindset but he appeared to be more focused on organization and detail and its absolute importance in a set-up.

I felt that myself and everyone in our set-up was well versed and drilled in that area and I showed Joe my folder and clip-chart from the Tipp game. I had worked on the detail all the way up on the train before fine-tuning it in the hotel the night before the game.

'Right, Anthony, you have ten points there,' he said. 'Firstly, did your manager Ger Loughnane use notes like that?'

'No,' I said. 'And I wouldn't have that on him. I wouldn't be able to make points off my head like Ger.'

'Did he make ten points?'

'I don't really know. I can't remember.'

'I doubt he did,' said Schmidt. 'Maybe he did over the course of a week but I'm sure it was two or three clear messages.'

He went down through my clip-chart. 'This is super stuff, but when did you deliver this?'

'In the hotel before we left for Thurles.'

'Right, mate. Two-hour bus journey to Thurles? Warm-up another half an hour? So you're talking about three and a half hours before the game? Would you remember it?'

'Probably not.'

'Why did you need the notes? They are all great points, but this is you covering your arse. They can't take in all those ten points.'

As he continued, I was hanging on to his every syllable. 'You gotta delegate more. I leave the psyching up to Paulie [O'Connell]. Surely you have a good sub who is a leader?'

Immediately I thought of Ruairí Trainor. Alan Nolan is another strong character. I mentioned those guys.

'Why couldn't you have left Trainor to make the point about the free-count? I regularly give Eoin Reddan obscure stuff about the backs, the front-row even, and ask for his observations from the stand. I hand over other stuff to other backroom members, which allows me to do my individual stuff with guys.'

We covered a huge amount of ground, from stats and analysis to motivation and tactics. Every last drop of information we could pump him for, in a polite and not over-the-top manner, we did. I asked Richie to take notes. When he sent them back to me with headings that evening on an email, he had narrowed it down to eleven different points we had discussed.

The only point Richie had forgotten was 'Smart-Edge'. I had written it down at the bottom of my clip-chart as soon as Joe mentioned the term because I was intrigued by the wording. Basically, it's a concept Ireland use to underline the importance of balancing the equation between discipline and destruction.

I told Schmidt about how we challenged Conal Keaney in 2013 on how we felt he was giving away too many frees. Keaney is a strong character who loves making big hits and breaking guys up in the physical exchanges but he came back to us and said that he felt we had taken away his 'mojo'. He didn't know how to play any other way. He played terribly the day after we challenged him and I told him to go back to the way he knew. I threw that at Schmidt.

'We have lots of guys like that, but it's not good enough,' he said. 'You can still have that edge but you have to be smart. The guys who aren't, I call them the outlaws.'

It was a super meeting and we got so much out of it. Richie emailed Mick Kearney afterwards to thank him, and to thank Joe for his time. He forwarded it to Schmidt, and Mick sent us on his reply. 'They were two very engaging guys,' he wrote. 'But I hope that they don't buy too much into our stuff. They have got to do their own thing.'

We were fully aware of that ourselves. When we sat down as a management team afterwards to review the information we'd gathered and advice we'd been given, we knew we were already doing a lot right. We weren't going reinventing the wheel, we just wanted the wheel to run that bit smoother. When you work with fantastic people like Gary Keegan, Declan Coyle and Liam Moggan, you always pick up something. There is always that tiny detail you can improve on, always something you can adapt or learn. We wanted to be as sharp as a blade, and Joe Schmidt helped sharpen the blade some more.

When Joe was speaking about 'Smart-Edge' and 'outlaws', I thought of an old maths teacher I had in Flannan's, John Finn. You wouldn't get away with it in school now but Finn had two terms for the guys who finished in the bottom two in the class – the Billy Dodo and the Nanny Dodo. I got caught once and I never wanted to get caught again. 'Now, for the first time this year, from the village of Clarecastle,' Finn would say in this concocted accent, 'Mr Antonious Ó Dálaigh, step up and join this side of the class.' It was harsh, but Finn was a great teacher and he knew what he was doing. By Jesus, you'd be ready for the next test.

It got me thinking. When we analysed our stats at the end of the league, there was a glaring trend from our free concession rate. Of the ninety-one frees coughed up, 45 per cent were for chops, pushes or technical fouls. 'I'm not talking about taking away yere manliness, or having to level a fella if ye have to,' I said to the players at the time. 'But can we stop pushing a fella up the hole when he is bending down to pick up a ball? Can we turn that forty-five per cent into twenty per cent? Those ten or eleven frees from that reduction would have had us comfortably in a league quarter-final. It might suit us nicely now because we're under the radar but that level of indiscipline won't win us the All-Ireland.'

I got Hedgo to get a whiteboard and we listed the six biggest offenders: Keaney, Rushey, Ryan O'Dwyer, Johnny McCaffrey, Peter Kelly and Danny Sutcliffe. They are possibly our six best men but they were also our worst outlaws. Out of the ninety-one frees conceded, they were responsible for 60 per cent. Keaney was the biggest outlaw of the lot, having conceded seventeen frees.

A couple of days later, Keaney went away and got six pink T-shirts and had the word 'Dodo' written across each one. The gesture summed up his immense character and leadership. It showed the type of person he is. He didn't sulk, he just took the initiative himself to address the issue. He never looked for the money for the T-shirts.

The six boys had to wear them in training on Saturday evening but their current status as GAA fashion statements will be reviewed after our next two challenge games.

'Look at the guys wearing the pink jerseys,' I said to the group before training. 'They would go through a wall for Dublin. But we all need to get a bit smarter.'

Smart-Edge. Love it.

Tuesday, 20 May 2014

After we played the U-21s in a challenge game in DCU, when we had eaten and the canteen had cleaned out, six of us – myself, Hedgo, Tommy Dunne, Shane Martin, Jenny Coady and Tony Griffin – squeezed down to the bottom end of the long table for a discussion which had been organized before-hand by Griff.

He didn't give us any feedback on how the mentoring sessions with the Dublin U-15s were to go but he kicked off the meeting with an observation one of his work colleagues – Tomás Harkin, who has worked with AFL clubs – had made during one of those sessions.

'How close are these guys to the summit?' Tomás had asked.

'Very close,' Griff replied. 'They're right there.'

'I don't get that sense. I don't get that confidence from them. Some of them have it but a lot of them don't.'

Whoa.

Why? In Griff's opinion, some of the main leaders had

stepped back in an attempt to allow others to take the lead. I could already sense that from Stephen Hiney. I knew he might feel undermined because he was unsure about his place but I was also aware that he firmly believed it was about time someone else stood up and did the talking that he had done for almost a decade. An attitude of 'Yes sir, no sir, three bags full sir, I'll sort it out for ye no matter what'. He was doing all that long before I arrived. Now it was someone else's turn.

I flipped that perspective around to us as a management team. 'If I shut my mouth when I was captain with Clare, if Seánie and Lohan said nothing, along with four or five others, Fingers was never going to get a fit of speaking. It wasn't in his makeup. Some people are happy leading and others are happier following.'

Griff stepped back in. 'You're spot on. Guys like Stephen and Johnny need to step their game up further and bring the boys with them. That is my synopsis, and Tom feels the same. And me, you Tommy, Shane, you Jenny, we all need to step up our game now too. There is only so much more they can take from Dalo, Hedgo and Richie.'

Me playing 'The Foggy Dew' on the bus is no longer enough to stimulate the players. I know they have an inherent trust in me because they know me so well. I have radically reinvented myself and my approach, but I think the greatest trust they have in me at this stage is that I can assemble a team around me to get the absolute most out of us. My focus now is on how I can get the most out of everyone, players and management, including myself. To make the apparatus even stronger than it is, to make the players believe that our framework is unbreakable.

Jenny is going to work on putting a video together. It will show a host of positives from training-ground and match-day footage before inserting a low of ninety seconds with footage of mistakes and missed tackles in the 2013 All-Ireland semi-final, alongside the devastation in the dressing-room after that game. Then Jenny will put the cherry on top of the cake by concluding with the absolute brilliance of Alan McCrabbe's goal against Limerick in a challenge game last week.

We are always looking to get across some message. After McCrabbe's goal, we seemed to self-regulate and check ourselves. It was almost as if lads said, 'Jeez, we're not meant to go 2-17 to 1-9 against Limerick, we'd better let them get a few points.' We take our foot off the gas, whereas the Kilkennys and Tipps of this world will bury you.

The core theme of the video is that we want to cut out these lulls in the middle of games. We want the footage to convey that message: this is us; this is what we can do; this is how we can fall down; but this is what we can also do. The decision is ours.

Lookit, you'll try anything.

18

Black and White Pride

After the 2006 All-Ireland semi-final defeat to Kilkenny, I knew my time with Clare was over. When I got home from Dublin on the Monday at 10.30 p.m. I was in an awful state. The stark reality of it hit me. We were gone. I was gone. It was over.

I got up the following morning and went downstairs for a glass of water. I didn't even hear the patio door open. When I turned around, Malty McDonagh, then chairman of the county board, was standing in front of me. I was wearing boxer shorts and a vest. I hadn't shaved since Saturday. Malty was immaculately dressed in a suit and tie. I was like a tramp.

'Well,' he said, 'are you gone?'

Immediately after the game, Malty had asked me not to make any rash decisions. I had told Seánie and Lohan that night but Malty wanted official confirmation. Now.

'Jeez, you told me on Sunday to take my time,' I said to him. 'Will you at least wait until about five p.m. I need to tell Eilís and the family before they hear it on Clare FM.'

By three p.m., it was Clare FM's lead story.

My name was hot news, but I was shuffling towards oblivion.

*

I have been lucky in life that I never suffered from depression but I could feel myself heading down that road. By October, I was on the floor. I was as low as a snake's belly. I was sitting on the beach in Spanish Point one evening, perched on the rocks, staring at the Atlantic Ocean, when Denise Martin rang. Denise had been involved with me as a statistician for three years with Clare and she could read my moods.

'You sound a bit down,' she said.

'I'm as low as hell. I'm just on the floor. The mundane is hitting me now. The high of being involved at that level, the cutting edge, I can't replace it. I don't know what to do with myself.'

I needed something to lift me from the darkness, and I could soon see a pinprick of light in the distance. It came from the most unlikely source but, before long, the light was shining like an orb.

I had got to know Brendan and Maurice McElligott from coursing in Clonmel. They were from Kilmoyley in Kerry and were hurling men to the marrow. The hurling part of north Kerry is also coursing territory and we had run the dogs over there a few times. I knew about the intense hurling rivalry there and it intrigued me. I had offers from three other clubs at the end of that October, but Kilmoyley just felt right. The car-ferry in Killimer that crosses to Tarbert in north Kerry was just up the road from Tullycrine. It was a refreshing outpost, but Kilmoyley are great people and I fell in love with them. Their warmth and generosity were unconditional. We had our disputes, like you would in any job, but you could never doubt their honesty and commitment. Their spirit crackled like electricity. For four years, it lit up my life.

They couldn't do enough for you. Ned Horgan, a great supporter of the club, ran his own meat distribution business and he'd regularly meet you at the gate with his standard question: 'Is your car open there, boy?'

'Sure, you're not allowed to lock your car around here,' I'd invariably reply.

When I'd go back to the car after training, I almost had to wrestle my way through a factory of gammon steaks, sausages and black pudding before I could sit in. It would have fed the Daly household in Clarecastle when there were eight of us. I'd be eating rashers for breakfast until they came out my ears.

They had unreal pride in themselves. They adored their club and their heritage. The first night I went down to Kilmoyley, I trained a minor team before a county final. Pete Young, who worked in Moneypoint, met me on the boat and acted as my human sat-nav. When we arrived at Ballinorig cross, I spotted a pitch and a ball wall. I was about to turn right towards the pitch when Pete stopped me in a panic.

'Jesus, don't go there.'

'Why?'

'That's Causeway's field.'

One of the first nights I stayed down there, I asked Shane Brick for a snapshot social history. 'Will you answer me one question? How do we have thirty lads on the field every night? There is a church, a school and a scatter of houses. And yet ye are gobbling up county championships.'

'Listen, Dalo,' he said, 'hurling is number one here. We get the absolute maximum out of that school. There is a massive tradition here and a massive pride in that jersey. And we all lap it up. We all want to hand it on.'

I immediately understood their culture and identity. 'I'm glad I came here,' I said to Shane.

They were super people – the Bricks, the McCarthys, the Murnanes, the Regans, the O'Sullivans, the Meehans, the

Godleys and the Youngs. Seán Murnane, the 'Bull McCabe' as I used to call him, was chairman for ten years. He was the face and the human spirit of Kilmoyley. He was rough and ready. He gave it to everyone straight. Including myself. I loved that rawness. Whenever I resigned, Murnane would be on to me before I'd be back on the ferry.

'Listen to me there now, boy, I lost it a bit there this evening,' he'd say in his thick north Kerry drawl. 'Sure, I'll see you there Thursday night and we'll chat it out. You'll be there, boy, you will, you will.' He'd hang up before I got a word in.

Then Maurice McElligott would ring. 'Did yourself and Murnane make it up?'

'We didn't. He spoke and I never got a chance to say anything. I'm fed up of him.'

I'd go back Thursday night and Murnane would be all smiles. 'It's mighty to see you crossing the boat, boy. There's a bit of grub coming tonight.' Next thing, his lady would land in with plates of sandwiches and chicken wings that would feed half of Africa.

Murnane reminded me of the great Clarecastle clubman Jack Moloney, but a large part of the appeal of Kilmoyley was the broad spectrum of similarities to Clarecastle. There was a cockiness there. They had won four-in-a-row under John Meyler at the outset of the decade and they expected success. I remember speaking to Meyler soon after I took over. 'Ya know, they get restless there very handy now, boy,' said Meyler in his acquired Cork accent. 'You're down there to win, boy.'

In my first year, 2007, we lost the county final to Lixnaw. A week later, I was buying a paper in a shop in Ennis when this auld fella nestled up beside me.

'Jaysus, you couldn't even win the Kerry championship,' he said.

'Funny enough,' I said to him, 'everyone else down there is trying to win it as well.'

I had to go back for another year to right that wrong but the whole experience felt so right that I stayed for two more. I could always relate to their drive and hunger for success. Everywhere you turned you could see shades of Clarecastle, and by extension my own character in them. They would fight on their backs for that jersey.

We played Kilmaley from Clare in a challenge game in LIT once and there was an awful boxing match between Colin Lynch and Tom Murnane. Lynch, in his gladiatorial tone, said to me afterwards, 'That was the type of match we needed. Good hard hurling.'

The championship never got out of hand in my time because they used to bring in high-profile referees from Cork and Limerick. But north Kerry league games were often a free-for-all. Against Causeway, Ardfert and Ballyduff, it was capable of kicking off any time.

It was always my ambition to bring them to Croke Park for an All-Ireland Intermediate final but it never happened. We lost to Blarney from Cork in 2008. The following year we were ahead by one point against Douglas with time up when Jason O'Mahoney awarded them a free against Colin Harris which in my opinion was never a free. Stephen Moylan slotted it and they beat us in extra-time. I was violent afterwards. The rest of Kilmoyley was even more violent, if you can picture that level of anger. I don't know how O'Mahoney got out of there alive.

When I was on *The Sunday Game*, we might be drinking tea beforehand and Pat Spillane would often ask me how I was getting on in 'bandit country'. It had that reputation, but we have holidayed all over Kerry and I would have far more time for the people of north Kerry than anywhere else in the county.

Their welcome was always genuine and heartfelt. Cratloe came down to play us in 2008 and the Cratloe bus pulled out of Maurice McElligott's pub in Ardfert at five a.m. And that was after Kilmoyley had given them a good hiding in the match.

In my last year, we lost the county semi-final to Lixnaw. The two clubs wore the same coloured jerseys and the 2007 county final was a joke because no one would give in to change. Coming up to that semi-final in 2010, we made a call and decided to wear the Clarecastle jerseys. We absolutely dominated the game but somehow managed to lose it. We missed seven goals. The Lixnaw goalkeeper, Martin Stackpoole, must have fallen into a bath of holy water beforehand because every time we tried to hit the net, we hit him instead.

It was the first part of a double-header in Tralee and it was the only time I ever experienced any personal abuse or vitriol during the game. 'Go home, Daly, and bring your fucking jerseys with you!' roared one fella. He could have been the biggest arsehole in Kerry but we were going for three-in-a-row and they were all getting sick of us.

It was the end for me, but it was a remarkable journey. Kilmoyley started out as therapy but it evolved into such a love affair that the club was my mistress for four years. Even when I was appointed Dublin manager in 2009, I couldn't extricate myself from the relationship. Fergal Hegarty and Tommy Howard did most of the coaching in my absence in 2009 and 2010, but when the evenings got shorter, I'd head across on the ferry. The breeze on the Shannon estuary would be pressing against my face and it felt like complete liberation. I'd pull out of Tarbert and drive to Ballylongford, then head for Lisselton before crossing the main Listowel–Ballybunnion road. After going through Ballyduff and arriving at Ballinorig, Causeway was to my right and Kilmoyley parish opened up to my left.

Driving in the gates in Lerrig often felt like arriving into Clarecastle. It felt like home.

I often think of that comment from my last game with Kilmoyley: 'bring your fucking jerseys with you'. It was even more hurtful to lose with the Clarecastle jerseys on our backs because the Kilmoyley lads knew how special that jersey was to me. The black and white colours always reached into our souls in Clarecastle. They reaffirmed how the love and madness of hurling define us as people.

Much of that mentality stemmed from our proximity to Ennis. Clarecastle and Ennis are so intrinsically connected now that the borders segue into each other, but the desire to retain our own unique identity fostered our spirit. When we'd often be hitching to town as youngsters, you might be picked up by some rep in a big car going to Galway. He'd ask where you were headed, and you'd say Ennis. 'Sure, is this not Ennis?' You'd be half tempted to tell him to stop the car and get out with the insult.

I'd like to think that it was always in me to cultivate that unique view of ourselves. When I was captain of the minors in 1987, I was sticking my hand up to be an U-12 selector. That sense of maintaining our tradition, which my father and uncles had carved before me, was so strong that some people in Clarecastle don't like me for it. There is always an element of begrudgery in how people view other people but I always tried to do the most I possibly could for Clarecastle. After the season with Clare was over, I tried to make every training session. I would always try to be the best player Clarecastle had. I just wanted the best for us.

Tradition and history demanded it. The 2003 county final against Ballyea was my last match for the club in Clare but I was an emotional wreck beforehand for far more reasons than the realization that the end was coming. Tommy Howard brought Hanly and Paddy and Mickey Russell in to meet us before we left Clarecastle. He even hauled Jim Lynch up from Kerry to the Coach House that day.

Jim was a legend in Clarecastle. He worked in Fenit in Kerry and used to cycle up to play with the club in the 1940s. We were reared on stories of how the village would wait at the Coach House for Jim to turn the corner before they'd all hit for Tulla to go to battle on ponies and traps.

Jim had to pedal his way from Kerry, but Philly Byrnes, who was married to my aunt, used to travel on a motorbike. Philly was a great player. He was from Ahane and he hurled for Limerick. My mother said they'd know that Philly was on the way when they'd hear the hum from his motorbike. A cheer would go up and caps would be fired into the air as soon as Philly would appear. Then nice and quietly, and without much fanfare, Jim might turn the corner after slaughtering himself on a rickety auld bike.

We were hot favourites to win that match in 2003 but I had to go off into the corner of the Coach House to hide because I was fierce emotional. The tears were still in my eyes when we passed Clareabbey on our way to Ennis. I was giving out hell to Howard. 'What are you after doing to us? That's OTT. I'm trying to clear my head before I have to run around after some young fella on the Clare minor panel.'

'I just want to make sure we win this match,' said Howard.

I won five county titles with Clarecastle. My father won two in the 1940s. After our third in 1949, we didn't win another one until 1970. And even that county title primarily stands as a landmark in an era of pain and suffering inflicted by Newmarket-on-Fergus. Newmarket won thirteen county titles between 1963 and 1981 and they beat us in seven of those finals.

With such a sense of longing and suffering in the club's heart and soul, we had our battles. There were some desperate rows with Newmarket. There was a brawl with Éire Óg in the late 1960s which I often heard Ennis people describe as the most vicious fight they ever saw. Around the same time, my father was stuck in another row after a semi-final against Crusheen in Cusack Park. He was a selector, and Tom Mac and his crew tried to break down the door with a telegraph pole. Clarecastle were in the final and didn't want to go fighting and get landed with a heap of suspensions. For a finish, they had no choice but to come out of their bunker like a battalion under siege from heavy artillery. My father, Patsy O'Loughlin, Paddy Russell and Packie Guinnane were the first four out. They had the hurleys cocked and they just started swinging. They belted all around them as they tried to clear a pathway for the rest of the players through a mass of Crusheen bodies. Barney Lynch still remembers it clearly. He was only a child, and his father caught him and threw him up on the old galvanized shed to get him out of harm's way.

We were reared on stories and tales of the hardship and bitterness of the 1960s and 1970s, the losing and the fighting, and the dream that it could one day be put right. When we got a taste of success, everyone saw that there was another way here, that we didn't have to fight our way to county titles any more. It took us a long time to shed that label, but we suffered so much in those two decades that those battles and wars stemmed from desperation to win. We didn't always start the rows but the 'one-in-all-in' attitude was a general tradition handed down to us because you never wanted to leave anyone isolated.

We probably don't think we're that clannish, but everyone

else in Clare sees that trait as our brand. We probably fight with each other more than anyone else, fellas arguing that this fella should be on the team and that lad should be nowhere near it. At this stage of my life, I nearly enjoy that now. There was a time when I'd always argue back. I had to be right. But my attitude now is to stop and take stock. 'Yeah, maybe it's the right call.'

Other teams regularly accuse us of always being on a war-footing, that we pack the line and try and intimidate the opposition. If anything, we just adopted that tactic from Sixmilebridge. When they started cleaning up at underage in the 1980s, they had a small army patrolling the line. We just decided at that time that we had to counter that strategy and it almost became club policy.

Sporadic battles continued to rage long after the 1970s had passed. The brawl against Ballybrown in the 1991 Munster club championship is probably the most infamous. It is still getting huge hits on YouTube. There was some desperate scutching, but we were the ones most sinned against. John Kenny – Kenny John as he was known – ignited the fuse and then inflamed it like a bushfire. The Gardaí had to try and break it up. There were kids on the field and it was something that nobody wants to see.

Expectation never takes a back seat in Clarecastle and we have always tried to drive forward and attain success. There have been plenty of occasions when we were prepared to do anything to get a result.

The blood runs high in all of us. In 1996, the Clare footballers were playing Cork in the Munster semi-final replay in Páirc Uí Chaoimh and the club decided to take in the match after a challenge game against Glen Rovers. The Glen had come up to us earlier in the year and we had given them a good hiding so they certainly weren't going to lie down on their own patch.

There was a real edge to the game. I'd had a run-in with

Deano Cooper before John Anderson arrived on to my patch. He began leaning in on me and I pushed him away with one hand. Anderson turned around and let fly. It seemed to me to be such an overreaction to a harmless altercation, like trying to kill an ant with a sledgehammer. He reefed me.

I put my hands up to my face and a pool of blood was gathering in my palms. Stephen Sheedy and Paraic Russell heard me roaring and came running. When Anderson saw them coming, he took off and kept going.

I thought I'd need plastic surgery and a sewing machine to stitch me back together but Johnny Callinan told me it wasn't as gruesome as I thought. Callinan was standing over me, but when I saw Anderson making his way back up the field, with the boys still hot on his heels, like Murty and Cillown Harbour trying to chase down a hare, I did everything to try and get up off the ground and join the chase for retribution. Callinan caught me by the two ankles and wouldn't let me go.

Anderson knew there was no escape. When the goalkeeper came out to try and protect him, Russell decked the keeper. So Anderson ran out the gate and ran to their club car park a couple of hundred yards away. A few of our lads gave chase but the gate was closed to keep in the hounds trying to hunt down the hare. Joe O'Leary, the former referee and Cork selector who was refereeing, had to abandon the game.

It was complete chaos. We thought we'd have to bate our way home to Clare but Callinan brokered a peace deal and I was sent off to a local doctor to get five stitches above my right eye. When I got there, Tomás Mulcahy was in the queue before me, waiting to get stitched up too. We had a right laugh at the whole commotion. Mul said that it was completely out of character for Anderson to do what he did.

We never went to Páirc Uí Chaoimh to watch the footballers.

We cut our losses and returned to Clarecastle. As the hours passed, the row was being described in *Braveheart* proportions. By midnight, it was like the Battle of Stirling. A couple of days later there was a full-page picture of me in the *Evening Echo* newspaper under the headline 'Split and Run'.

We lost that 1996 county final to Wolfe Tones but we atoned for the defeat a year later by beating St Joseph's Doora-Barefield in the final. That November, we had our greatest day, when Martin Sheedy brought the Munster club trophy back to the village, a side managed by three great Clarecastle men – Rodgie McMahon, Oliver Plunkett and Ger Ward. We had great days, but our quest to live the ultimate dream perished on a cold spring day in 1998 when we lost an All-Ireland club semi-final replay to Birr, one of the greatest club teams ever.

The Clare club championship was like a bear pit back then and the disappointment of losing to Birr was sharpened by the realization that we might never get another chance to go the full distance. We never did.

We are still chasing the dream. We have a new talented generation coming and that's why I have kept a hand in. Despite my other commitments, it is my duty to do what I can for Clarecastle, when I can.

I seem to have a habit of making the front page of newspapers and creating headlines for the wrong reasons. In October 2012 there were twenty-six people killed in a tornado in New York, yet on that Monday morning I was plastered all over the front page of the *Irish Independent*.

Like the last time I featured on the front page of a national daily paper, it was one of the real low points in my life. It was actually worse than my previous appearance because I'd had control over my actions this time around.

Clarecastle were playing Kilmaley in the Clare Minor A final. Tommy Howard and Niall Romer got involved in a scuffle. When I saw Howardy's glasses flying, something snapped inside me. I sprinted to his defence and struck Romer.

There are no excuses or dispensations for that kind of behaviour, but you forget yourself. It was a county minor final, the game was tight and tensions were high. When everyone else started getting stuck in, you were forced to try and defend yourself. Dick Pyne from Kilmaley eventually got a hold of me and said it was time to stop the madness.

I didn't realize the scale of the fallout until I saw traces of black ash and debris all over Facebook and Twitter that evening. A photograph of me throwing a punch at Romer was all over social media like a rash. I knew then that this was going to be big news. I was Dublin manager, Dublin sell newspapers, and this was a bonanza for a quiet time of the year.

It didn't fully hit me until I saw the papers on Monday. It was desperate. I tried to justify my actions on the reflex of going to a lifelong friend's aid but I was still angry with myself for not showing more restraint for someone in my position. The kids were old enough to know what was going on. I was hugely embarrassed for them and Eilís and the rest of my family. I was even embarrassed thinking about how it must have looked to the Dublin lads. I had already agreed to go back with Dublin and I rang John Costello to try and offer some kind of explanation.

'What are you at, you mad lunatic,' Costello said down the phone.

John knew there was no badness or malice in my actions but those actions still caused so much hurt on so many fronts. Eilís is from Kilmaley. Her four brothers are steeped in Kilmaley hurling. Her father is a fanatic. Her nephew Paraic was playing on that minor team. We always had a good relationship with

Kilmaley. A couple of Kilmaley lads had even played on the Clarecastle team of the 1940s. The collateral damage and fallout are always felt most by your immediate family.

My three girls were at the match, and that was no example to be setting. Orlaith was going to a Feis the same day and had to be in the West County Hotel in Ennis at five p.m. She left the match with Eilís with ten minutes remaining and the timing of their exit was ideal for those with an eye for detail and an ear for thunder.

'Even his own wife left the game because of the violence,' it was reportedly said. 'She even took the children with her.'

Úna and Aoife stayed until the end with Eilís's sister Siobhán, but that was conveniently omitted for effect. 'Sure, they must be separated again.'

I was getting it in the neck from every angle. A small ex-Kilmaley player from the 1980s was perched on the hill in Sixmilebridge, singing like a canary.

'Come on the sky-blues! Come on the sky-blues! Some year for you, Dalo, boy!'

The same guy himself was always a mouthpiece on the pitch. I was half tempted to walk into the crowd and get stuck into him, but I was in enough trouble by then.

I got an eight-week suspension, which I had no problem accepting. When we went into the subsequent county board meeting, I came completely clean. 'I'm not going to tell any lies,' I said to the disciplinary panel. 'Of course I hit Romer a box.'

We held our counsel and refused to single out any of Kilmaley's crew involved in the row. We completely held our hands up. The county board didn't go to town on us but some of our own were sticking the knives into our backs at that stage.

Over the weekend of the incident, we felt that some people in the club didn't back us in the way they should have. Some of the executive wanted to suspend Howardy, Sheedo and myself for starting 'a riot' and setting a bad example to young kids. The chairman of the senior club, Ruairí Concannon, and Fergie O'Loughlin, chairman of the minor club, didn't entertain that option for a second. 'If yere talking about suspending those three men,' Concannon said, 'ye'll be looking for a new chairman.' Ruairí provided huge support to us but I still found it very hurtful that some of our own wanted to bury us. We did wrong. We completely accepted that fact. But it was as if all our decades of service to the club, our blood and sweat and tears, had disappeared in a puff of smoke after one short-circuit.

A month after that game, we met the minor panel. We apologized to them personally about our behaviour, and asked them to apologize to their families on our behalf. We told them that if they were willing to have us back as a management, we would come back and try and make up for the disappointment and letdown of 2012.

We won a brilliant championship in 2013. We brought Fergie O'Loughlin and Kieran McDermott on board and they were a huge addition to our backroom team. We trained harder than ever. We ran into Kilmaley again in the final and for the second year in a row it was the best underage game in Clare. We won an epic match.

It was emotional seeing Bobby Duggan lift the cup, but coming out of Shannon that day there was nearly more a sense of satisfaction of having proved a point to those in Clarecastle who had doubted us twelve months earlier than in beating Kilmaley.

When we met Newmarket in the 1992 championship, the gun had been emphatically turned from when they'd routinely pistol-whipped our ancestors around the hurling fields of Clare. We were reigning county champions, they had been in the doldrums since 1981. It was our chance to trample more dirt down on top of the shallow grave they found themselves in.

When we lost, half of Clarecastle wanted to dig a big hole and bury us inside it. They wanted to decapitate me first before they threw me in because I was skank bad. I was walking down the village a couple of days later when I passed a man I knew. 'Well Ger,' I said to him. He turned his head away as if I was a leper.

By that stage, the word was out. The previous week the Clare footballers had won their first Munster title in seventy-five years and myself, Barney Lynch and Padraig Russell went back to Doonbeg on the Monday night to join in with the celebrations. The captain Francis McInerney was the Clare captain and it was their last stop-off so we felt it was the place to go, especially when it was early in the week ahead of our match.

We drank very little. We just wanted to drink in the atmosphere of a Munster title success and what it really felt like. The few drinks we did have had absolutely no impact on our performance, but some fella spotted us and it provided rocket fuel for those in Clarecastle who wanted to run us over when we lost to Newmarket.

A couple of days later, my poor widowed mother was coming up from the shop with her groceries after ten o'clock mass when a woman shouted across to her: 'Tell him to go back to Doonbeg and burn his hurley in the bonfire.' My mother didn't know what she was talking about, but it was just vintage Clarecastle. The character of Clarecastle is largely formed and framed from how we all look at one another. There are spleens and divisions all over the place, yet most of the people in Clarecastle would fight to the death to protect its name and honour.

Some crowds just don't like each other and I try to be in the middle of it all. There are more lads who don't like me because

I stand for certain principles. They'd say, 'We're not good enough for him, he shagged off to Dublin and Kilmoyley, and he hasn't trained the seniors yet.' They conveniently forget that I trained the team in 2002, but I have gone beyond caring what they think. Sure, if a guy doesn't like himself, how could he like me?

I just accept the dynamic and culture of Clarecastle for what it is because I know the place and its idiosyncrasies so well. There is a tolerance of a few pints and fellas being who they are. I'd often sit in the middle of a group of fellas in Navin's and agree away with what they have to say. I could be sober, and lads would ask me afterwards, 'How do you stay listening to that shite?' I just love the banter.

It's down to the way I was reared. In Madden's Terrace, there was no one more important than the next. You had the same sized house as everyone else and you weren't long discovering that everyone had the same problems – young families struggling to make ends meet, too much alcohol in some houses, a young girl getting pregnant.

When I moved to west Clare, I was also moving to a completely different culture. People would be asking you questions about you and your family, more out of kindness and consideration than anything else. In Clarecastle, they'd want to know a story about someone else and see if they could knock some craic out of it. Clarecastle people have a unique sense of humour. They are just completely open. My mother's house was always an open house. Anyone could be inside in your front room, almost to the point that you'd sometimes nearly want them to clear off so you could chill out. On the day of my wedding, Martin said in his speech that he was staring down at faces he had been looking at all of his life inside our house.

It's that kind of comfort and connection which always links

you to your own people, even when the chain sometimes gets broken. About three years ago I had a row with Barney Lynch, a stupid altercation over politics while we were out one night. One word led to another and we both said things we regretted. Myself and Barney are great friends. Our family histories have been interlinked for decades. My uncle John was Barney's father's best man. Eilís and myself often stayed in Barney's house. The whole of Clarecastle thought we had fallen out, but I rang Barney the following day and apologized.

'Forget them all and what they're saying about us, will we meet for a pint?' I asked him. 'Let them say what they want.'

We went to Powers and sat at the counter. We had settled our differences within minutes, but I wanted to let everyone else know that while politics had warped us the previous day, we were still unbreakable.

It was almost a neat metaphor for Clarecastle.

19

The Captain's Prize

Monday, 2 June 2014

No sleep. Zero sleep. I tried everything. Read. Watched Sky Sports News. I even texted Ray Finn at three a.m. Unsurprisingly, he texted back. I had asked for a four a.m. wake-up call at the Castleknock Hotel but there was no need for the receptionist to bother. When the call came, I was already showered and ready for road.

I was sitting in the lobby for ten minutes before Christy O'Connor arrived downstairs at 4.30 a.m. We chatted for a short while before Shane Martin's car pulled up outside. Daylight had already pierced through by then. The air was crisp and fresh, warm even. Our nutritionist Crionna Tobin was sitting in the front seat so Christy and I fired the bags into the boot, sat into the back and Shane sped off in the direction of the airport.

We were flying at 6.20 to Faro in Portugal for a training camp. Tony Griffin was already in the airport by the time we arrived. I got Shane to scan my ticket and passport at the express check-in kiosk but we still had to queue to drop our bags. The crowds were animal and the clock was ticking. Eventually, a call came over the tannoy for anyone flying to Faro to go to Desk 35 for an express-baggage drop. Saved.

It was just after ten a.m. when the taxi-bus ferrying the five of us pulled in the gates of the Amendoeira golf resort, just beyond the town of Silves. Against the backdrop of the Monchique Mountains, with orange and lemon trees dotted along the brown landscape, the taxi-bus turned right four hundred yards down the driveway and towards the training centre. As it drove past the dressing-room area and veered left, we could see the lads in their sky-blue tops on the training pitch, the sun glistening off their foreheads. You could even pick out Hedgo's face, his skin already toasting from one day in the warm sun.

The bus continued along a narrow paved path, the brown-coloured slabs faded to a yellow hue, diluted by the sun's strong rays. We chugged along beside the big white marquee on our right, packed with weights and physio tables, before snaking our way past baby palm trees and purple flower beds as the path led to the entrance to the training pitch. As we pulled up, we drove over a cable connecting to a fridge beside the pitch, which Ray Finn was stocking with crates of bottled water.

A speed/acceleration session had been planned for between 9.15 and 10.30 and Ross Dunphy was controlling that part of the session. The players were lined up in groups of sixes and had to sprint no more than fifty yards. As a form of competition, the winners were being announced as either north-siders or south-siders. Tommy Dunne concluded the session with a couple of sharp striking and accuracy drills.

It was only after ten a.m. but it was warm, really warm, hitting for thirty degrees. Before the lads made their way to the outside pool for a recovery swim, Hedgo and Ray were handing out bottles of sun-tan lotion like bottles of water. There was a football on the pitch so as the lads were making their way towards the bus to ferry them to the pool, I started kicking it around. The World Cup was only days away. I was so hyped up, I felt like I was preparing to play in it.

It was our third time in Portugal for one of these camps. When I went on one of Bernard Flynn's GAA Legends Charity Golf events to Cyprus in 2004, I spoke to Joe Kernan about how he had taken his Armagh squad to La Manga on a training camp the year they won the All-Ireland in 2002. It sowed a seed in my head and I brought the Clare lads to Portugal for a camp in 2005. Colin Lynch approached me before we departed for home and thanked me for allowing him to live like a professional athlete for a week. We almost won the All-Ireland title the same year.

I knew the benefits, but Dublin weren't at that stage in their development in 2009 that we could be aiming for a warm-weather training camp. We had planned to go to Portugal in 2010 but we had to cancel when that volcanic eruption in Iceland belched out black ash which drifted over western Europe and disrupted flights. We switched to Castlebar at short notice and it served its purpose fine. We went to Portugal in 2011 and 2012 but I didn't feel we were entitled to ask for a trip in 2013 so we bedded down in Castlemartyr in Cork instead for a training weekend.

For our previous trips abroad we had gone in April, but I had it in my head at the end of last year that we might go on a camp as late as we possibly could in 2014. I first raised that point when we went to Mullingar in September 2013 for a management think-tank.

We had had a good year in 2013 but I didn't want to rest on our laurels. So we booked into the Mullingar Park Hotel on Saturday morning and tore each other to shreds for the day.

Frank Rock, an independent facilitator, whom Richie Stakelum had sourced, chaired a meeting which lasted nine hours. It was relentless. Twelve of us sat around a boardroom table and you could say whatever you thought. Nobody held back.

Richie, being the man and the strong character he is, challenged me. We were all searching for that critical edge that might drive us over the line and win us an All-Ireland, and when I scanned my mind back on the season, I felt I could have given more to the cause. There were a couple of nights when I'd felt like turning back for home. It was just the monotony of the long winter roads beating me and my enthusiasm down, but when you're trying to tip the balance of the scales, every grain counts.

I opened my heart about how I felt we were in trouble after Tipp hammered us in the league semi-final. I'd had the health scare the previous week and I was probably mentally fragile and unable to firewall all the viruses from my system, but I still should have been setting a more confident and definite tone.

There were other times during the season when I'd doubted myself. One evening before the 2013 All-Ireland semi-final I decided to cancel training and bring the lads kayaking in Dún Laoghaire harbour. I had spoken to John Allen, Limerick manager at the time, about the difficulty in handling the five-week lay-off after a provincial final and he said that less was as beneficial as more.

That prompted my decision to go kayaking that evening and we had some craic on the pier. The players nearly drowned me. It was one of those beautiful, spontaneous evenings when we felt really alive and on top of the world, and ready to take on the world, but Niall Corcoran said to me afterwards that he was mad that the players hadn't come up with the idea first. In other words, the players wanted to show that they were taking on more responsibility. Corco was just mad that I beat them to the idea.

I was delighted with Corco afterwards but mad with myself. Was I still dummy-feeding them too much? Was I still not prepared to hand over more responsibility to them? We had established a leaders' group, but was that covering enough bases? Would we really have gone kayaking if I hadn't initiated the move?

It may have been me being over-analytical and self-critical but I was determined to learn from the season and to make myself and the group even stronger again in 2014. It was at that think-tank that I floated the idea about going to Portugal in early June, two weeks before we would go straight into a Leinster semi-final as a seeded team.

I knew it was a risk and that if anything went wrong everyone would be lining up to gun us down – that it was too warm; that we went too close to the match; who did we think we were, Real Madrid?

I didn't care. I knew we could get a massive amount of work done, both on hurling and tactics. And now we're going to do it.

When I played with Clare, there were no training camps in Portugal. We went to Killarney in 1995 for a training weekend but we'd been conditioned in Crusheen and the hill in Shannon, penal institutions where the beatings continued until morale improved.

The first time we were out of the country was the team holiday after we won the 1995 All-Ireland. When we boarded the plane in Shannon that December, a TV camera followed us and Loughnane gave an interview. 'I said to our tour operator, Tom Mannion, take us somewhere where they know nothing about hurling,' said Loughnane. 'So it was either Tipperary or Thailand.'

Only Loughnane. We went to Thailand.

We had a team meeting before we went. There was a vote taken on whether or not we should bring girlfriends and the outcome was that only wives would travel. And there weren't too many of them around in 1995.

Some of the lads, and their girlfriends, were very put out but it allowed us to focus more on the team dynamic. Instead of couples going out in small groups and largely sticking together in that company, we were able to take over some bar and spend as much time together as possible.

It was a crazy holiday. We spent three nights in Bangkok and ten nights in Pattaya. It was a mad world. I never saw anything like it. Most of us had never been further than a sun holiday in Spain or a few days in a caravan in Lahinch. We were like a typical crowd of young Irish lads just let off the leash. We stuck together like a posse and 'Fingers' O'Connell invariably led the charge.

Fergal Hegarty and I were going back to the hotel one night in Bangkok on the back of a tuk-tuk bike. I was wearing flip-flops and I stretched out my leg to tell the driver to hurry up. 'Speed it up there, Jack, you're taking us out the Long-Mile Road to fleece us, ya bollix.' The tour guide had warned us to treat the head as absolutely sacred and never to touch the locals in that area. And then I go and kick one of them into the head.

The flip-flop slipped off my foot and clipped your man on the back of the crown by accident. He instantly jumped off the tuk-tuk and I told Hego to run. We were just thankful that he wasn't some Bruce Lee wannabe because he would have been entitled to chase after us and kick the shit out of us.

When we got to Pattaya, we continued to do what we liked.

We were staying in a five-star hotel and would normally arrive back around five or six a.m. There was a twenty-four-hour Italian restaurant on one of the floors and we'd descend on it like a crowd of ravenous wolves. We'd be eating pizzas and drinking wine while people were going downstairs for breakfast.

One morning, one of the lads signed the cheque under the name of Tom Mannion, the tour operator. We were after hoovering up eight bottles of wine and enough pizza and pasta to feed half of Rome. The threshold had been crossed, the die cast. Pat O'Donnell got the next blast the following evening. Then it was back to Tom again in room 241. By the end of the holiday, half the squad were going by the name of Tom Mannion and Pat O'Donnell.

We had cleaned out Sparrow's mini-bar one evening, but this was lunacy. You'd nearly have bought a house with the digits we were clocking up. The day we checked out, we were all told to settle any outstanding bills owed. We were all sitting in the lobby when Pat O'Donnell and his wife arrived at the desk. About fifteen papers instantly went up over our faces. Suddenly we were all fluent in Thai and immersed in the literature section about Thai culture.

Our concentration was soon broken with this screech.

'I never ate a pizza in my life,' Pat said to the receptionist.

'Well, you're down here for sixty-three of them, mostly pepperoni,' she replied.

That was only the half of it. He also owed for eighty-seven bottles of wine. And Pat and his wife Marilyn never touched a drop of drink in their lives.

Johnny Callinan, who was with us as part of the holiday committee, had been tipped off. He had a credit card that would draw money out of the holiday fund for emergencies. Callinan knew the story. He put his solicitor's hat on while he reasoned with a raging Pat. Callinan turned around and stared at this chandelier in the hotel lobby, diamonds and rubies sparkling from its frame. It was probably worth a couple of hundred grand.

'Can you imagine if we brought a rugby team here, Pat,' said Callinan. 'Can you imagine the bill we could be paying out then? It's only a few bottles of wine and a handful of pizzas.'

Good man, Johnny. To defuse the situation, he was discreetly telling Pat that he was lucky that we hadn't been swinging off that chandelier, pulled the thing off the roof and had to be bailed out of jail.

Callinan slipped the card to the receptionist and paid the bill. He had to deal with a similar reaction from Tom when he arrived, but Callinan let that play out too. While Tom was waiting for his bill to print off, there were reams of pages coming out the side of the printer. By that stage, it was hard not to crack. We were falling off the chairs in the lobby. In fairness to Tom, he saw the funny side of it too.

I was lucky I even made it home from that holiday. Lohan nearly killed me with a jet-ski. He had Hego above on the back of it and he lost control. I had just fallen off my ski and Lohan missed my head by about a foot. If he'd hit me, I'd have been killed stone dead. Having Hego on the back was totally against the rules but we were a law unto ourselves.

Fergie Tuohy and Stephen Sheedy decided to be more adventurous. We were told not to go beyond the bay on the jet-skis, but just like at school, the two boys had to bend the rules. They disappeared off into the distance like two dots. You could go about a mile on the jet-ski before it would run out of diesel but it looked like they were headed for India. And Sheedy couldn't even swim.

Sure enough, the boys were soon stranded like apes. They

managed to chug-chug the two jet-skis in close to some rocks until they conked out and collapsed on their side. They had life-jackets on and Tuts dragged Sheedy in to the shore. They cut their feet to ribbons on the rocks and found themselves in the middle of nowhere, hardly able to walk.

By this stage, your man who rented out the skis was going bananas. He tore over to us and asked where they had gone and we just shrugged our shoulders. Your man kept pointing at the fuel gauge on the jet-ski and saying, 'No, no, no.' Deep down, we were worried sick. We were picturing the two boys at the bottom of the ocean or being torn apart by some shark for breakfast.

The jet-ski operator took off on this speedboat. A few minutes later he arrived back pulling the jet-skis behind him, but no sign of the two boys. Holy Jesus, total panic set in. It looked like Jaws must have had a right feast.

As time passed, the fun was well siphoned out of the chat. Loughnane arrived and started reasoning with your man, asking him could he go back out on the speedboat again looking for the lads. Lo and behold, next thing we heard Lazarus behind us.

'It's a fucking rip-off,' says Tuohy. 'Twenty quid for those yokes and not enough diesel in them.'

Himself and Sheedy had stumbled upon some construction site and got a lift back to the hotel on the side of a lorry. They'd left a trail of blood on the pristine polished lobby floor before smearing the manicured lawn at the back of the hotel as they made their way back on to the beach.

Sheedy was hardly able to walk but Tuohy had to have the last word. When the jet-ski operator saw him, he nearly made a run for him. He tore the life-jacket off himself and Sheedy. Then he told us all to clear off, that he never wanted to see us again.

The county board hardly expected us to go to museums or the

theatre and we hit the town so hard we hardly saw the room at all. We weren't in the mood for much else, only drinking and chilling out, but one of the highlights of that holiday was a soccer game we played against a local team, which was arranged through one of the players who worked in the hotel. They were a serious outfit but they couldn't handle our physicality and we beat them by about four goals.

Thousands of miles from home, with beer sweating out through our pores in buckets, we refused to let up. Mike Mac always had this famous saying: 'Every year, thirty men will win a Munster championship.' Mac was our manager that day and he just altered the words: 'Every year, thirty men will win an auld half-arsed soccer match in the middle of Thailand.'

No matter where you are, no matter what you're doing, the camaraderie of the group, the sense of common purpose and friendship, is always the stitching that binds everyone together. When we were in San Diego in 1997, the lads were going off looking at whales one day. I had no interest, and neither had Lohan. We took a notion to go horse riding, even though the only horse I'd ever been on in my life was one of Jimmy Flynn's asses. Eamonn Taaffe said he'd come along. So did Brendan 'Mousie' McNamara, who thought we were going horse racing, not horse riding.

Mousie got some shock when we turned up at this cowboy ranch. We went for a trot and I nearly lost my life when Lohan's horse took off for a gallop and my lad followed him. As we were trekking back to the ranch through woods, Mousie put on his Peter O'Sullevan accent and started commentating on a mock Grand National. When we returned to the ranch, we broke out some tins of beer and sat around a camp-fire with the cowboy. We spent hours chatting and shooting the breeze on an idyllic evening. It was unplanned but perfect. I would have had great time for Mousie and Taaffe but that was the first time I ever really spent quality time in their company. I got to know them better. I found out more about their character. To me, that's what team holidays should be all about.

We won't be jumping up on any jet-skis or horses out in Portugal but the training camp is as much about building that kind of friendship and strengthening that bond between the group as it is about working on our hurling and developing our tactics.

When you go into battle, you will always fight more honestly and valiantly if you're doing it beside good friends.

The keys to our apartments were in a white envelope, which included a resort map and a two-page schedule of the week, with the Dublin crest on the top of the first page.

Just below, it read:

> The Objective of this training camp is to be READY FOR BATTLE on Saturday June 14.
> In order to do this, we must focus on ourselves, maximize OUR potential and prepare tactically for our opponents for the most important game of the year.
> Recovery, Rest, Nutrition and Sleep are key elements and should be taken where possible.

On that Monday at six p.m., the day we arrived, we had a full-sided fifteen-on-fifteen game, twenty minutes per half. It was electric. Super stuff. The B team were wearing our grey jerseys and some of the lads stood out so much they could have been dripping with luminous green paint.

After dinner in the golf clubhouse, there was a meeting arranged in one of the rooms, which was facilitated by Tony

Griffin and Tomás Harkin. I never really know, or want to know, what is said in those meetings but it came back to me through one of the players later about the immense contribution Colm Cronin had made. He had spoken about how much he looked up to some of the older guys. Yet when he had misplaced a ball during that training game, he couldn't believe the amount of abuse he got from three or four of the older fellas. He didn't think it was right. Colm didn't think that was part of our brand, or that it should have any association with that brand.

The lads were apparently blown away by how well Colm articulated his point. It was such a powerful moment that it triggered the older lads into adopting a new philosophy regarding on-field communication during matches.

Weeks and days like this are about searching for those few extra granules, those few extra grains which might tip the scales. At the start of the week, we might have already begun tipping the balance more in our favour.

All week we kept loading more grains, more granules on to the weighing scales. Before we played our second fifteen-on-fifteen training game on Wednesday morning at 10.30, we went through our three gameplans once more. It came back to us from the players' meeting on Monday that not all the players were fully clear on the adjustments that needed to be made when we tweaked formations. Jenny Coady has brought our stats and graphics to a whole new level and when we went through the three gameplans in more detail in the players' meeting room that morning, Shane Martin was able to move players around on the screen like Gary Neville on Sky Sports.

At a management meeting on Monday evening we had discussed coming up with a fourth gameplan but we decided to leave it out of our plans because we didn't want to over-complicate matters. Just to make fully sure that everyone was clear on what we wanted, I marched the players to the small Astroturf soccer pitch behind the main pitch before the training match began on Wednesday morning. We lined out the team, explained once more what we wanted when going with a particular gameplan, and off we went. It was another electric match.

We had another recovery swim planned for afterwards and an afternoon trip to a water park, 'Splash & Slide', was on the schedule sheet for between two and 5.30. It was optional but Shane Durkin was collecting the money and organizing the numbers and most of the lads were on board. Ross Dunphy wasn't too keen on spending over three hours out in the blazing sun so we narrowed the time to two hours.

Ross had also insisted that lads leave T-shirts on to prevent any sunburn or overexposure to the sun, but that didn't fit with the park's policy. Ray and Hedgo were frantically handing out the bottles of sun-tan lotion but Keaney and a couple more lads didn't need much sun-block because they had skin-tight training tops, which were allowed. Those garments were a shield from the sun but they were also useful as an aid to build up more speed.

Within minutes, lads had hunted down the best and most hair-rising slides. The ones with multiple lanes were the biggest attraction because five of them could race against one another at the same time. The competition was nearly more intense than the training matches back at the Amendoeira resort. I was going up against the best of them and I probably had an extra advantage coming down those plastic tubes with my added girth. Some lads, though, were just cruising around at their own leisure, dipping in and out of the jacuzzi pools or sauntering down the less adventurous slides. Joey Boland, who had picked up an ankle injury, was just paddling around in one of the shallow pools trying to soothe the damaged ligaments.

By the time everyone else had taken the pace down to that level, we all went to a small café to drink tea and eat ice-cream, before Eamonn O'Reilly took the lads for a stretching-core-mini-yoga session on the lawn just in front of the park's entrance.

Going to the water park was as important as any training we did back at the resort because it provided another opportunity to cement the bond within the group. Given that we were playing Wexford nine days after arriving back into the country, this camp had to be more than just having the foot pressed to the floor for five days, trying to cram in as much training as we could, like gorging at a buffet because the opportunity is there. We worked hard, but everybody had plenty of time for recovery and chilling out.

When we'd been away on training camps before, we always had something arranged, a fun element that would loosen the pressure valve associated with training so hard in such a short timespan. One year we organized a mock-play. Noley was impersonating Hedgo so he cut out a red cushion and stuck it on his head. Paul Ryan was mimicking me. Another year they did a sketch where they dressed Chris Thompson up as Ian Paisley. I nearly keeled over from laughing.

We didn't arrange anything like that this time round because lads had more downtime on their hands, but of course they used that downtime as an opportunity to mobilize and rip the piss out of other lads. Paul Ryan is a brilliant mimic and he put his skills to good use. A load of them gathered in one of the apartments one evening and Ryan went to work. One of them recorded it on a phone.

Tommy Dunne was the first target. Ryan claimed to be some fella, with a dire country accent, from Parnell's in Dublin, a club which became flush with cash after selling a load of prime-location land during the boom time. When Alan McCrabbe started rubbing his index finger against his thumb to prompt Ryan to discuss a potential fee, Tommy was very diplomatic and he didn't engage in that discussion. Tommy probably knew something didn't add up when Ryan started talking about helicopters and flying him from Toomevara to Dublin for training.

The boys worked their way through a list of potential targets. Seánie McClelland was an obvious one, because if you enlist, you must drill with some of those boys, and Seánie is a great lad for the craic. There were golf buggies around the apartment complex and Seánie had driven the shite out of one of them. Ryan rang him up, pretending to be me, and he cut loose, claiming that he'd trashed one of the buggies and that the hotel management were 'freaking out'. Seánie was on his way to see me when Chris Crummy told him to come back and not to make an ape of himself.

They left the best call until last. Ryan dialled Michael Carruth's number, summoning the best English accent he could manage.

'Michael, hi, this is Jimmy Carlisle from Sky Sports. How are ya, mate?'

'Jimmy, how's things.'

'Michael, obviously Sky are covering the Dublin-Wexford match in a couple of weeks and we'd like to do an interview with you about the team. The fact that you're an Olympic champion an' all that, ya know what I'm getting at, mate.'

'Yeah, that's fine Jimmy, no problem at all.'

Over the next couple of minutes the air was rank from the amount of bullshit Ryan was spewing. He nearly gave the game away a couple of times because the boys in the background were struggling to contain themselves. At one stage Ryan asked Carruth about the hamstring concerns of 'Liam Rushey'.

'Ah he's fine, Jimmy, he's coming on good.'

It's an honour for us to have an Olympic gold medallist working with us. Michael is a huge character. Having him on board shows the immense depth of character we have around the place. Nobody would mess with Carruth, but Ryan has a neck for anything. His wind-up was so impressive that Michael never copped a thing.

He sat down beside me at the breakfast table the following morning, delighted with himself. 'I'm awful media savvy me, ya know wha' I mean.' I knew exactly what had gone down and I was struggling to keep a straight face. Amendoeira is really a golf resort, with a top-class course, and as Michael began discussing the round of golf he had planned that afternoon with Sean Shanley, he was completely unaware that 'Jimmy Carlisle' was sitting directly behind him at another table.

Back in the 1990s, we used to drink in this pub in Ennis called the Rocks. After league games we'd head to the Diamond Bar on O'Connell Street before making our way up the longest street in Ennis, past Ennis Cathedral before crossing Clare Road at the top of the street and settling in for a night of celebration or post-mortems.

The place was run by Sean Hartnett and Eamonn and Gerry Fitzgerald. They were big hurling men and it was a huge kudos and benefit for them to have us drinking on their premises. They knew the potential value but they also appreciated the custom. When Eamonn Fitz heard that we were going to Killarney on a training weekend before the 1995 league final, he wanted to treat us to a round of drinks. He gave me a cheque for £250.

It was a nice wad of cash. It would have bought a decent round of drinks, but the money was ultimately going to end in a urinal. I wanted it to have more value so I presented the lads with two options: we could either piss the money down the toilet or put it on ourselves to win the Munster title. For once, it was a no-brainer. Lads could buy their own drink.

I cashed the cheque in the bank and hatched a plan. I heard Lifford Racing were offering odds of 8-1 on us, and I fancied it. I just didn't want to lay the bet myself and draw unnecessary attention on ourselves. Eilís wasn't that comfortable with the idea of going into a betting shop but I had frequented the place a couple of times and had one of their betting slips at home. So I wrote it out for her in unmistakable bold lettering: Clare at 8-1 to win the Munster championship.

Eilís walked in, handed the cashier the slip and slapped the money on the counter. He wouldn't give her 8-1 because those odds were only offered for bets of less than £50. He offered her 6-1, and Eilís, mortified and in a panic to get out of the place before someone recognized her, took it and ran back to me in the car. If anyone saw us, they'd have thought we were part of a Malaysian match-fixing syndicate.

I went in to training the following night and told the lads that 6-1 was the best price I could get.

'You fucking eejit,' said Tony Considine. It was typical Considine.

'Here,' I said to him, 'you hold on to it so. There is luck in you.'

On the night we won the Munster title, we knocked some craic out of Considine on the bus home. 'Give me back that docket,' I said to him. 'Who's the eejit now?'

Of course, he had to go in and collect the winnings. I'd say the place was barely opened the following morning when Considine arrived in the door. When the guy behind the counter saw him, it soothed some of the pain from the payout. 'Jeez, I was hoping it was someone connected with the team,' he said. 'Because it was an unusual bet.'

'That was Dalo's girlfriend,' replied Considine.

We set up a bank account and that was the beginning of the famous holiday fund. Loughnane put a committee together – Gerry 'Diamond' Kelly, Johnny Callinan and Seamus Hayes – to administer and control the fund and over time it became more than just a resource to provide the money for team holidays. If Loughnane needed to send someone abroad for physio or special medical treatment, the backup was there. It ensured that Loughnane never had to go with a begging bowl to the county board and it covered a wide range of requirements. If a player had some misfortune, he could call into The Diamond and plead his case with Gerry Kelly.

For years, the account funded our annual golf outing. It was finally closed in 2013, but almost two decades after it was first opened we still meet once every year to play a round of golf and just hang out together. A group of fifteen or sixteen lads normally play the golf but another crew who have no interest in belting golfballs will arrive afterwards and we'll spend the evening rekindling old stories and stoking the embers from distant days when we felt like kings.

The numbers have often dwindled but some lads have made a great effort to keep it going. Frank Lohan and Barry Murphy have been brilliant in recent years. There was a time when letters would be sent out, but Frank has everybody's email address and the planning takes far less time now than it did in the early days.

Before we all retired and started getting fat, those early group golf outings were mostly restricted to team holidays. They were always great craic but some of them were pretty saucy too. We went to the US West Coast and Hawaii after winning the 1997 All-Ireland. The first part of the trip was five days in San Diego, and we went golfing on one of the last days.

We had planned to tee off around eleven a.m. but Loughnane and Considine wanted to get on the course far earlier. They said they would make their own way down and play themselves. We had a draw to pair golfers with a handicap alongside guys who rarely played and everyone handed in their scorecard at the end. Loughnane and Considine just handed in their scorecards as we were heading out.

When the beer started flowing back at the hotel that evening, we decided to gong the two boys. We didn't feel the need to justify it because they hadn't paid us the $20 for prizes and they hadn't been part of the draw. As sure as Jesus, when we totted up the scorecards, Loughnane and Considine had the best combined score, four points ahead of Fergie Tuohy and Barry Murphy.

When we were in the bar later on that evening, Tuts was doing MC and he dressed it up like he was presenting the Green Jacket at Augusta. He got two blue jackets off two waiters and got Seánie McMahon up to slip them on them. Loughnane and Considine meanwhile were stewing away, in full knowledge of the score which had won.

As Murphy modelled the jacket, Tuts picked up the microphone again. 'And we'd really like to thank everyone who participated, everyone who played today and made it such a memorable round of golf.'

The following day, Loughnane and Considine were barely saluting lads. They were giving everybody the silent treatment for about three days.

When we were flying to Hawaii two days later you could have

sliced the tension at the airport with a machete. When Tuts asked Loughnane for his tickets, he almost threw them at him. Before we boarded the plane, a couple of lads were talking about the whole episode in the toilets, about how Loughnane and Considine would want to cop themselves on. And then, like in one of those movies, the toilet flushed and out walked Considine from one of the cubicles. All that was missing was the dark background music.

When we went golfing again in Hawaii, we did a draw for pairs and I pulled out Loughnane's and Tuts' names together. Just try and picture the look Tuts gave me. They were teeing off before me and I was barely able to stop myself from keeling over with laughter. There was still no talk out of Loughnane by this stage and Tuts shanked his first drive from the lingering tension. I almost collapsed into the bushes.

They were talking by about the fifth hole but Loughnane was on a roll by that stage. Tom Mannion, God rest him, had got us into this Jack Nicklaus-designed course, a real posh place. There was a strict dress code but it was a roasting day and Loughnane whipped his shirt off after about the second hole. One of the rangers tore down on a golf buggy.

'I'm sorry, sir, but could you put your shirt back on, please. I'd really appreciate that now, sir.'

Loughnane put it back on but the ranger was gone about a hundred yards when he took it off again. The ranger came back about four times before he issued his final warning to Loughnane.

'Sir, if you don't put your shirt back on, I'll have to eject you from the course.'

Loughnane was the law. He had no real interest in golf around that time. He had less interest in abiding by rules. It was just as well the ranger wasn't following Loughnane around the whole time. You were supposed to keep the buggies on the margins of the fairways but Loughnane drove his straight up the middle of every fairway.

Our golf outings now are restricted to once a year and it's a fantastic way for the players to keep in touch. Mike Mac always turns up and has always been a huge supporter of the event. Unfortunately, Loughnane and Considine don't come any more, but we'd all love to have them back with us again. Just like old times.

Everything about the week in Portugal was almost perfect. We all felt like a real group because everybody worked so hard. Even Crionna was brilliant. Her week extended far beyond taking hydration samples and measuring body fat because she even did cooking demonstrations with the young lads. One afternoon they made healthy muffins. I was just about to take a bite out of one of them when I asked Crionna who had baked it. I left it back on the plate when she said Seánie McClelland.

I've only really got to know Seánie in the last year but he has already developed into a real character within the squad. He's one of the young brigade, and a guy with the potential to become a real leader for this team going forward.

Crionna was also there on the Tuesday evening when we held a management meeting in the restaurant after our evening meal. The meeting was part of the original week's schedule but it became much more than anyone intended, or expected, it to be. It became so personal and heartfelt that it was almost an emotional letting.

A lot of stuff came out. Ray Finn got emotional because of how much all this means to him; he spoke about how much satisfaction he gets from working in such a professional set-up with his best friend, Hedgo. Tommy Dunne is a complete professional in everything he does but you could hear the strains of emotion in his voice and read it in the contours of his face as he spoke about how much Dublin had restored his confidence since departing from the Tipp backroom team in 2012. When I first rang Tommy in 2013, he was on the floor. Tipp means so much to Tommy but the manner in which it ended for him the previous year had flattened him. Coming to Dublin, and thriving within the set-up, was a form of rehabilitation which he was extremely grateful for.

Tommy articulated as much to the players when we had our last meeting, our last exercise of the week, just before we departed for the airport. The meeting was facilitated by Tony Griffin and Tomás Harkin but because it included everyone and the numbers were too big to host it in the players' room, which included a pool table and table tennis table, they had to hold it in the restaurant. The difficulty with that venue was that other people were eating in the far section of the restaurant and the big beige curtain which was pulled across to close off our section couldn't muffle the background noise.

Griff had a flip chart and whiteboard up against one of the bay windows but he had to pull the group in tighter on two occasions because everyone was struggling to hear him. His exercise focused on the concept of the 'Hero's Journey', a pattern of narrative identified by the American scholar Joseph Campbell that appears in drama, storytelling, myth, religious ritual and psychological development. It describes the typical adventure of the archetype known as 'The Hero', the person who goes out and achieves great deeds on behalf of the group, tribe or civilization.

In more common terminology – I certainly don't want to describe us as heroes – the basis of the exercise was to summarize how we were returning home to our ordinary lives after an extraordinary week, wanting and hoping to bring something with us that would help transform our fortunes as Dublin hurlers.

Griff took out a roll of masking tape and stuck some to the ground, forming a straight line parallel to the long beige curtain. Every person present then had to cross that line and state what positives from the week they would bring home to help make us a better and stronger group. Then that person had to pick out somebody from the main group, speak positively about them and why they had selected them, and he in turn would speak before selecting another person to cross the line to join them.

Ryan O'Dwyer was the first to speak, and it was obvious after about an hour how intense the exercise was becoming. When Simon Lambert was called across the line, he broke down. He was barely able to speak. Simmo is a huge part of our panel, a massive character within the squad who has been recovering from a cruciate ligament injury all season.

'This is my team,' he said, fighting back the tears. 'My team. I don't care, whatever I'm asked to do for this team, I'll do it. Whatever it takes, I'll do it.'

One of the most surprising elements of the exercise was that guys didn't select the team-mates you'd have expected them to. Colm Cronin, one of the younger crew, chose McCrabbe, who he said he'd looked up to since he'd presented him with an underage medal the year he won his All-Star in 2009. I thought it was powerful because McCrabbe probably expected to be called out by Noley or Budgie (Ruairí Trainor).

The room was so emotionally charged that the exercise was taking longer than expected, and since we had a plane to catch Tomás Harkin told the speakers to condense their contribution and to stop selecting other players. Now, once the speaker had finished, someone else just had to cross the line and make their contribution.

I was the last to cross that line. I got emotional too. 'Simmo has probably set me off,' I said to the group. 'Ye know how much ye all mean to me. We are involved in high-stakes stuff but what I want most of all for ye to bring back home is to realize how important it is to cherish what we have. Even when you hit the lows, you have got to cherish what we have created.'

When Griff ripped the masking tape off the floor, after we'd all crossed that line, I stood in the middle of the floor and everyone gathered around me in a huge huddle, arms linked tightly together. I hadn't anything prepared to say but I could hear the commotion from just beyond the curtain where a golf group were having a small presentation of prizes.

'That's the mundane out there,' I said. 'You can have the mundane for long enough when you've packed up hurling. You can worry then about the captain's prize and the bit of crystal and all that shite that goes with it, but what we're involved in here is serious, serious business. There were times we weren't sure if we were good enough. Were the other teams just better than us? Did tradition go against us? But we know now that when we're right, we're as good as anyone.'

As we left that room and got ready to pack for home, I was convinced that whatever Wexford threw at us in nine days' time, we'd be ready for it.

20

Nemesis

I woke up this morning and the weather mirrored my mood. Sunny. Warm. Fresh. Excited. I thought about going back to the Pollock holes in Kilkee for a dip but I was craving some madness so I travelled further north up the coast to White Strand in Doonbeg. A farmer was driving his cattle across the road to one of his fields near the beach and he gave me a funny look as I sped past him and his herd in my trunks. I kept going at a high pace before flinging myself head-first into the Atlantic Ocean, the cold water instantly jolting my senses and coursing through my body like an electric shock. 'WHAAAAAAH!' Brilliant. Once my body readjusted to the temperature, I could have stayed in there all day.

The minerals and nutrients in the sea water are a great cure for any physical ailments or pains but I find it provides balm for my mind as much as anything else. Fr Harry is friends with Seán Boylan, the herbalist and former Meath manager. In my final days with Clare, when we were trying to keep some of the older lads fresh and their muscles stress-free, I asked Harry to probe Boylan for his advice on recovery for lads who were nearly bollixed.

'Sea water,' said Boylan. 'Plenty of sea water.'

We used to encourage the lads to go to the sea as often as they could. Seánie used to regularly travel back to the coast for the biggest ice-bath possible but he'd often run into Brian or Frank Lohan or Colin Lynch, cooling the lactic acid in their legs and releasing the stress in their minds. When I hear the Dublin lads complaining about the cold water in Portmarnock during recovery sessions, I tell them the Irish Sea is incomparable to the Atlantic. 'What are ye talking about? Sure, with Sellafield over the road, this is like bathwater.'

I don't do this every morning but today is going to be a long day. We're training this evening and I felt like starting the day as I mean to go on. Buzzing. Energetic. Jumping out of my skin with anticipation and excitement as Kilkenny loom on the horizon.

This forms a small part of my preparation for Sunday, but this craic is other people's daily routine. There's a guy from Kilnamona, just outside Ennis, who runs back to Lahinch 365 days of the year, jumps into the ocean, swims around for ten minutes, dries himself off and thumbs a lift home. It's like he has a fleet of taxis booked every morning because everyone on the road into Ennis from Lahinch knows him well by now.

I won't go to those extremes but I do up the ante on weeks like this. I'll jump into the sea again at some stage. I'll do the cliff walk around Kilkee a couple of times. I might even try and fit in the trek around Kilrush, Cappa and Aylevarroo. Some people think I've a great life but the reflex response in my own mind is that Sunday against Kilkenny is a bigger week's work than a lot of people put down. I don't want that to come across as condescending, but trying to put Leinster titles back to back for the first time in seventy-two years is a big deal for a lot of people and I want to be as prepared for it as I possibly can be.

Because you have no real control on the pitch I get more nervous as a manager than I did as a player, but I absolutely live for weeks like this. Everything is building up to four p.m. on Sunday but it's almost like you don't want that time, that anticipation, that buzz to come to an end. It will be all over by 5.30 and hopefully it will be elation, but preparing to try and create that feeling is almost as pure as living it when it actually happens. As Loughnane said after the 1997 Munster final, it is the feeling you never want to end. But it is still over and you're already moving on.

I often wonder what Brian Cody does on weeks like this. How does he prepare, what is his routine? I'm sure he doesn't go to the same extremes as I do. I certainly couldn't imagine Cody jumping into the Nore in his trunks anyway.

Kilkenny project this image of everything being low-key and basic. You never see Kilkenny going on warm-weather training camps. They probably hear about us going to Portugal and wonder what we can be doing in the Algarve that they can't do in Nowlan Park, but it's not that easy to measure. They have hurlers falling out of trees in Kilkenny. They don't have the distraction or lure of football. Winning is their culture, their heritage. We just have to work so much harder to try and create that culture and develop that mindset.

All I know is that Cody and his players will be gunning for us after last year and we have to do everything we can to be ready for that onslaught. The first time I ran into Cody in the championship as a manager was in 2004 when Clare met them in an All-Ireland quarter-final. I couldn't believe what he had got away with in their previous game against Galway. He was like a man possessed. He hounded and berated the referee and the linesmen and anyone else who got in his way. I felt Galway completely rolled over to him, and I said to myself, 'I'm going standing up for myself anyway when we play them.' Everyone had seen how hyped up Cody was that day and I wanted our boys to know that none of us was going to be walked over, including myself on the sideline.

Early in the first half there was a confrontation over a sideline ball and Cody cleared his throat. I was ready for him.

'G'way to fuck, that's a Clare ball.'

'Go way, Daly,' said Cody, 'that's a Kilkenny ball.'

'I don't care what you've done, you won't fucking bully me,' I responded, half hitting him a dunt in the chest with my shoulder. 'You got away with that the last day, you won't get away with it today.'

That was the end of that set-to but I wanted to lay down a marker to more than just Cody and my own Clare players, and my hunch was confirmed as the years passed. I felt that a lot of the officials genuflected before Kilkenny when they were on the throne for so long. For most referees, their main ambition is to do the All-Ireland every year, and since Kilkenny were in the final almost every season it wasn't in any referee's interest to get on their wrong side.

Maybe it's paranoia on my behalf and I'm reading that wrong, but I understand the human element too of referees targeting big games and having to play the cards that might facilitate that ambition. They don't want one of the successful county managers saying to Ned Quinn, 'Make sure that fella isn't refereeing the All-Ireland final.' Loughnane got hammered for saying that Cork didn't want Johnny Ryan refereeing the 2013 All-Ireland, and while Cork and the refereeing body denied the claim, there was substance to Loughnane's core message of how county boards and managers try and have a say in these matters.

When we didn't get some tight calls over the years, I often asked myself, 'Did we not get that decision because it's unlikely we'll be in the All-Ireland final?' I felt there was certain intimidation going on along the sideline. I don't know what was being said in the referee's room at half-time but I'm sure the referee was fully aware of Cody's wrath.

There wasn't a word between Cody and myself when we met again in the 2006 All-Ireland semi-final, and the two of us had a great chat in the tunnel afterwards. He made a great speech in the dressing-room and we didn't cross swords again until we met in the league in Croke Park in 2011. Hailstones and heavy rain were spilling down on top of us but it didn't quench the sparks, which ignited into a flame.

It was over another contentious decision, and I didn't back down. He was probably taken aback by my brazenness in 2004, but when I lost the rag with him a second time he didn't take it lying down and we nearly came to blows.

'You're a long time trying to bate me now, Antnee,' said Cody.

'Sure, my mother would train that team, Brian,' I shot back. 'They train themselves, anyone would win with them, g'way will ya. How did you lose one or two of those All-Irelands with those players?'

'We're bating ye anyway, and you better believe that we'll keep bating ye,' he snorted back. 'And we'd have beaten yere [Clare] team as well.'

'Wrong there, Brian. I'd love to have seen it but ye wouldn't have been beating us.'

That was the end of it. The match ended in a draw and we both smiled as we made our way towards each other afterwards with our hands outstretched.

'We went a bit over the top there, Dalo,' said Cody. 'I suppose we'll get sense at some stage.'

The Dublin footballers were playing after us and we shot the breeze while we walked across the field to the dressing-rooms under the Cusack Stand.

We beat them in the league final a month later, but the championship was another matter. When we finally should have beaten them in the 2013 drawn Leinster semi-final, when T. J. Reid scored an injury-time equalizer, my emotions were in a spin but I still had to smile at Cody afterwards.

'Jesus, will I ever bate you,' I said.

When we finally did a week later, Cody delivered kind and gracious words to us in the dressing-room, about how he'd been saying for a long time that we were a very good team and how our performance had confirmed what he had always believed.

'I've seen this coming for a long time,' he said. 'And I'm genuinely delighted for ye as well. But ye and I know that today is no good unless ye win next week. I suppose ye are carrying the Leinster hopes now. We let the Bob O'Keeffe cup out of Leinster last year and it's not something we're proud of. Ye are the Leinster team left now and I wish ye the best of luck and we might see ye before the year is out.'

When I went into the Kilkenny dressing-room, I told the players that I never thought I would get to talk to them as a winning manager. 'It is very easy to go into a winning dressing-room, and I've had to do that so many times against ye,' I said. 'It is a weird feeling and I certainly hadn't prepared for it, but I know Tipperary are coming to yere town next week and I'm sure there will be a backlash. I don't know what today means long-term but all I know is that it means a hell of a lot to our boys down the corridor. It was always our ambition that some day we would beat ye in the championship.'

Kilkenny have been exceptional, but they have come back to the pack and the rest of the teams have come up a level.

Kilkenny are no longer able to stroll through June and early July any more. Galway took them out in Leinster in 2012. We beat them after a replay last year. Galway took them to a replay last weekend. When Munster had that ferocious competitiveness over the last decade, where teams were slaughtering one another, Kilkenny could put their feet up before stretching their legs in August and September.

That still doesn't take away from their achievements, and I'm in awe of Cody and his success. I have always had great respect for him, and I've had great craic with him too on the line over the years. I had a great night with him one year at the All-Stars. He and his wife Elsie were having a few glasses of red wine and Cody started telling some great yarns. He's ruthless and is like Loughnane in lots of ways. You can see the similarities between them, and there's a fun side to Cody too that you rarely get to see.

Mick O'Dwyer and Kevin Heffernan are GAA legends, but to me, Cody is the greatest GAA manager of all time. I had a cut at him that day in 2011 and said what a lot of people think, but we all know too that it's not that simple. We had great players too in Clarecastle. We feel we should have had four or five more championships but we didn't always handle our talent as well as we should have. Cody had a uniquely talented bunch who were defined by an insatiable hunger, but managing that talent and continually maintaining that calculated instability, that edge which generated their relentless drive, is Cody's greatest legacy.

Sunday, 6 July 2014

I got up at seven a.m. At 7.50, I handed Orlaith my phone and said, 'Take a video of this.' I poured a glass of water and dropped in a couple of spoons of wheatgrass, an organic powder containing nutrients for nourishing and detoxifying the body. It tastes like shit and looks like a slimy cocktail only a tribe in the jungle would swallow but I've been taking it since Griff introduced me to the stuff in Portugal. I threw it back as Orlaith held up the phone with the recording button on. 'Battle juice taken,' I said into the camera. 'Ready for war.' Then I smiled, and Orlaith turned it off. She uploaded the recording on the squad's Facebook page. It was my goggles-and-swimming-hat moment to try and lighten the mood and get ready for battle.

We're ready for it. Kilkenny had two games against Galway but we're coming in fresher. When the heat came on against Wexford, we responded manfully. The only real move we had to make on the line was to switch Paul Schutte on to Conor McDonald. The lads took care of all other business themselves. It was the kind of leadership we've been looking for all along.

I drove to Dublin with Eilís and Orlaith and met the squad in Parnell Park. As soon as I sat in the bus for the journey into Croke Park, I got concerned. It's a short journey from Parnell and the level of noise was far louder than it should have been. I never talk on those journeys. I was the same as a player: I would hardly open my mouth between Cashel and Thurles. I glanced back at one stage and a lot of guys had their headphones on but there was still too much yapping for my liking.

When we got into Croker, we went out to look at ten minutes of the minor game, which was going horribly wrong because Kilkenny were hammering Dublin. I had spoken to the minors on Wednesday evening and I didn't like the portents.

I went back inside and met Tony Griffin in the warm-up area. I asked him what he thought.

'I'm a bit concerned,' he said.

'So am I.'

Griff expanded on his concerns. 'I didn't play in too many

Munster finals but I can't imagine it being this relaxed. This level of relaxation doesn't seem right.'

I fully agreed with him because I had just made a similar point to Ross Dunphy. 'I was letting it go earlier on because you don't want fellas too worked up either,' I said. 'But guys need to be worked up to a certain level.'

I called them in around me and delivered some hard reality about what was facing us. 'We can't just switch this on when we go out on to the pitch. We need to set the tone early. We need to be mentally ready to set the tone.'

We weren't.

Kilkenny 0-24
Dublin 1-9

I walked up to Cody at the end of the match and shook his hand.

'Well done, Brian, the scoreline was an accurate reflection of the match.'

'Ah, I don't know about that, Anthony,' he replied. 'Ye were still in the game there with fifteen minutes remaining.'

'No, Brian, an accurate reflection on the result. Well done.'

The shit was beaten out of us.

There was bound to be flak flying around after the performance and most of it was sure to be aimed in my direction. I couldn't honestly tell you where the shells were being unloaded from or who was manning the rifles because I kept my head down and stayed away from the crossfire. I knew what would be said: we were listless; the gameplan was all wrong; what were we doing leaving Jackie Tyrrell loose? What were we doing full stop?

Perspective is your only guiding light when that darkness

descends. Watching the Clare championship matches last October and November, teams without some form of a game-plan were deemed prehistoric. Jimmy Barry-Murphy was almost laughed at for playing conventional hurling, even though he nearly won an All-Ireland.

Clare were deemed the leaders of a new hurling revolution with the panache and precision of their style but, ten months on, Clare couldn't beat Wexford home and away, while we've been ridiculed for trying to play with a gameplan. JBM said after Cork beat Waterford in the Munster quarter-final replay that desire and workrate will always far outstrip tactics and gameplans. Jimmy was bang on. Whatever gameplan and tactics we had against Kilkenny wilted from our lack of desire and workrate, and in the heat from their greater intensity.

Our tactics looked off the wall on the day, but it was our diluted desire that was a wall, and it prevented us from getting close enough to Kilkenny. The basis of our gameplan was Colm Cronin coming out the field but using his athleticism to make runs through the space vacated. He got in for one goal and almost had a second, while the two-man full-forward line was to hold inside. It didn't make any difference because so many of our players were off the pace.

The week was a scramble for answers, a frantic search for the origins of the meltdown. My head was fried. Twelve days before the game we played one of the best training matches we'd ever played. We were absolutely on fire, scorching the earth with the pace of hurling. Kilkenny and Galway had played out an epic draw in Tullamore a couple of days earlier. 'I hope it's another epic, epic, epic the next day,' I roared to the lads when I blew the final whistle that evening. 'If we play like that, we'll eat either of them alive.'

When we met in St Anne's Park on the Wednesday evening

after the Leinster final, we tried to shine a torch into the collective soul and mindset of the group, on the darkness which had enveloped us against Kilkenny. Keaney is often the most accurate gauge and Griff addressed him late in the meeting.

'Conal, I know you're hurting,' he said, 'and I'd like to hear from you.'

Keaney said he didn't know what to say because he struggled to understand why he and the team had underperformed. Yet what he did say was very revealing. 'I do know that you said to me, Dalo, over in Portugal, "Get yourself ready for Rossiter." And I had said to myself for ten days before that match that Keith Rossiter was not going to finish my career below in Wexford Park. He is the same age as me, if not older, and that was the dominant thought in my psyche.

'Maybe in the meeting last Wednesday night, when I said that it was all about going out and playing the game, that we all have Leinster medals, that we'll either be in the All-Ireland semi-final or quarter-final on Monday morning, and the season will go on regardless, that maybe I let that creep into my head. Maybe that took the edge off me.'

At the time Keaney made those comments before the Kilkenny game, I thought, 'Great, they're not anxious about the occasion, they're nice and relaxed.' When he tried to put some meaning on the effect that mindset may have had on the performance, a light went on in my head.

We had put so much into Wexford, starting with all the effort in Portugal, I wondered if beating them triggered a release valve in all of us? We were definitely in the last six from that moment on, maybe in the last four. Maybe we forgot about going toe-to-toe with Kilkenny and savaging into them.

Then again, maybe that's just speculation and us searching

for answers in the black hole we now find ourselves in.
Everything in life is merely speculation because nobody knows
what's going on in other people's heads.

21

With Your Shield, or On It

Sunday, 27 July 2014

Icollected Tommy Dunne in Nenagh because we were meeting in the Curragh. When we arrived, the setting was perfect. It was peaceful and tranquil, just where we needed to be before we crossed into Munster for the mayhem and madness of battle.

I didn't bring the lads back to the Curragh for the same purpose I wanted it to serve before we played Wexford in 2009, to rekindle memories of the hardship we'd experienced there months earlier. We had done some of our hardest fitness work in the gym in the Curragh with Ross earlier in the 2014 season but we're in a different place now to where we were in 2009 and I just wanted somewhere isolated and quiet and closer to Thurles.

After the meal, lads went off to do their own thing for an hour before Tommy addressed them downstairs in the gym. He spoke about their integrity and honesty and how much he loved working with them. Tommy had trained most of the current Tipp squad under Declan Ryan between 2011 and 2012 but our whole approach on the day was to stay away from talking about Tipperary and to focus on ourselves. To try and exorcize the demons which had stalked us since the Leinster final.

Ross had a room prepared for us upstairs, where we went through our tactics, which were not complicated. We had three match-ups at the back: Shane Durkin on 'Bubbles' O'Dwyer, Stephen Hiney on Noel McGrath and Niall Corcoran on Lar Corbett. The other three defenders were to try and hold their positions as much as they could.

We didn't focus very long on tactics and gameplans because this was all about fighting the fight. When I spoke to them upstairs, I used the analogy from the film *300*, the fictionalized retelling of the Battle of Thermopylae where 300 Spartans go into battle against the Persian 'God-King' Xerxes and his invading army of more than 300,000 soldiers. The film falls within the genre of historical fantasy; the Spartan tradition saw them carry their war-dead home from the battle on their shields. You never want to equate hurling with war and killing. There is enough destruction and death going on in this world without trivializing it in this way. But some of the lines from that film were applicable for the mindset I felt we needed to have against Tipp.

'Come home with your shield or come home on it,' I said to the lads. 'Whatever about winning or losing, don't anyone appear in that dressing-room afterwards without your shield.'

I knew most of them had probably seen the film or heard of the legend, but I wanted to be specific to hammer home the point I was making. 'Just in case anyone in this room doesn't get the meaning of what I'm trying to say, I'll explain it again. If you want to get out of the battle early, throw away your shield. If you do, you'll be coming home without your shield and with the pain and shame we had after the Leinster final. So come home with your shield or be carried home on the fucking thing.'

After we warmed up in Dr Morris Park, I gathered all the

players around me before we made the short walk down to Semple Stadium.

'With your shield. Or on it.'

With ten minutes remaining, that chant, that thudding war-cry, something that first laid siege to my eardrums in 1993, was raging all around Semple Stadium again.

'TIPP, TIPP, TIPP, TIPP, TIPP, TIPP, TIPP, TIPP, TIPP, TIPP, TIPP . . .'

The rain was coming down in sheets but the sun, which had been sporadically shining earlier, was peeking back out from behind the rain clouds, beaming panels of sunshine down on the hills in the distance around Upperchurch and Ballycahill.

I was standing in my polo shirt, my arms folded, almost oblivious to the rain drenching me, my mind stoking the dying embers of a game that was gone from us. I had my index finger on my chin when Rushey scored our last point in injury-time, my hands on my hips when the referee blew the final whistle just moments later.

Richie Stakelum patted me on the back. I stood briefly for a moment before making my way down the sideline. Johnny McCaffrey had his head down as he meandered his way through the Tipp supporters, heading for the tunnel. He didn't see me as he crossed my path so I just touched him on the shoulder. James Woodlock, who had been substituted late on, shook my hand before I gripped Eamon O'Shea's hand and wished him all the best for the semi-final.

As I ambled for a couple of seconds, I tapped Noel McGrath on the back before a Tipp supporter in one of those old-style jerseys commiserated with me. I was heading for the dressing-rooms through the emerging Tipp throng when Tipp selector Michael Ryan came chasing after me and we spoke for a few seconds. Then I made my way down the tunnel, my head bowed, Jack Dougan in front of me, McCrabber behind me.

When you get beaten by thirteen points, a bigger margin than the Leinster final, the easy assumption to make is that we threw away our shields again, that we arrived home in pain and shame. Again. I honestly don't believe that we did. We were always chasing the game but I felt we battled. There was a stage when Tipp were in control of the game but we had great chances that we didn't take, which might have put a different colour on the game's complexion, or even altered its direction, in the last twenty minutes.

The result defines everything, but there is too much lazy journalism and analysis out there now to really bother finding out who did throw away their shield and who arrived home with it, or on it. Because 'Bonner' Maher could have had two goals, the general impression was that he got on top of Rushey. He didn't. I had put it up to Rushey all week: 'You or Maher? Who's a better man?' I thought Rushey was magnificent, especially in the second half.

Some lads didn't perform but I thought everyone at least tried. Conor McCormack was a doubt coming up to the match and we probably shouldn't have played him. He got a belt against Limerick and didn't train in the lead-up to the Tipp match, but Eamonn, the physio, said there was at least half an hour in him. Conor tried his best and battled for twenty-five minutes but the injury curtailed his efforts.

Our touch just deserted us again. Despite all the ball-work we had done, despite our touch being adhesive and glue-like in training for the past week, it was undermined by anxiety, and anxiety to do well. It paralysed our hurling. We just can't find that happy medium between being wired and being able to flow. Declan Coyle has a great phrase: 'Throw out the dirty petrol, put the boot down and just go for it. Play with freedom.' We tried to do that, but we just didn't. Somewhere in between is where that Dublin team plays their best hurling.

Tipp's hurling flowed but you could sense that they weren't up for it. I felt Lar wanted it handy. When Rushey blocked him down in the 30th minute, I roared, 'He's fucked now, drive into him Corcoran!' Lar was right beside me and he didn't even bat an eyelid. He could say that he was in the zone and my presence or my words didn't matter but I can guarantee you if I said it to one of the Limerick fellas, who riddled Wexford in the first quarter-final, I'd probably have got a wallop.

I felt our match-ups worked well. Bubbles got man-of-the-match because he got 2-1 from play but he was in the right place at the right time for the two goals. They were struggling to pick a man-of-the-match and Shane Durkin did well on him. Shane was probably our player of the year for consistency. Everyone was questioning our decision to put Corco on Lar when Lar got two points in the first few minutes but Corco got to grips with him after that and Lar wasn't on the ball once in the second half.

Corco had adopted a defensive mindset early on when he was told to go with Lar. I could understand him having a few early doubts, but it was his first start of the year and his response to Lar's two early scores summed up the man he is. Hiney's display said as much. Similar to how he had done on T. J. Reid in the Leinster final, he had Noel McGrath in his pocket.

Before we played Kilkenny, we wanted to show those guys how good we were but we forgot about process and performance and the bottom line. Against Tipp, we went back to reality and tried to fight for everything. We were seven behind at half-time and had the wind to come. We felt we were still right in the match.

'I haven't delivered again,' Keaney said at half-time. 'But there comes a time for every team when the gun is put to your head and you have to face it down. We didn't win many of the individual battles against Kilkenny but we're winning a lot of them out here.'

Rushey's contribution carried a similar tone and the general feeling going out for the second half was that we were going to have a real cut. We were putting Paul Ryan in as an orthodox corner-forward, going fifteen on fifteen, and putting it up to every man to win his own individual battle.

Even though we had beaten Kilkenny and hadn't beaten Tipp, Tipp aren't Kilkenny and we had no psychological hang-up with them. I wasn't deluding myself, of course I have to keep positive, but I felt we were right in the game in the third quarter. Ryaner had a penalty saved in the 47th minute but we had it back to six with twenty minutes remaining and had generated serious momentum. When Mikey Carton won a great ball and was fouled for a free in the 51st minute, I leapt up for the first time that day. I turned round to the boys. 'We have this crowd!'

Mikey tried to play a quick free to Mark Schutte, who had made a great run, but he just overcooked it and the ball went out over the line. Tipp took a quick sideline cut, worked it up the field and engineered an overlap, Peter Kelly had to come, Séamus Callanan slipped the ball through to Bubbles, who drove it past Noley, who nearly stopped it. Nine points down. Game over.

The easy conclusion to draw was that we choked again. I'm man enough to admit that we did in the Leinster final. I have no doubt that if Colm Cronin had stuck the ball in the net with fifteen minutes remaining against Kilkenny to bring the deficit back to two points, we would still have lost the game. But we didn't choke against Tipp. We didn't play well. There was no rhythm or flow to our hurling, but we kept trying, kept battling. Nobody embodied that more than Keaney who battled manly with Padraic Maher, their defensive talisman. That first goal just drained the life out of us and there was no way back.

The dressing-room was a sad place. 'I know Tommy mentioned integrity today and don't let anyone question yere integrity,' I said to the lads, the sombre mood enveloping the whole room, the disappointment so thick it was dripping off the walls. 'It was an absolute honour to work with ye. There are no ends that I asked ye to go to that ye wouldn't have gone to, both for me and the backroom team.'

When I finished speaking, I went round and hugged the heads off every one of the players. I wasn't going to speak to every one of the thirty-five – I'm not Gandhi – but some of the exchanges were heartfelt and poignant. A few of the lads were emotional. So was I.

After I embraced Niall Corcoran, he pulled me back and thanked me for the opportunity, for having him as part of this odyssey. 'Nobody would give me a chance in Galway to prove myself,' he said. 'You gave me a chance. Some of the days against Galway were the days I proved myself the most.'

My exchange with Hiney was one of just absolute and total respect. 'Warrior,' I said to him. 'I never met the likes of you.'

I played with, and managed, a lot of great characters, but Paul Ryan is one of those figures you rarely meet. He has an unreal sense of humour, a personality a lot like myself. 'Ryaner, you were probably pissed off with me at times, kid, but when I remember nobody here, I'll remember you.'

Martin Quilty was one of the last players I embraced. 'Quilt, I'd say you hate me. I'm sorry for not giving you enough chances. Just when things were going your way, you picked up that injury.'

Quilt lifted his eyes to meet mine at the same level. 'Ah Jeez, no, Dalo. No way, never think like that.'

I know there are lads in the dressing-room who probably don't like me. Well, they're probably pissed off that I didn't give them more game-time. We used a lot of the same players this year throughout the league and championship and it could be thrown at me and the management that we didn't trust our panel enough, that we didn't always reward training-ground form.

On a Friday night in Bray, nine days before we played Tipp, Martin Quilty and Eamonn 'Trollier' Dillon had excellent games. Before we trained on Sunday in Clondalkin, I told the squad that we were picking the team on the form from the A versus B match. Quilt and Trollier were on the A team that day but they hardly got a puck between them.

Like Quilt, Trollier is a super fella. He's young, has great pace and a brilliant attitude. I had guaranteed him coming up to the Tipp match that he would feature and he did. Both of those fellas will be huge players for Dublin going forward, but every player at this level has to consistently perform if they want to survive and prosper in this cut-throat arena.

On the first night I met the players in Parnell Park in 2009, I told them that I had loyalty to nobody. That there would be no favouritism. Mark Schutte was on the absolute periphery of the panel at the outset of 2013 but he ended up featuring in every match in the championship. One of our big plans against Cork in the 2013 semi-final was that we would spring Mark to win the match for us, and then maybe start him for the final.

The primacy of the collective over the individual and the absolute suppression of ego are the values you want to define your culture, to define your squad. Players will always be annoyed with a manager but every player has to buy into that culture and to understand that a manager's conviction is part of the culture too.

Before I finished speaking, I thanked the board and I mentioned the lure of football because I was conscious of the presence of John Costello and Andy Kettle. 'I know it would have been easier for some of ye to go off playing football, but ye stuck with us. Keaney coming back to us from the football was one of the pivotal turning points in us winning Bob O'Keeffe.'

There is still a brigade in Dublin who believes that we didn't fight hard enough to secure the services of some of the young dual players who opted for football. When this argument was raging last year, we won a Leinster title for the first time since 1961. We could have won an All-Ireland. We secured three All-Stars. Yet the Dublin footballers did win an All-Ireland and those young players never even considered choosing hurling.

I didn't see *The Sunday Game* the night of the Tipperary match but Loughnane and Donal Óg Cusack were reportedly banging that drum about Dublin being manufactured hurlers and the county needing to insist on dual players deciding at fifteen or sixteen which game to play in the future. The consistent argument is made that we need to make hurling a more attractive option, but we are the only top-ranking hurling county in the country playing second-fiddle to football.

I wouldn't entertain that argument for a second because the lads we have are the lads we want. They would give you everything and that's all you can ask. What had I to sell to the young dual players at the outset of 2013, when most of them made their decision to choose football? We were after coming off a disastrous season in 2012. The footballers didn't win the

All-Ireland that year but total domination looked within their compass.

For the lads who felt that I didn't push hard enough to try and win over the hearts and minds of those young players, what was I supposed to do? Resign? Threaten to resign unless I secured the services of dual players? Meet them for coffee and try and brainwash them? If I, or anyone else, thought that tactic was going to work, the only one I'd be brainwashing was myself.

I know how this thing works. On the Clare team I played on, five or six of those lads would have walked on to the Clare football team – which was a serious outfit – at that time, if they'd had a mind to take football seriously. Hurling was just the more attractive sport to play in the county so there was no decision to make.

If Loughnane or Cusack are saying that Dublin needs to ensure guys pick hurling ahead of football at fifteen, that's fairly rich coming from the both of them. Ger is a hurling purist from Feakle, where football has no place or order. Although he apparently was a decent footballer, I'm sure Cusack would be ordering boxes of pen-knives if football ever became a serious imposition on the hurling culture in Cloyne.

Did Loughnane ever entertain the notion of a dual player in Clare? Frank Lohan came on in the 1997 Munster final against Kerry but he hardly trained with the footballers and was only given leeway because the game was played three weeks before the All-Ireland semi-final against Kilkenny. So it's a bit rich for Loughnane and Cusack to be banging that drum with the force of a sledgehammer.

To me, the real issue here has been totally missed. If you look at the Dublin panel, the squad is packed with players from just four clubs – Ballyboden St Endas, Kilmacud Crokes, Lucan

Sarsfields and Cuala. Apart from Dotsy, there is nobody else from Tallaght. We have nobody from Finglas, no one from north of Craobh Chiaráin – which is another massive population area. If you take just Tallaght and Finglas alone – just two areas of Dublin – that's one senior hurler out of around 120,000 people. If there's any more there, I haven't seen them. And I've looked.

If Dublin really want to start reaching All-Ireland hurling finals and winning them, they have got to start finding players from those hurling wastelands. There also has to be a revival in some of the traditional hurling clubs which have fallen on hard times.

Everyone talks about the huge money which has been pumped into developing Dublin hurling. There is great coaching going on but, outside of certain clubs, where is it really developing? And all the while the Dublin football culture is thriving. They are hoovering up All-Irelands at all levels. The football revolution is spreading like wildfire.

With the exception of Joey Boland and Martin Quilty from Na Fianna, there is no other club outside the big four which has more than two players on our squad of thirty-five. Na Fianna would have three if Tomás Brady hadn't joined the footballers after four great years with the hurlers. I was disappointed, but I don't blame Tomás because I understand the reasons for his decision.

Na Fianna are doing superb work and they'd seven players on the starting Dublin minor hurling team in 2014. Yet one of the club's best young hurlers, Conor McHugh, also happens to be one of their best footballers. He was man-of-the-match in the All-Ireland U-21 football final against Roscommon but he was – allegedly – told that he'd be dropped off the Na Fianna senior football squad if he went playing with the county U-21 hurlers.

Square that one. And let somebody come back to me when they've solved it.

I remember a fella in the pub saying to me after we lost to Antrim in 2010, 'Where are you going with those Dublin fellas, sure they hardly even have the basics.' The night we won the league final the following year, I went into the pub for a pint. Your man was there and the lads gave him an unmerciful slagging about the basics.

When we scored 2–25 against Galway in the 2013 Leinster final, nobody was talking about basics. Some of the hurling we played in the All-Ireland semi-final against Cork was as good as anything seen in Croke Park during such an electric summer. It was another shootout. Surely you need shooters and good players to play in those kind of games? Yet all of a sudden, now we're only seen as 'manufactured hurlers'.

I had retreated into the bunker at home after the Tipperary game when Richie Stakelum sent me a text and told me to look up Cody. In an interview he'd done that week, Cody had rejected the characterization of Dublin's players as 'manufactured hurlers'.

'The same people were saying six months before that they were capable of winning the All-Ireland final, so it was a huge change in how people looked upon them,' said Cody. 'I would consider Dublin to be a top team, an absolute top team. I've been saying this for a long time. They're much better than they looked on both days [against Kilkenny and Tipperary]. They performed badly on the day – as many teams have done before – and the same level of remark wasn't passed upon other teams who have also failed to perform in given situations. There was nobody questioning their natural ability over the past couple of years whereas it's easy enough to hit them with that now. But it's completely wrong as far as I'm concerned.'

I'd never texted Brian Cody in my life, but I took out my phone and tapped a few words on the screen: 'Brian, just want to say thanks for what you said during the week. It was appreciated.'

'Just thought it was a load of rubbish, Dalo,' he texted back. 'All the best.'

How do you manufacture hurlers? Is it that you don't manufacture them in time? Do Dublin lads not play U-8 and U-10? Are they not applying certain nuts and bolts on the early stages of the production line, which ultimately produces a less natural product?

It's always easy to stereotype a team's identity in sport, especially in a game like hurling which carries so much tradition and history. After we lost to Tipp, the consensus was that we didn't have the wherewithal to live with Tipp's natural class. It opened a debate about natural hurlers and manufactured hurlers with the preordained conclusion that Tipperary is a place where hurlers are born, not made.

Yet where was this debate last year when we could have won an All-Ireland and Tipp were gone from the championship in the first week in July? Jeez, don't get me started. We were listening to that shit too for long enough in Clare.

When I got off at the Curragh, Mikey Carton asked me to come with the lads for a drink. I told Mikey I'd consider it as long as it wasn't somewhere where you'd get the eardrums blown off you with disco music. I had planned to go for a drink with Shane Martin but Mikey texted me later on: 'Upstairs in Keoghs, we'll have it to ourselves.' Spot on.

When I arrived after 10.30, six of the lads were sitting around one table. Most of the rest of the lads arrived before midnight. Lads laugh and smile away after a while. I do too.

Lads always get emotional with drink taken. Nobody was saying anything but you could sense the emotion in the air, the sense that this might be my final stand with this group, our final hours together as one unit. They probably got that vibe from my words and my body language in the dressing-room.

I love this job and this group of players, but I think it is the end, that it is time to move on. I don't know what the future holds but I'm suppressing any thoughts of end-games and new beginnings for now. The low and the first strains of mild depression can wait for the car journey home to Clare on Monday afternoon.

At the end of June 2014, Tullycrine primary school, which our three girls attended, closed down. The numbers just weren't sufficient any more to sustain it so it merged into Kilmurry-McMahon National School. Eilís had worked there. Similar to the Principal, Mary Lynch, Eilís was incredibly sad when they were taking down posters and packing up boxes at the end of June, when the end-game finally arrived and everybody was preparing to move on.

The voyage and the crossing we've all made with Dublin has been comparable to the journey our whole family have taken through that school. There were a few ups and downs but it was mostly an impeccable experience, a memorable and defining time among all those that make up the great odyssey of life.

There are and always will be obstacles and challenges, often accompanied by sadness and hard decisions. You just keep on keeping on. Keep going. Keep trying. Keep searching.

At the outset of July, Dublin hurling looked set to launch into a different orbit. The minors, U-21s and seniors were all in Leinster finals for the first time together. A month later and we were all out of the championship after suffering hard defeats.

Hurling in the city may be in a better place now than where it was when I first arrived in 2009 but summers like 2014 force you to ask yourself if we really have got any closer to getting the rock pushed up the hill.

I know we have.

'Look, the minors were unlucky enough today [beaten in the quarter-final by Waterford],' I said to the assembled media after the Tipp game. 'The U-21s were in the Leinster final too, minus all the lads that went at minor level. Four of the forwards from that minor team went off to play football. What do you do, like? Do you give up and leave it to football? And everyone concentrate on winning All-Irelands? Or do you keep going? And I'd like to think they keep going.'

Dublin just have to keep pushing that rock up that hill. Keep pushing until they can't push any more.

Epilogue

Live It, Love It, Embrace It

Timmy McCarthy didn't score in the 1999 Munster final but he cleaned me out. At one stage in the second half Timmy got a run on me and was through on goal. I was desperately trying to get back when I heard the ground pounding behind me.

'Get out of my way!' roared Ollie Baker.

He hunted down McCarthy, got goal-side and blocked him down. Baker was on his knees when the ball broke but he got his hurley on the ball and got it into his hand. Baker was almost covered in black soot from putting out all the fires but I arrived back on the scene with sirens blazing and he handed the ball out to me. I bate it the length of the field and there was this collective roar: 'Aboy, Daloooo!'

I went out the field after the ball and Baker passed me out.

'Isn't that fucking awful,' he said.

'That's teamwork, kid,' I replied.

Those are the kind of memories which stand out more than victories and cups and medals, those days when the adrenalin rush is fired from the brotherhood of the dressing-room, the days when you're pumped up on the narcotics of delirium. As alive as alive can be.

Winning is the drug we all chase but it can never be all about cups and medals and trophies. The most memorable match I ever played was a game we lost. We were All-Ireland champions when we went under to Limerick in the 1996 Munster semi-final but it was an eternal day. A day of days, one you rarely get to experience.

We warmed up in Ennis before getting a Garda escort into Limerick. As soon as we crossed over the brow of the hill in Clareview, heading down towards Ivans in Caherdavin, we couldn't see the road. It was blacked out with a tidal wave of people. The bus journey from there to the Gaelic Grounds took us the same time as it would have taken to row the same distance through an angry ocean.

Loughnane went to the top of the bus and grabbed the microphone. 'Lads,' he said, 'take a look out. This is the stuff that your fathers and grandfathers told you about. This is the Munster championship.'

As soon as Loughnane stopped speaking, I let out a roar. Twenty more lads started roaring after me. It was like a war-cry, a call to arms for one of the biggest battles of our lives.

On our way to the dressing-rooms, Clare supporters were leathering us on the back. It was primal stuff. Tom Ryan, the Limerick manager, had stirred it up that week about how we'd timbered them in the previous year's Munster final and how it was now time for retribution. It felt like the whole county was going to war and we were the frontline warriors.

Before we left the dressing-room, Loughnane held up a Clare jersey and spoke about how Tom Ryan had disrespected it. The hairs were standing on the back of my neck like spikes. The atmosphere was like nothing I'd ever experienced before.

The heat was ridiculous. The pitch was like a cauldron.

We should have won that game, but it's funny how all the inches can add to the difference between winning and losing – between winning and dying, as Tony LaMotta says in *Any Given Sunday*. Mike Houlihan hit Baker with a loose pull in the second half, and broke his cheekbone. I remember even Kirby giving out to Houlihan afterwards because Seánie slotted the free. Houlihan snapped back at Kirby, 'Do you want me to let him hammer us?'

Colum Flynn, our physio, wanted to take Baker off but we wanted him on the field. We should have gone in and decked Houlihan – well, you'd want to be a brave man to take that challenge on – but we thought we were in a good position and there was no point losing the head. I told Baker to get up off the ground quickly, not to let them see him sprawled in a heap. When Fitzy took a late puckout, just after Limerick had equalized, Ciarán Carey caught it over Baker because the man could hardly see. Carey slalomed his way up the field to land one of the greatest points ever scored.

Inches. When Carey was charging up the field, Seánie was roaring at us to hold our ground. 'Hold, hold, hold!' – like William Wallace in *Braveheart* as the English cavalry approached. Carey was coming between Seánie and me but Carey was hoping one of us would charge out and bury him and Kirby would slot the free. Hego was on his heels and had the pace for him but he tripped on Carey's legs and Carey had time to get the shot away just before he reached Seánie. Before we knew it, the game was over and they were belting out 'Sean South From Garryowen' like a war-dance.

It was our fourth year in succession meeting Limerick in the championship and the rivalry between the counties during those years was absolutely savage. Anything went. It was often a free-for-all. When 25,000 turned up for a league game in November 1994, there was a thirty-man brawl. The same day, Jim McInerney locked horns with the Nash brothers. Jim Mac and Declan Nash were sent off with blood streaming down their faces.

We hated each other at the time but they were a team I really liked as a bunch of individuals. They were a shower of hard bastards but they had some unreal characters – Houlihan, Davy Clarke, Steve McDonagh, T. J. Ryan, Mark Foley, Carey. They'd give it to you on the field but you could have a pint with them afterwards. When they lost their two All-Ireland finals in 1994 and 1996, I wasn't too disappointed. Looking back now, I genuinely would have loved to see those guys win their All-Ireland medal. They deserved it for the contribution they made to that golden era.

That day in 1996 is a standout memory, but a hurling life is framed from a million little pixels that create the grand picture, most of which are formed by people.

When we beat Cork in the 1993 Munster semi-final, Tuts got the decisive goal in the second half. He was poxed lucky to get it. Ger Cunningham made a brilliant save and as the ball squirmed along the goal-line, the sliotar only ended up over the line when Tuts kicked it with his trailing foot after a fresh-air swing. He high-fived Sparrow on the way out with the neck that suggested it was akin to Jimmy Barry-Murphy's iconic strike against Galway in 1983.

He got some slagging in work in Roche afterwards. When they organized a table quiz not long after to raise funds for the social club, Tuts asked them if they wanted a spot prize. All the while he was slipping off his shoe under the table and, quick as a camera flash, he planted it on the table. 'The boot that sank Cork.'

The week after we won the 1995 Munster title, we went on this 'Magical Mystery Tour' of the county. Myself and Tuts ended up staying in Mike Mac's in Scarriff on the Thursday night. His wife Marie cooked us up a fry that morning and we had to hitch it back to Ennis because we were back training that night. This guy who I knew from the bank, Gerry Lynch from Tulla, picked us up. He drove us home but he insisted we stop in to his place first to meet the wife and kids. His wife made tea and cut us two massive wedges of cake. At training that evening, five hundred people turned up and Mac put on a show. The drink and the cake steamed out through our pores.

There are a million grains in the great picture of life and each one really is a picture in itself. The time Len Gaynor asked me to captain Clare was one of the proudest days of my life. Clare hadn't won a championship game in four years but being chosen to lead the senior hurlers bestowed an honour that went beyond results and the hope of success, instilling an immeasurable pride. It was an incalculable privilege.

Any county title you win is special but the 2003 medal was sugar-coated in glory and honour after being told the previous year that I could no longer play sport. In the dying moments of the 2013 Leinster final Dublin got a point to push us eleven clear and I spotted Hedgo coming up the line, doing a little jig as the ball sailed over. It was pure raw excitement from Hedgo, decades of hurt and longing washed over by elation. It was a magical, beautiful moment which I could completely relate to.

We had often spoken about winning Bob O'Keeffe and when it finally did happen, seeing Jimmy Gray, who was part of the 1961 Leinster title-winning team, present the trophy to Johnny McCaffrey was magic. I had got to know Jimmy through the Friends of Dublin Hurling golf classic and he almost seemed like the perfect thread to connect the past to the present.

What made that day even more magical was celebrating it with Eilís and my three girls, all decked out in sky-blue jerseys, each one of them having invested as much in Dublin's success through my commitment to the cause. Only Eilís was around when I was lifting trophies with Clare but the girls finally got to sample the beautiful fusion of euphoria and delirium wrapped up in satisfaction at the end of a long hard road.

My girls grew up at the same time I grew as a manager and the Dublin players grew as a group. It's amazing to see your family growing up, watching relationships and identities develop, observing how powerful a force sisterhood actually is. Orlaith and Aoife are very tight but Úna is developing her own independence from the other two ordering her around.

The day of the Leinster final was tough, but the days afterwards were even harder because Orlaith was back in hospital. Six weeks earlier she'd been given a date to return to Temple Street for more tests; it just happened to be the day after the Leinster final. When I returned to meet Eilís and Orlaith in the hotel that evening I was racked with pain and shame, but that soon dissolved with a dose of reality, the sharp realization that health and family will always take precedence over a game that defines me.

Orlaith underwent the usual battery of tests and scans and procedures that week. They tried to bring on a seizure once more but nothing happened. It was positive that they couldn't. Orlaith had completed her Junior Cert exams and she did fine. She hadn't had a seizure in months, and when they released her that Friday at eleven a.m., Orlaith's doctor, Dr Amre Shawan from the neurology department, was satisfied that she was now seizure-free. The neuropsychologist advised her to do Transition Year as opposed to going straight into fourth year and she won't have her next check-up with Dr Shawan for six months.

A month after she got that good news, Orlaith went off to Cork with five of her friends on the train. If she had asked for that permission six months earlier, neither myself nor Eilís would have been able to contemplate or grant it for a second. Orlaith is going into Transition Year, which will be less pressurized, and having a year under her belt in school in a more relaxed environment should be of real benefit. You hope her life will be easier from now on, but it already is with the reduced medication. She used to suffer from headaches and severe drowsiness in the morning, all side-effects from swallowing a small hospital of pills. But Orlaith is in a good place now and we have so much to be thankful for.

Maybe it was the oscillating trend of that week, which started so low and ended so high, that caused my mood to crash again the following weekend. Orlaith had taken my mind off the game for most of the week and I went to training that Friday night on a complete high. It was a great session, which lifted my mood even more. At the team meeting on the Wednesday night after the Leinster final I promised the lads a match every night in training, and the game that evening was a dinger.

Eilís and Orlaith had gone home earlier that day but I stayed up on Friday and Saturday night because we were training again on Sunday morning. I was mentally beat up from the week and I wanted to take an extra return journey from Clare out of the schedule. I spent all day Saturday on my own, and once I had time to think and to brood, I caved in. I got so low that evening, the pain and the shame from the manner of the Leinster final defeat was sticking into my skin like needles.

To alleviate the pain, I started writing. What had we done wrong? What had I done wrong? Where were we as a squad at the moment? Where are we going? The answers didn't provide much antidote to the pain. I was just as low on Sunday after training. I had thought about going straight to Cork for the Munster final afterwards but I just couldn't face it.

I was just as bad after the Tipperary game. Win or lose, I had planned to go to the Galway Races in Ballybrit the following day. When the time came, I couldn't face the races because I couldn't face meeting anyone. I didn't think the defeat would bate me up that badly, but it did.

A few weeks later, I watched a fly-on-the-wall documentary on UTV on Ryan Giggs's four games as manager of Man United at the end of that 2013/14 season. United won two, drew one but lost to Sunderland at home. Despite the truck-loads of cups and titles he had won, that Sunderland defeat trailed Giggs like a black dog.

That's me. The winning days pass over me so quickly. The losing days invade my system like a virus and linger. Losing hurts me like I can't describe. Losing like we did in the Leinster final tears me to pieces.

I have had a lot of bad days with Clare both as a player and a manager. I've had my dog-days too with Dublin, but being manager of the Dublin team has been a humbling experience for me as well. With due respect to Gaynor, Loughnane and Cyril Lyons, I don't remember ever having the forum as players to criticize the manager. With Dublin, the culture we created was that nobody was immune from criticism or evaluation or introspection. It has been good for me that I have had to look long and hard at myself at times. To face up to a truth that there is no hiding from.

It might not always seem from the outside that you have made any improvement but you know the deficit that had to be made up and the gains that were made. Ultimately, we didn't make enough gains in 2014 to take us to where we wanted to go, but you can't let the road beat you down either. You gotta keep going. Keep positive.

The characters, the people you meet and work with along the way, keep you strong. When I was driving home from the Cork–Tipperary All-Ireland semi-final in August 2014, I got a text from Gary Maguire: 'The "manufactured hurlers" from Cork never showed up today.' Classic Gary. Super guy.

Gary has been a brilliant player for Dublin. He has really grown into one of our main leaders, but he had a difficult summer. He broke his thumb in May and the injury took so long to heal that he wasn't fit for any of the championship matches. Noley came in and had a brilliant championship but Gary was always there as a beacon of support within the squad.

I will really miss all the lads but my journey had come to a natural end and it was time to move on. The county board offered me another three-year term but nine years would have been far too long to stay in the job, especially with the mileage I was clocking. We only had six years with Loughnane as manager and he won two All-Irelands.

The enthusiasm of the backroom team, some of the players and the county board for me to remain did force me to agonize over the decision for a few weeks but I had already accepted in my heart that it was over. It is time for a fresh start, for all of us.

Already it feels weird. There is a vacuum in my life. Uncertainty can often be an uncomfortable companion. You just accept that reality in this game, and I have always been prepared to roll the dice. If I'd wanted certainty I would have stayed in my solid pensionable job with the TSB Savings Bank nearly two decades ago.

I don't fear the future because I know what my priorities are. I have three girls to look after, to put through school and hopefully send to college. That's a challenge every parent has to face, and I'll fully back myself to do the best for them.

Winning the game of life is the ultimate victory. You live life and love it because you never know what's going to meet you around the corner. I have seen home devastated twice through death. That has coloured my life a lot. You often hear stories about how people become liberated when they're on their deathbed, and how sad that is. They spend so much time worrying about what other people think of them that their lives almost pass them by.

I spend a lot of time in this life worrying and fretting over hurling, but it still frames my life and defines me as a person. I might not still be bating the ball the length of the field after Baker's done all the hard work but I'm vicariously bating that ball up the field with Mikey Carton and Stephen Hiney. Hurling will always be the ultimate expression of who I am and who I always will be.

The game follows me everywhere I go. Before every big game, I would visit the graveyard in Clarehill where my father, Paschal and my uncles Haulie and John are buried. Paschal is just inside the gate. My father, Haulie and John are buried side by side. I'd go to my father's grave first before turning to the others for a chat. 'Lads, ye might cut me a bit of auld slack today.' Then I'd call to my mother's house for the holy water.

I'm certainly not the most religious person alive. All that's in Clarehill now is the bones of my people but I feel that connection to the spiritual world. I talk to them. About the day ahead. About what's on my mind. The clear, cold freshness of the cemetery clears my head and does me good. It helps me cherish every day.

When we were in primary school in Clarecastle, we were always daring each other. One day our headmaster John Hanly overheard someone daring me to sleep in a graveyard. I said I wouldn't.

'Why wouldn't you?' Hanly asked.

'That would be scary, sir,' I replied.

'Hi, it's the living you have to fear,' he told me, 'you've nothing to fear from the dead.'

He's right. Even when we weren't playing a big match, I'd regularly head up to Clarehill and browse around. My grandfathers are buried up there. So is my uncle Seán, who resides in the old part of the graveyard. My sister Patricia had twins, the first grandchildren in our house. Padraig survived but the other baby didn't. Patricia also lost another baby. The infants were never named so I'd often amble over to their little grave and say a prayer for them, over the tiny little headstone with the inscription 'Glynn Babies' (Patricia's married name).

Sometimes I'd spend over an hour in Clarehill, looking at the names on the headstones. There are a lot of familiar names there now, old, and not so old, some of them Clarecastle hurlers who I heard about or who I once dreamt of emulating. When you are young, all the tenants seem so old. When you get close to the age of forty-five, they don't seem that old any more.

I cannot hurl any more but hurling will always remain at the core of my life while I'm still on this earth. I always try to live life as fully as I can but Martin Sheedy often says to me, 'Tony, it's time to realize now that you're forty-four, not twenty-four.' I don't feel like forty-four. You have to change and alter the pace of your life but I don't feel like slowing down. I'd be full on in most things I go at. Even in the screw-ups I make, I'm full on with those too.

There is an element of abandon about me. I will make a balls of myself at something again. I have made lots of mistakes but I'd never be afraid of trying something. Taking on Dublin

appeared crazy from a logistical point of view. I took on an age-
ing Clare team. I went down into the bear pit of north Kerry. I
always like the challenge. I continually want to test myself.

There will always be challenges ahead, and whatever I go
at, I'll do it with Len Gaynor's words of advice ringing in my
ears.

'Live it. Love it. Embrace it.'

Absolutely.

Acknowledgements

I was a lucky man the day I met Eilís Murphy. I want to thank her so much for all her love and support over the years, and for allowing, helping and enabling me to chase my dreams and fulfil my ambitions as a player and a manager.

To our three beautiful daughters, Orlaith, Aoife and Úna, who are the lights of our lives and who give us so much joy in watching them grow and developing into young ladies. Every day with Eilís and the girls is a day to be cherished on this earth.

To Michael, Marian, Patricia, Lucia, Martin and Stephanie for always being such wonderful brothers and sisters, and for being so good to my mother while I was away so often. We had some tough times as a family but we always stuck together and the bond that remains between us is something which I will always treasure.

My mother was the glue that kept it all together. When times were tough, she always found a way. Her attitude and her approach to life was often a neat metaphor for my playing and managerial career, that when difficult days descended, you just had to drive on and try and forge a way through. My mother has always been an inspiration and she still continues to be.

I want to thank Bishop Willie Walsh for being such a massive early influence. And to other great friends – Martin Coffey, Michael Vaughan and Gerry Kelly – for always providing so much help and assistance over the years, and in turn helping form the person I am.

To my Clare team-mates and the Clare management of the 1990s, comrades for life, I want to thank ye all for the greatest days and years of my life. To the Clare players between 2004 and 2006, I want to salute and acknowledge ye all for giving me, Fr Harry, Alan Cunningham and Ollie Baker everything ye had. We didn't achieve what the team of the 1990s did but we still created something special, which will always have a special place in my heart.

The Dubs will hold the same place, and with the same affection. The last six years were a rollercoaster of emotions but we had some fun and the greatest craic of all time with a group that gave an inhuman level of sacrifice for the cause. We didn't win the All-Ireland we dreamed about but we won more important stuff than trophies and titles along our great journey together. I sincerely want to thank Richie, Hedgo, Vinny, Johnny, Shane, Tommy, MK, Ross, Jim, Tony Griff and all the extended staff for their honesty and loyalty over six great years. I would also like to say a special thanks to John Costello and the Dublin county board for allowing us to make it all happen.

On the long road through life, I have travelled to many places but one of the greatest welcomes I was ever extended was in Kilmoyley and from the people of north Kerry. They always embraced me with huge warmth, whether it was with a bag of sliotars or a greyhound. On the subject of greyhounds, I'd like to thank Gerry Holian and George Gallery for just giving us great dogs.

Along with the hurling and the dogs, I also had a soccer career, which never garnered much attention but which always gave me immense satisfaction. I played with Turnpike Rovers in Ennis from when I was about fourteen to thirty and I want to say thanks to the Pynes and Jamesie Gormley for all those great days. When I had packed up playing with Clare, Tullycrine Celtic filled a void. I shared great memories with great people, especially the four Neylon brothers. They might not have been big days with big crowds but the memories they created will last just as long.

To Christy O'Connor, it was a pleasure working on this book with such a talented writer. We were rivals for so long with Clarecastle and Doora-Barefield but we were a real team on this project. It was made even easier by the fact that we were so long on the road together, so many great chats on that long road home. Christy spent six years with me in Dublin as goalkeeping coach so I also want to thank him very much for the brilliant job he did coaching Gary Maguire and Alan Nolan.

To everyone at my publishers, Transworld Ireland, I want to say sincere thanks for all the help and support, especially to Brian Langan and particularly to Eoin McHugh. I would also like to pay a big debt of gratitude to Eoin Conroy, who was always there as support in the background, and who provided me with huge guidance throughout this project.

To Olivia and the boys, to Joan O'Connor for often feeding me, to Denis Walsh, to Carolan Lennon in Eircom, I would also like to offer my sincere thanks. And I would like to say thanks to Eilís's family, the Murphys from Aildavour in Connolly, for all their support over the years.

To my close circle of tight friends – ye know who ye are lads

— ye have been like brothers to me and the sense of brotherhood we have formed has been unbreakable.

Finally, I will leave the last word to the Magpies, the men and women of Clarecastle who made me who I am. They are too numerous to mention so I won't even try and name them because I would need another book to include everybody. Ye infused me with the unique Clarecastle spirit and wit, a passion and love for hurling and craic, an appreciation of our rich heritage and tradition that is embedded deeply into my DNA.

No matter where I go, I will carry that spirit with me.

Anthony Daly,
Tullycrine, September 2014

Picture Acknowledgements

Every effort has been made to contact copyright holders where known. Those who have not been acknowledged are invited to get in touch with the publishers. Photos not credited have been kindly supplied by Anthony Daly.

Section one

Pages 2/3: Dean Ryan finalists, Flannan's, 1985: courtesy of Michael Daly.

Pages 4/5: AD and Barry Foley, Munster Club final, Clarecastle v Patrickswell, 07/12/1997: © Patrick Bolger/INPHO 10277; Munster champions, AD with Ken Morrissey and Fergus Tuohy: courtesy of John Power; County final action, Clarecastle v Ballyea, 2003: courtesy of John Power; AD and the 'Cannon', Clarecastle, 2003: courtesy of Francis Power; AD, Munster Club quarter-final, Clarecastle v Patrickswell, 26/10/2003: © Matt Browne/Sportsfile 126327.

Pages 6/7: Clare Council Civic Reception for Murty's Gang: courtesy of Michael Daly; Murty's Gang, Navin's bar, Clarecastle, February 2002: courtesy of Francis Power.

Page 8: AD and Eilís on their wedding day, 20/09/1997: © Aidan Sweeney at Aidan Sweeney Photography.

Section two

Page 1: AD, Man of the Match, Munster semi-final, 1993: courtesy of Michael Daly; AD, All-Ireland final, Clare v Offaly, 1995: © Lorraine O'Sullivan/INPHO 506155.

Index

INDEX

ABOUT THE AUTHORS

Anthony Daly is one of the most respected and dynamic hurlers and managers of his generation. He has enjoyed success as captain of the senior Clare hurling team throughout the 1990s, and more recently as manager of the Clare and Dublin teams respectively. His playing career saw him winning two senior All-Ireland medals, three Munster provincial medals, and three All-Star awards. At club level, he holds five county club medals for Clarecastle, and a provincial medal in 1997. Daly managed the Clare senior team from 2003 to 2006, and was manager of the Dublin team from 2008 to 2014, culminating in Dublin winning the Leinster Senior Hurling Championship in 2013, for the first time in fifty-two years.

Christy O'Connor is a freelance journalist based in Ennis in Clare. His first book, *Last Man Standing*, was runner-up in the Boylesports Irish Sports Book of the Year in 2005. His second book, *The Club*, won the William Hill Irish Sports Book of the Year in 2010. A McNamee award-winner for print journalism in 2011, O'Connor was also a team-mate of Anthony Daly for four years during his time on the Clare panel. He also worked with Daly as a goalkeeping coach during Daly's six seasons with Dublin.